EDITED BY
KATY GARNER & PEACE MITCHELL

First published in Australia in 2020
by Karen McDermott
Waikiki, WA 6169

Interior design: Ida Jansson
Edited by Dannielle Line
Proofread by Tracey Regan

National Library of Australia Catalogue-in-Publication data:
Back Yourself/Katy Garner & Peace Mitchell
Success/Self-help, Business Stories, Self-help/Motivation

ISBN: 978-0-6450371-9-7 (sc)
ISBN: 978-0-6450520-7-7 (e)

To the women who dream of something more, the ambitious ones, the creatives, the ones who do things differently, the courageous ones, the ones who wish they were braver, to the innovators, and the ideas girls, the ones who won't keep quiet, the unsung heroes, who dare to be different, who break the rules and rewrite them, the curious ones, the thinkers, the ones who wake up every day with purpose and passion, the risk takers, the adventurers , the ones who never give up and the ones who want to change the world. This book is written with love for all of you. It's your time so keep following your calling, keep dreaming big and keep striving to back yourself!

Peace and Katy xx

CONTENTS

Introduction 7

Part One

Kylie Mort 11
Brenda Keane 23
Emma Allen 39
Leanne Murner 55
Heidi Jonsson 66

Part Two

Laura Elizabeth 83
Louise Lugg 95
Davina Borrow-Jones 105
Rachael Ferguson 117
Vanessa Fiducia 131
Emma Heuston 143

Part Three

Karen Mc Dermott 159
Katrina Wurm 168
Yona Signo 180
Rachel Neate 193
Nicola Le Lievre 206
Kristy Moore 219

Part Four

Katy Garner 231
Candice Meisels 243
Peace Mitchell 255
Elle Likopoulos 268

Part Five

Rebecca Corbett 281
Lana Kruger 294
Cherie Gregory 307
Lynda Pedder 323
Sarah Walkerden 336
Sandra Spadanuda 349

Introduction

What does it mean to back yourself? It's about believing in yourself and reaching for the stars!

And yet, why are so many women resistant to putting themselves forward, to promoting themselves or to following their dreams? Why are so many women holding themselves back from playing bigger, from dreaming bigger or from allowing themselves to do all of the things that they want to do and know they are capable of? Our playing small serves no one. It's not easier. It's not safer. And yet? So many women are playing small and too afraid to truly back themselves and go for their biggest dreams!

Believing in yourself is an incredible force of power that starts with you. Whether you want to change the world, invent an incredible product, take on the big brands, inspire people, take your business global or start a movement there's never been a better time to get started!

This book is for anyone who knows there's more for them. Anyone who knows they have the power and potential inside them to achieve their goals and for anyone who knows that it's time to step up and back themselves.

Written by 27 women who have learnt how to do it, they will guide you through the steps to back yourself and reach your dreams whatever they may be. Combining inspirational stories and expert business advice, this book shares the life-changing power of what can happen when you learn how to back yourself.

Back Yourself gives back

This book gives back! Proceeds from the sale of 'Back Yourself' go to providing women in business with scholarships to enable them to receive support, mentoring and education through The Women's Business School.

Aligning with the United Nations goals for sustainable development, The Women's Business School scholarships are awarded to women in remote and rural areas, Indigenous women, migrant women, women with disability and those facing financial hardship.

We believe that investing in women is the most powerful way to change the world and these scholarships provide opportunities for deserving women to participate in Ignite a 6 month incubator program for early stage startups and businesses and Accelerate a 6 month accelerator program for high potential and experienced entrepreneurs ready to scale their companies and expand globally.

You can read more about the work of The Women's Business School Scholarship Program and how they're changing the world by investing in women here:

thewomensbusinessschool.com/scholarship

Part One

The Importance of Passion: Why Your Niche Needs to Be You

KYLIE MORT

To say one cannot see the forest for the trees is to assume one knows what a forest looks like. Yet what if our preconception of what a forest is fails us? Recently I discovered something so impactful, it has completely transformed my modus operandi. The beauty of hindsight; finally viewing the journey through the beginner's mind and therein lie the clues. What was once so invisible is now starkly telling. Proverbially, you do not know what you do not know, until you know it. If only you could have recognised what you could not envisage. So where is one to start?

Being an entrepreneur necessitates courage, fortitude, and resolve. Yet are these ultimately the *foundations* of success? I am the granddaughter of a highly educated dutchman who survived the P.O.W camps of World War II. The daughter of an entrepreneurial father cruelly erased from my journey all too soon. What have I learnt from my linage of visionaries? To back myself, using inner strength and determination to conquer adversity and aspire ever higher. Yet what sustains me? The tenacious and inspirational forebears? No. It is the little voice that whispers to my heart that I cannot give up on something that is an integral part of who I am. What I can now elucidate clearly is so much more precious to you, my dear reader, because you already know it.

'Follow your passion.
It will lead you to your purpose.'
OPRAH WINFREY

Internal motivation is the difference between those who dream and those who do. The driving force behind the ambition and the magic creating a future held steadfastly in the mind's eye. It is your own unique vision, and be it celebrated or denigrated, it remains unquestionable: no one will ever see what you see. You can paint a picture; illustrate it with vivid aspirations and an entire rich palette of ideals, values, and outcomes. Yet in the end, you are attempting to explain the inner mechanisms of the whirring entrepreneurial mind. To hold faith in this vision and stay true to the purpose rooted herein, you must anchor in the unbreakable resilience of undeniable passion.

The adage says with *age* comes wisdom, yet it is *time*; time to recognise your journey, to recognise your influence over that journey and inevitably, time to heed those who have journeyed before you. In this way, it is not ageing that matters, but the time taken to *truly see yourself.*

It took me many years to recognise my journey. Surveying now, the road that stretches out toward my distant childhood-self, I see unfamiliar gorges I do not recall surpassing and craggy outlooks that now overlook alternate landscapes. For too long I focused on besting my adversaries, lording over my conquests, and all the while plagued by a siege mentality that made a mental prison of my success. Now I see myself, unfettered, empowered and free.

Your mindset is your most powerful weapon, but to wield such a weapon is dangerous if you are not fully aware of its power to manifest the pathway that rises towards your feet. What are you creating with your inner monologue? What narrative do you construct?

Most importantly, focus on that which you control, and contextually, as the camera of your narrative zooms out, and the detail of your career and family shrink, ultimately, there is only you. You control that which you hold inside you, fuelled by the passion of your soul. Therefore, a business plan starts with a Vision Statement portraying the mountaintop you seek, followed by intricate mappings of the Mission Statement, each step you will take skyward. Specifically, though, they map your purpose, the *why* behind the what. A business that fails to plan, plans to fail, and the quickest way to get lost in the convoluted valleys and peaks of the commercial landscape is to forget where you were going in the beginning. Your Vision and Mission Statement anchor you to your truth, reminding you of why you started. Because in the end, if you have passion you have a gift, and who are you not to share it with the world?

'In order to be irreplaceable,
one must always be different.'
COCO CHANEL

Many businesses begin with a need an entrepreneurial mind has the motivation to meet. In many cases, filling a required niche is enough. Yet I have found through my own diversified rise to owning multiple award-winning companies that to truly inspire, it needs to be something only you can give. What is it that you alone can offer the world? What makes you unique? It is not enough to convince someone to buy what you offer; show them they cannot see a future without it.

There are those among us who have the intrinsic art of persuasion. The captivating, who hypnotise not just with strategy, but personality itself. I am not this person, yet still I have people flock to me. I have a waiting list for my mentorship and loyal referrals. Consequently, I need not convince people of anything; I have no marketing budget or sales funnel, but I know how they work.

A dear business mentor insisted on equipping me with these commercial skills. This coaching was so similar to my academic mentoring: taking the sales call and inverting it just as I do the essay structure, chipping away the broader detail to reveal the precious contention lying in wait. Illuminating the perception that has been there all along, like the pearl so successfully secreted away in the dynamic organism of the oyster shell. However, where I tailor arguments in the tapestry of essays, my mentor's artistry lay in revealing pain points to the consumer. Exposing to their cognisant sensory system the critical absence, and how indeed, now they are conscious of this lack, the solution is at hand within this newly discovered niche. The shucked shell of the oyster allowing one's innate wisdom to reconcile itself with the need for the proffered solution.

His skilful manipulation was mesmerising, as over and again he personified the business proposition. I revelled in the simplicity but found it superfluous to my goals. Why didn't I need the dynamism of his mastery? Because selling a service is not my purpose. My mentorship is my passion and as thus, it is not a job, not something to espouse and solicit clients for, but to provide to those who seek me. When you find your purpose, when you harness your passion, it is not something you leave outside the business hours of 9-to-5. I am consumed by it and constantly ruminate on new ideas; jolted with epiphanies and seeking new knowledge for a more holistic approach to what it is I offer in its own rareness. My strength comes from my passion, and my success, from my obsession with it.

'Just be yourself, there is no one better.'
TAYLOR SWIFT

Thus far I have instructed on envisioning your passion and building a pathway to monetise it, yet it would be disingenuous of me to claim this is what I did. This is what I *now know*. You build your authenticity and congruency on past versions of yourself. So much of my own story is found in the psychology of adolescent minds, not only as a mentor, but as an isolated child that lacked one. I base my passion on the need to understand that time, to analyse mistakes and recognise pathways that portend the same fate. Strengthening individuals with knowledge that will assist them in being their best self and making choices that will build their personal confidence and capabilities to live their best life.

For such a long time I could not see the forest for the trees and my pre-conceptions failed me. I cannot rewrite my past, but I can understand the territory. The adolescent mind is rapidly developing and irrational, biologically unique and stereotypically uncertain, as young people struggle with the question: who am I? The inherent characteristics burgeoning are but seeds in the wind, not yet earthbound, not yet identifiable as the mighty oak to be, yet with the clarity of hindsight, the signs were there. The inclination, the fire, the passion was always there. Stay true to that authentic seed and you will remain effortlessly congruent.

Many of us remain limited by the perspectives of those who have known us. Those who, because of once knowing a version of us, will consciously or not, maliciously, or not, entrap us with a label that announces to the world that this is who we *are*. Yet the complexity that is you, will, and must change, as you evolve and adapt to new knowledge. It is consistently your responsibility to shape your future with that which you now know. Every morning you can set the intention for what you can achieve. What is stopping you? You can defy the odds and defend your position and be anything you want to be! But that is just the point, isn't it? Do you want it? What is it that lights your soul on fire? Sometimes, if we are honest with ourselves, when someone proclaims, 'go back to what you are good at,' there is no need to be defensive, reactionary, or defiant. You may achieve extraordinary things, but perhaps they see it is not your passion and not where your destiny lies.

And now, dear reader, you may be confused. Perplexed by the way I have energetically asserted for you to seek your passion. Discover yourself! Start the journey! Stay the course! And now? Give up? Go back? And yet… you already know, don't you? In your heart of hearts, you know we are all on a different pathway. Just as you could be the stifled soul who has never trusted herself to fly, you could indeed be in juxtaposition, the one who is lost in the expanse of an enterprise which does not feed your soul. Someone who has forgotten the Vision and Mission of her passion. Someone who needs to reconnect with her why.

It matters not where you find yourself because you are exactly where you need to be. Wherever you are, whoever you are, start now:

REIMAGINE yourself. You are not who they see; you are not your actions, nor your past, nor a helpless product of your immediate environment. Reimagine your life.

REDESIGN yourself. The beauty of self-actualisation is that it comes from within, you need not wait for someone to tell you it is time. Envision a melding of the pathway that brought you here and the new path you will take. Turn up the colour, the volume, the intensity and redesign your life.

RECREATE yourself. You are uniquely you, and your life thus far has been a lesson; the situations, the people, the places; whether they empower you, drain you, or threaten to break you. Be grateful for the lessons that created the unique design. You, that could only come from the journey, are the epitome of your own success. Recreate your life.

'It's time for you to make the contribution you were born to make.'
MARIE FORLEO

Empathy is understanding the emotions of another, and any teacher must also be the student, to embody the adversity, the doubt, and the imposter syndrome, as at one stage, we were all beginners, and we cannot lose touch with this. All experiences are teachers, and this moment is what you need to experience. Recognise the lesson. As for all learners of all ages, every growth edge is of critical importance. Do not back away from the challenge, do not surrender to the fear. Lean into it. Celebrate your feeling of not knowing, this is what will build you and inevitably, it will provide the opportunities you need.

REFRAME. The one voice always with you is your own, so do not let it work against you. Train your inner monologue to be your ally, as the subconscious mind is always listening. Reframing to find the positive is such a seemingly inconsequential step, but has the power to manifest a wholly different future.

REFLECT on the teachings you have been given. Each day, every challenge and every assistance are a teacher of equal measure. What can you use? What can influence the decisions you need to make?

How have you grown and what have you still to learn?

REFOCUS. Be flexible, yet more than reacting to uncontrollable external factors, stay true to the inner vision you control. As an empowered individual, you can evolve at any time. Give yourself permission. Continually evolving means we can adapt to any situation and overcome all obstacles. Your focus creates your future and even if you do not know what to focus on, remember what *not* to focus on. Manifestation is our one true constant, whether you are conscious of it or not.

Mindfulness is the state of recognising your awareness. The human brain can analyse, recognise, and automatically react within seconds. Known processes are stored and replayed without consciousness, creating space for ever more activity. Herein lies the oversimplification, though; are you habitually proceeding with blind commitment? We are fallible creatures, and reactionary prevalence is not advantageous. Successful past responses may not still serve you now. Do not let blind commitment derail your conviction. Be as resolute as a mountain in your vision, but as flexible as the waterways you will navigate in your mission.

> *'I don't have to prove anything to anyone. I only have to follow my heart and concentrate on what I want to say to the world. I run my world.'*
>
> **BEYONCE**

You are uniquely gifted with the determination to achieve the most wondrous accomplishments. Yet remember, just because you can, does not mean you should. If I have learnt anything from my own tumultuous journey, it is that the only true goal is peace, and with this comes fulfilment. She who has a passion not realised will not be at peace, just as she who toils at that which does not feed her soul will feel an unexplainable emptiness. We find peace when priorities and passion align. What do you want to say to the world? Everyone has their own reason for penning the narrative they choose. You must recognise this choice and own your voice. If you could end every day with a sense of accomplishment, what would you do to create that? What would you give to create that? There are the dreamers and the doers. The difference lies in the effort given to intention.

Academic clients and I discuss at length the concepts and themes surrounding a text. We unfurl the world of the novel, revealing thematic implications and perspectives that abound amongst limitless interpretations. We then spend just as long scaffolding the essay, as after revealing the multifaceted depths I then need to guide my mentees back to a concise and powerful contention. One cannot clearly articulate their vision if they are meandering haphazardly through the complexity of the narrative landscape. One must focus on a clear objective, leading the reader on a journey that will feel autonomous, yet driven artfully by a powerful intention. This is essay mastery. How powerful is your intention? How consistent is it? How reliable?

More importantly, is it the direction you chose? Is your current course aligning your priorities and your passion? Is this direction serving you? The world is one of endless commitment and activity. We are constantly bombarded with stimuli and the speed at which we keep pace with our environment can detract from our ability to turn inward and seek the unparalleled knowledge we hold within us. A knowledge, so intimate and intuitive, that if we spend enough time referring to it, we'd realise the answers were with us all along. Take the time to seek your truth, avail yourself of the guidance of wise individuals, but always remember your true path begins inside you. You will find your most valuable perception by meditating on your own vision, contemplating your unique mission, and aligning with your passion.

Within the pages of this book, I have sought to guide you back to your own strength, build on the lessons from the past, heed the teacher in every situation, and lean into the grow edge of new knowledge. Do not be afraid to reimagine, redesign and recreate yourself and your life. Remember as you reframe, reflect, and refocus, that there is both strength and weakness in consistency; be aware of when each will apply. Have empathy for others by truly seeking to understand their journey and seek fulfilment through recognising what will bring you peace, as this is your sincerest goal.

If I may, I would like to leave you with advice from a yoga teacher who has found peace and fulfilment in stillness. A stillness she knew was missing, knew would be beneficial but never truly realised was so extraordinarily vital. Yoga is an ancient knowledge, passed down for thousands of years, based not on a pliable body, but a flexible mind. Surprisingly, there are many correlations between the blistering speed of my commercial investment training and the enlightening stillness of my role as the student-yogi. Through *Shoshin*, harnessing the inquisitiveness and openness of abandoning pre-conceived ideas, I went on a journey of self-actualisation and found *Santosha,* contentment. The map is not the territory. All we perceive, we view through the myriad of filters we have accumulated along our journey. If you are to see the forest, to truly awaken and view the entire landscape you must be still, still enough to perceive the little whispers that have been there all along. The tiny clues that have blown along the winds of time, guiding you to where you now sit, contemplating your role. Do you feel your power? Your passion? Sit comfortably, with a straight back, roll your shoulders back and breathe deeply, now, close your eyes, and listen…

KYLIE MORT: Author, educational mentor & performance coach

In essence, I am a teacher, not only the qualified and registered teacher of multiple industries, but a teacher at heart. It has always been my passion. I became a teacher after surviving the terrors of an unhappy and abusive journey through childhood and adolescence.

My career began as a secondary school teacher of English, Literature, Humanities, Business and Commerce. I was acting Year 12 Coordinator at a rural secondary college when I resigned in 2009; my vision - *to help more.*

Since 2005, I'd been growing the first award-winning company, however, it was in 2010 when I began my second company that my purpose and passion aligned. I was a finalist in the Micro Business and People's Choice Awards in 2018 and after huge commercial expansion, a finalist in the AusMumpreneur Leadership Award in 2020.

In 2019, I joined a collaboration of inspirational businesswomen, writing for 'Empowered Women Empowering the World,' a cathartic journey of self-awakening, realising the potential I had to support others through analysing my own path.

Early in 2020, I wrote for 'Amazing Women of Influence' and was interviewed by Serena Carcasole, the founder of the Amazing Women Entrepreneurs Network, about my role as a woman of influence.

2020 also saw my acceptance to be an Executive Contributor for Brainz Magazine, a global magazine featuring industry leaders and expert coaches. I was also selected for the Brainz 500 Global list of 2020, a list of companies, entrepreneurs, and influential leaders worldwide, recognised for entrepreneurial success and dedication to helping others.

And in 2020 I wrote for *'Back Yourself.'* Contributing herein, I focused not on the power of my narrative, but the sharing of my gifts as a teacher. Abilities I continue to strengthen through my current study and research into Psychological Science at Deakin University.

Always the entrepreneur, always wanting to find a solution and fill a need, studying Business and Sales Mastery under Aaron Sansoni was a natural progression. However, it was when I trained in Neuro-Linguistic-Programming, Ericksonian Hypnosis and Performance Coaching, certified through the Global Speaking and Coaching Authority, that I realised I needed to realign my purpose and my passion.

Securing my qualification and registration as a yoga teacher, I have now come home to passion writing as an international author and for global magazines, and tailoring bespoke mentoring packages for individuals, supporting academic, physical, and personal advancement and success.

www.kyliemort.com.au

How to make a difference with your business

BRENDA KEANE

I can't really say where it started, this feeling I often felt of needing to give back, but I can say it was something I saw in our house as we grew up. We didn't have a lot of money when I was young, but my dad always gave back what he did have and that was his time. He coached young kids of legacy in gymnastics and coached footy teams on weekends. My mother was a foster mother for babies waiting to be adopted in the late 60s early 70s. Over the years, they've also fostered children overseas through World Vision, where they gave a regular amount each month to the charity for a child. We would receive updates with photos and stories of their lives, which fascinated me. These kids were always happy.

For me, I just know I came to a point in my life where I felt a strong need and a want to give back to my community.

Leaving a mark, or making a difference to your own community, or maybe if you're thinking big, the world is not for everyone, but it is something that is important to me. Additionally, not everyone wants to use their business to give back. Their Business goals may be to make as much profit as they can, to retire early and do what makes them happy. We choose our own destiny and I believe as long as what you do brings you joy, then that's ok.

There is, however, scientific evidence that altruistic behaviour releases endorphins to the brain, producing the positive feeling known as the "Helpers High." Just one of many benefits to being philanthropic in your business.

A 2008 study by Harvard Business School professor Michael Norton and colleagues found that giving money to someone else lifted participants' happiness more that spending it on themselves. (Despite participants' prediction that spending on themselves would make them happier.) Happiness expert Sonja Lyubomirsky, a professor of psychology at the University of California, Riverside, saw similar results when she asked people to perform five acts of kindness each week for six weeks.

PART 1

Values, Visions and Mission Statements

If you are going to include giving back or donations as such, then this should be included in your mission/vision statements, or be included as a Value.

When you had your business idea and then created your business, you will have had an idea of the product and/or service you will provide and what the purpose of that product and/or service is. For example, let's use my Business - active wear. You will have some values around the product, how it will be made, maybe where, and some values which are just a part of who you are. Are you kind? Are you vegan? And are you religious? Did you get treated well growing up? etc., The generosity you saw from and to others, these will all form part of your values, and some will become a part of your business values.

We can separate them as you don't have to have all or even any, but it helps others understand what you're doing and what you stand for. It can even sometimes remind you about what your purpose is and whether you are heading down the right path.

Your **Vision** is where you see the business going, where will the business end up, what are, for want of a better word, the goals of the business. This will also assist team members to see where the business wants to go and ensure they are also working towards achieving the same outcome.

The **Mission** statement for a business is often is woven in with the vision statement, but for me the mission statement is the reason for the business or the objective/purpose of the business. It tells my customers and the team what we are about and why we are different. Why they want to buy our product and not someone else's. It will tell them what we do as a brand, how we do it and what we care about and want to be known for.

If your mission is to give back through your business, then including this in the mission statement is as important as the need to have an overall mission and/or vision statement. Along with a list of values for your business, which are available to your customers and your team.

These will help to stay focused on the end goal, a reminder of what we are in business for and although not spelled out, one of our missions is to include making a living for ourselves.

Our Mission statement is:
BeKeane Activewear will create a range of activewear for EVERYbody accommodating their functional needs. Our products will be high-quality fabric, ethically sourced and excellent craftsmanship. They will always be fun, functional and inclusive. They will make everyone look and feel fabulous.

BeKeane activewear supports diversity and inclusion in sports and endeavours to give back to those lesser-known sports. We also support causes which have impacted us personally. We work to raise funds and awareness for these sports and charities that provide a safe space for everyone.

If you are interested to know what we see as our values, these are ours. We always strive to be

- kind
- patient
- honest
- genuine, allowing everyone to be their true self
- work with suppliers, manufacturers and other brands with similar values

And our vision is:
To see BeKeane Activewear as a global brand, and household name/go to for inclusive, quality activewear! To be able to continue to give back through the sale of our activewear and make a difference one pair of leggings at a time!

To support our mission statement, our range goes from a 6-38 for ladies, 4-14 for kids, and an XXS - 6XL for men. Additionally, we also make bespoke garments for Paralympians, longer and shorter legs on request. This is an example of how we are meeting our mission of having activewear for EVERYbody. We live our values every day. Our visions work is being done through leggings campaigns which I will talk about later.

PART 2

Determining the end goal

If you have decided you want to give back in some way, it's important for you to determine what format that will take. Even if you don't think it's for you, you can still think about the things that keep you up at night or get you bounding out of bed.

Understanding how you want to make a difference is the key to ensuring you don't overwhelm yourself in the early days. What are you passionate about? Is it an ecological thing? Is it donating money to charities? Is it volunteering? Is it giving clothes or products to the needy? There are so many formats giving back can take.

Take some time to think about the things you are passionate about and really feel you want to change in that particular area.

Something I did was to think about what things I felt strongly about and things which had affected my life already. Even things I didn't want to happen to anyone else, and also things that brought me joy, and so I wanted to help others feel the same way. I knew I was passionate about women helping women, supporting them and lifting them up, giving them a voice and making sure they understood their strength and resilience. I knew I didn't want anyone to be in a violent marriage with no voice and nowhere to turn, believing they were worthless. And I knew I felt a woman's body was her own business and beautiful in all its shapes and sizes and the amazing things we as women go through and can achieve. I also knew I wanted everyone to feel included and never be excluded for any reason whatsoever.

So, I knew anything along those lines would sit well for me to give back to and make a difference.

I also thought about how I could give back, being realistic about what I would have available easily in the initial few years.

I didn't have a lot of time at the start as I was just launching my business, working fulltime, and a mother. I had previously given time, working for the Salvation Army cafe in the Melbourne CBD once a month serving breakfasts and lunches. This was fun, and as I had nothing else to give, it made me feel good about myself as a person. But it wasn't practical in my initial business years and so I decided early on that it would need to be through the sale of product, or donations we could give back.

Once you have found the thing/s you're really passionate about, and if maybe there is more than one, that's fine. Probably best to decide which will be your first project. I started small in the first couple of years as I needed to allow time to let the business find its rhythm and grow. You will find the right time for you too. Sometimes an opportunity just arises when other businesses or local community groups approach you and you're off and giving back to the community before you know it.

When you have something you are passionate about, and really want to make a difference, you will put together a plan on how to make it work. It could be just as simple as a list, or it could have dates you want to achieve things by. Always ask others how they have done things. People are always happy to share, but just know what the end result is you're looking for and ensure that is where you are moving towards. This will help you focus on a desired outcome.

PART 3

Surrounding yourself with the "right" people

You may be just starting out and thinking to yourself, *'I can barely afford myself, let alone the right people,'* and then adding to the mix the giving back part. So, let's talk about what I mean by the right people. Who are your supporters, your customers, the people who make or deliver your product and/service? If and when you have them, your team members and your peers must be the right people too.

Ensure people you work with or who work for you have the same or similar values as your business. Those who support your mission and think in a similar way to you about the things you are looking to make a difference in the world with. They are the people you need to choose wisely.

When working with your suppliers/manufacturers, tell them about your plans for giving back. If you have chosen the right people, they may even be interested in being a part of it, which is a bonus for everyone.

An example is when I wanted to create a range of kids' leggings to give back to Taryn Brumfit's "kids embrace" documentary. I spoke to my designer and explained what I was doing and how the leggings had to convey body positive and just positive in general messages and how a percentage would go to the campaign. She told me how much she loved Taryn and her messages about body positivity and wanted to do the design as part of her donation to the campaign, so it was a win-win there. She found a way to give back, and we could give even more. Share your ideas as many people want to participate but are often not sure how to.

I have always chosen people to work with who have been recommended to me. I feel this recommendation ensures the person will have similar values. I also ask about what's important to them, and ensure they understand our values and mission and feel they are also comfortable with our end goal.

I made a few mistakes when I first started out in thinking it was more important to get runs on the board and a product out, even if I felt uneasy about some of the work being done. In the end, I realised it is not worth compromising your values, or your mission for a faster outcome, if it is not to the standard you really want. You will not be happy; it will not bring you joy and it can tarnish your reputation.

If, like us, it's important your product is made ethically, then you need to have the hard conversations about how they work, the hours, the payments, the ages, the diversity of their employment practices, and above all respect, for especially women. If you're unable to visit, ask for photos and check what is going on, ask for references. Ensure you are comfortable and your values are being met. If you want to be looking after the environment, again, ask questions that will satisfy the values you have about waste, recycling, fabrics, carbon emissions and footprints... Whatever is key to your core values, ensure you do the research before forming any partnership for team or supplier/ manufacturers.

I think it's important to remember we are all human; we all make mistakes or errors in our judgement. Once you know your values have been compromised, then it's more than ok to cut yourself off from or stop trading with people who you are not comfortable with or who are not a fit for your business. This includes people who you may feel you need at the time or can't do without. There is always a way.

PART 4

Judging when will you be ready to make a difference

Once you've decided what you want to do regarding giving back or making your difference to your chosen passion, doesn't mean it has to be immediate. You may have a mission statement to give xyz to charity or donate X number of hours to a charitable organisation a month, but you choose when it begins.

It means you have a plan that at some point you will make this something that is done in your business.

It may not be done in your first year of Business or your second or third, but it is there and it is something you know and your team and customer, suppliers all know you are working towards.

I started quite small and in my first year I gave donations to some charities that were making handbooks for the local community about programs available for youth. It meant I had my logo in the handbook as a supporter. I sponsored the local Auskick sausage sizzle, which meant they put our name and logo in the newsletter and announced us as the sponsor.

Always get to know your chosen charity. Obviously, Google is your friend, but also call them and talk to them about what they do, how they do it, do they get other funding, how long have they been going, what do they need. Not all charities need money. Then make your informed choice about where you will put your energy into raising funds/awareness and time.

In our second year, we would donate a door/raffle prize when we were approached by local groups (maybe a women's gym, local schools/kinder etc.) This got our name out also and again gave something to help others raise funds. We also gave away discount vouchers and buffs for women's events so they could provide participants with a goodie bag for their attendance. We also kicked off our kids' embrace leggings, where a percentage of the sales go to the charity. This is a fun one as the buyers know they are giving back too.

We now have several legging designs where some profits are donated to different charities dependent sometimes on who the artist for the design chooses or in some cases we have chosen. These charities have all been chosen because of personal impacts and growth, and being able to give back to them gives us joy and releases the happy natural high endorphins.

When you decide how you are giving back, if it is a product or service, ensure you are realistic about how much of the profit or sale you want to give back. Any charity will be more than grateful for any amount, and whilst we want to make a difference, you do not want to put yourself out of business either. Then no one wins.

PART 5

When the effort didn't feel like you made a difference

Sometimes you can put a lot of time, resources and effort into project or collaboration. But when the results come through or you are hit with roadblocks along the way you can feel a little flat or disappointed that it wasn't really what you had hoped for or planned for.

This happened to us this year. We partnered with our biggest Charity to date "The Hunger Project." You may have heard of them. Their Mission is "*To end hunger and poverty by pioneering sustainable, grassroots, women-centred strategies and advocating for their widespread adoption in countries throughout the world.*"

I'd already donated some money to the Hunger Project through another business owner and came to know more about what they do. I loved the way they worked and that they don't just hand out money to communities struggling with poverty and starvation, but they teach them how to be sustainable and support themselves. They teach the women, which again was a big tick for me, and they give back the dignity to these communities as they become so proud of what they have been able to achieve.

So, we partnered with them and worked on a design for our THP leggings which would raise money for this cause. We found people like to get something for their donation, but also know that part of the purchase is going to a worthwhile cause. The launch date had been set, and it had taken us almost six months during a global pandemic to come to fruition.

We almost did not make this launch date. This is why I say pick a charity or cause you are passionate about and truly believe in as we could easily have just given up and said it's too hard.

Our manufacturers shut down, so we had a design and a launch but no product. Our manufacturers knew how important this was to us and so once they could, with a skeleton staff, they made us enough leggings for our booked in photoshoot. We had models from the THP team and our community. We had a photographer, and a videographer booked, and then (because we are Victoria-based) were locked down again. So, no photoshoot, no gatherings, no deliveries. Our leggings are now in transit who knows where?

Again, we could have given up, but this was important. We decided we would get all the models to take their own shots, deliver them each prop, and organise a zoom party to bring us all together and take some fun photos and videos. We hired an accommodating videographer, not our original, and once we had taken all our shots and videos, sent them to the lovely Nick to piece together for our launch.

Oh, and did I mention the shoot date has arrived and still no leggings, which led me to begging and pleading with DHL to allow an approved courier on site on a Sunday to pick up our delivery. Which they had to find at the depot and deliver so my husband (they come in handy sometimes), and I could hand deliver all over Melbourne to our models in time for the launch party.

This almost stopped us but we decided nothing could stop strong determined women who believed in the charity and the reason we were doing this in getting together, having fun and sending their message out. If we were that determined then surely, we could be part of ending hunger by 2030.

Knowing the work that THP does and hearing stories for the differences that have been made in people's lives makes us proud to be involved.

Being so passionate about this project and working on the launch for months, when we launched on International Friendship Day, I really felt we would sell hundreds of leggings. When the initial sell through was only 21 pairs of leggings and two crop tops, I was very disappointed.

It meant our donation to the hunger project initially was $389:00.

I really felt we had let them down, but my amazing team at THP swiftly reminded me of what a difference just $20 makes.

$20 could train 16 community members in Maternal and Child Health and Nutrition in Africa. By teaching mothers about how they can feed their children nutritious food that is locally available, mothers can ensure their children avoid malnutrition.

This reminded me that Little by Little, a little becomes a lot.

It's so important to remember it doesn't matter how big or small the effort or amount, every little bit makes a difference to someone. We are so proud of our efforts and will continue to give back through THP and our other charities and feel the joy of making a difference by giving back through our business.

Conclusion

As you think about what we have talked about and decide for yourself if you want to include giving to charities or giving back your time or something else altogether, I suggest you consider:

- Who you can ask questions of? Do you have a network of women, or peers? There are loads of Facebook groups with entrepreneurs always available to provide advice or steer you to how they may have done things or charities they have worked with.
- What are your values? Do you have a vision or mission statement that includes giving back?
- Should you give back through your business? Is it really the

right fit for your business, or even you? Not everyone chooses to give back.

- How do you want to give back? What is the format for you? Is it money, time, resources? Perhaps something you make and donate? Whatever you decide, it needs to be right for you.
- Are you surrounded by the right people? If not, how do you change that?
- When will the time be right for you? Do you have a plan to help you determine when you will be ready? And if not now, it can be something much further down the track.

If you have started your business, congratulations! That was the hardest decision and took courage now go forward and I hope you make a difference with your business in the world somehow.

BRENDA KEANE

I am a mother, wife, sister, aunt, daughter, niece, a friend, an employee and a Business Owner.

I am also a Personal Trainer (PT) and a curvy woman. As a PT and a bigger woman, I was tired of seeing luscious curvy women trying to exercise, or even get out for a walk in activewear, that rode up, fell down or both, was not made from quality fabrics, boring black and not put together well as not being designed for ample bosoms, yummy tummies and bootyful bottoms.

In 2007, a mum of four children (one of my greatest achievements, besides my business) , working long hours as a Project Manager, and with all the other hats we as women often wear, I felt that I did not have the time and certainly no money to start a business. I continually thought that someone else would come up with the idea and make an Australian plus size activewear range . Surely someone is noticing all these women who need to be catered for, surely someone with the money and brand power would do something.

There are some brands who have come on to the market since I recognised this was a problem needing an answer. None of the options goes above a size 24, none of the retailers carry very many of the larger sizes so they sell out quickly and not too many are Australian.

I recall the angst of trying to squeeze into a LJ or a Lulemon, body spilling over the top and out the bottom, barely able to breath, bend or squat and I still had this desire or should we say dream to create this range. the range for me and all curvy women like me- of activewear for everyBODY which would accommodate all of our functional and aesthetic needs. Which was Fun, Functional and

High Quality.

You need to know that I am not a very confident person. I am what is known as an extroverted- introvert. I manage depression, PTSD, High Blood Pressure, Migraines and Diabetes, but do not allow these to define me. I have very low self confidence, and don't believe in myself or my abilities, I have a voice constantly telling me that I might fail, or I can't do things, to the point where I have named her Elzabeth and I just tell her to mind her own business, and to believe in Be Keane activewear as much as I do, as the product I have created is brilliant! To add to the self doubt initially and I do not have a fashion industry background, which Elizabeth reminds me of when we have a setback, I am from grocery retail, and IT.

I have been through the whole, why would someone buy my product?, how will I make a product?, Where will I get money?, how will I sell that product?, and the list goes on, but I have also learnt that you don't have to have all the answers. At a weekend called Live Brave, run by Margie Warrell I pitched my idea to a room full of women, who were supportive and backed my idea 100%. They too were amazed at how no one else had done this, and their enthusiasm reinforced what I knew, and so I decided to back myself and kick off Be Keane Activewear. I did learn from this weekend that women together can do amazing things and the continued support of these women has been invaluable.

It has taken three years to bring me to where I am now and it's been a fun ride, ups and downs, and we have widened our range due to popular demand, we started off from a 12-38 and now we start at a 6. We now also have mens tights and kids and our Maternity range will be launching in November.

I get up every day because I want to hear about the women who love to wear our leggings and feel and look fabulous. This is what brings me joy everyday. Giving back to the community I live in and people not as fortunate as me, also brings me happiness and I have managed to ensure that it is one of the missions of BeKeane activewear, giving our products even more purpose than just a piece of clothing or self care products.

This is me warts and all and I am so Proud of my Brand and the difference a pair of leggings can make to many lives.

Be Kind

bekeanehealthyandfit.com.au

Carving your own pathway

EMMA ALLEN

If you asked me in my senior year what I saw myself doing a decade or two later, there's no way I could describe the life I live today. I'd be able to tell you my most important values, like family and justice, but I couldn't explain how things would play out in my life or career. All I knew was that for me to be happy, I had to do something I loved; to grow, I had to embrace every opportunity; and to succeed, I needed to show up every day ready to give everything a go.

My mentor at university, Dr Lydia Levleva, is a renowned sport psychologist. She once told me that 'there is no such thing as luck, it's merely preparation meeting opportunity.'

I live by this mantra because it puts us in a position to choose and influence the pathways we create for ourselves, even if we don't exactly know how it will unfold.

Some of us may recognise that we want to change direction but it's easy to fall onto a pathway that's expected of us. It could be our family's strong will, our own self-doubt or society's expectation for women to be primary carers and at the same time advocates women should forge a career. How many mothers are still the first phone call from the school if a child is sick? At some conscious level, we have to say, 'Hang on, this isn't what I want,' and have the courage to plan a new path.

The concept of carving your own pathway works on a personal level to create a way for the important things in your life to co-exist. From a business perspective, we must guide our businesses with clear direction and forward momentum. Therefore, the notion of carving means that with the tools we have available to us, we can persist day by day and move closer to our goals. That could be as simple as having the flexibility to actively participate in school activities, or upscaling your business.

Whatever your reason for starting business, you have everything at your fingertips, even if you don't know it yet. It doesn't matter if you were not born here, if you're twenty or even fifty. (My mother started her most successful and fulfilling business at fifty. See what I mean?). You don't have to be a male university graduate to be a business owner. Take every lesson that's strengthened your character and project that into your business.

"My definition of freedom is knowing who you are and then being it, no matter what anyone else is doing." - Pink

When you carve your own pathway, it may be different to what others envisage for you, so you really need to 'back yourself' and act on it. Things won't always go according to plan, but that doesn't mean you can't make it work. Set yourself free, make the most of what you have and *carve your own story!*

CLARITY OF DIRECTION

Where are you heading?

Alice came to a fork in the road. "Which road do I take?" she asked. "Where do you want to go?" responded the Cheshire Cat. "I don't know" Alice answered. "Then," said the cat, "it doesn't matter."

ALICE IN WONDERLAND

I started my first business in my 20s. It was incredibly exciting to be a 'business owner', so I perfected my product and invested in new equipment, logo design, website and all the things I thought I was supposed to do. I was focused on what I was going to deliver, but I didn't have a plan on how I would take it to market or the avenues which people would engage with me. Why wasn't my phone ringing off the hook with orders?

People kept talking about a niche. Wouldn't a niche mean I'd turn away potential paying customers?

When I launched Active Property Investing (API), it was more than a decade later. I had a strong career in corporate and business development behind me, and this time the business had a different focus. API was built on a distinct and solid 'why'.

People were buying property to make money, but did they know how to assess the risks, costs and more importantly, if it was feasible for their family? API is a bridge of fundamental steps to move people from thinking about investing to understanding, identifying, and successfully purchasing property that fits their objectives. I was tired of real estate being about 'selling' and wanted to shift the power to the buying process, so we developed a framework which upheld the high level of quality you need for a strong performing investment.

Consistency leads to stability and trust.

When you start your business, consider what you want the brand to stand for? API stands for quality; from the partnerships we have all the way down to the printing of our educational workbooks. What message do you want to send to your customers? We want them to know that they're important. What is the look and feel of your business? And how will their interaction be consistent with your messaging?

With a clear understanding of what we represent, we will move towards achieving our business goals in a way that aligns with our messaging. Being a brand of quality means that we don't engage in randomly cold-calling people to convince them to buy property. Instead, we aligned with well-respected professionals who have a similar ethos to educating people around finance and wealth creation. Nor do we utilise hard-selling tactics and fear mongering. Instead, we promote education and understanding.

Once your business is up and running, your strategic direction will also evolve. It's easy to direct a business in a market that is booming, but what happens when the environment changes? If the source of your customers dries up, then you might have to look for new ways of reaching leads. Turn to simple things like refer-a-friend, which costs nothing and is often an untapped source.

Find ways to connect with your audience like collaborating with other businesses or services that complement yours. There will come a time where you must be flexible, and maybe even adapt or pivot quickly, but there are values at the core of your business that you may never want to compromise. Stick with it as the quick, easy win may be money in the short-term, but the undoing of your hard work later.

A leader with clarity and one who acts with purpose creates an environment that is engaging, trustworthy and inspirational. Be brave and bold to stand for what you believe in and think about what legacy do you want to leave on the world?

RESOURCEFULNESS

Making the most of what you have

'It's not about how much you have, it's what you do with it that matters.'
EMMA ALLEN

If you're just starting your business and feel overwhelmed, remember we all had to start somewhere. There are countless businesses that started in someone's garage or stories of entrepreneurs who could only afford to produce one small batch of stock. What's important is that you are resourceful in utilising whatever you have access to.

My greatest inspiration has always been Mimi, my mother. Not only did she establish her Argentine Tango school at age fifty, she had the ability to dream up a concept and transform it into an event that was memorable and touched the hearts of hundreds of people. For many years I was by her side helping her ideas come to life. I especially loved the lead up to Christmas and the annual Tango Ball as its one of the largest events in the calendar and she poured so much soul and vision into it. Mimi didn't have the means to hire a staging company. Instead, her resourcefulness meant creating an atmosphere with the budget she had. She used her ingenuity to create ambiance through lighting, décor and her genuine warmth and love of people. She had a great talent for connecting ideas and promoting these events in a way that tickled people's imagination. I'm certain that she was actually in the business of creating memories and moments.

It's great 'entrepreneurial spirit' to create something out of nothing.

When you think you don't have enough to continue, be resourceful to move yourself forward along your pathway. Stop for a minute and challenge yourself to think outside the box because there's always more than one way to do things. For example, how many uses can you think of for a clothes peg? The beauty of carving your own pathway is that you can make the most of what you have without rhyme or reason.

You get to decide what you want to spend your time and money on, but when resources are limited, then prioritise based on what will get the best outcome for your objective. Hint: set smaller objectives to reach bigger goals!

During the last property downturn, we had to restrict our spending to sustain cash flow for an unknown period of time. We needed a quick and direct way to generate new exposure, so in recognising we had a stream of 'satisfied clients', we created the client journey that documented how everyday people were succeeding using our method. It was quick, simple, and engaging, so it was relatable and worked beautifully as a piece of free marketing.

There's no one type of investor, just like there isn't one type of business owner. It's commonly thought you need to be wealthy to invest in property, but in fact, it's quite the contrary. Property is the vehicle that makes people wealthy.

Our clients come from all walks of life with individual dreams and aspirations. They also have different professions with varying incomes, but this isn't to say that if you earn a moderate income, you can't utilise the vehicle of investing. It's a matter of making the most of the deposit and borrowing ability you have, then to modify the property search to identify an investment that will work for you. What's important is what we do with what we have, and that's why I named my business 'Active' property investing, because you need to be actively doing it to reap its rewards.

Think of abundance and keep an open mind when you look for ways to optimise what you have. There's no point being wasteful. Instead, allocate your resources based on what outcome you need at that time. With limited resources, it may take you a little longer, but you will get there with persistence.

Resourcefulness is an important skill in property investing, as it is in life and business. Making the most of what you have means that there is always a way, you just need to find it.

FINDING AND CREATING NEW OPPORTUNITIES

'If opportunity doesn't knock, build a door.'
MILTON BERLE

It's interesting how the world perceives success. Opportunities come hard and fast when you're already established, yet as a start-up, they seem harder to come by.

As business owners, we need to sharpen our awareness to recognise opportunity and be ready to even create our own ways of moving the business forward. Thinking back to the concepts earlier in this chapter, knowing what direction you are heading in and capitalising on everything you have is relevant to identifying opportunities.

To see opportunity, you need to look at the world through entrepreneurial eyes.

If you talk with people from different industries, their attention is attuned to the field they are most familiar with. For example, if you had a night out with friends and went to a restaurant, four people would notice different things. The foodie will be tasting every ingredient in the meal, and the marketer would have viewed the website prior to arrival. The interior designer would either be cringing or delighted about the décor, and the entrepreneur might be more interested in how smoothly the operation could deliver. Whatever we're wired to see will become more noticeable.

As business owners, we can develop our eye for opportunities by increasing our awareness of how things are connected. We can do this through close observation. - Be curious to how things impact the customers experience, and be open to exploring new avenues, starting new conversations and learning about other people and businesses to find ways that can help you move forward.

Opportunities can come in many forms. They could be new ways to improve your product or service; new channels to reach potential clients; partnerships where you have services that can dove-tail each other; expanding your offering; or an improved system or process that increases your efficiency.

Where you can see a connection, leverage the opportunity.

I noticed more and more young professionals were struggling to get into an already expensive property market. It's hard to save a deposit for a home when the median price is over ten times the average salary. Yet few people knew about *Rentvesting.* The concept of Rentvesting means they can continue renting where they want to live whilst capitalising their savings and investing where they can afford. It inspired me to write an eBook with practical tips for these investors, and we delivered workshops for the growing interest around this strategy. It was a simple value-add for people to learn and then engage our service to execute the strategy.

In more recent times, things like the pandemic place undue pressure on business and entrepreneurs. It means potentially tough times, where we could buckle or take this as an opportunity to evolve ourselves and our businesses. It can be incredibly stressful when you have salaries and overheads to pay but open your eyes and heart to doing things differently and carve a new path if you have to. All the while staying true to your core values and service philosophy.

Developing an eye for opportunity is about finding ways to keep you moving forward, but to also stay relevant and at the forefront of your industry. Everything is an opportunity! We just need to see it and act on it.

FOLLOWING YOUR INTUITION

'Follow your instinct, that's where true wisdom manifests itself.'

OPRAH WINFREY

Have you ever met with someone, only to walk away thinking, 'Gee, that didn't feel right.' Some of us get strong vibes. Others have to work a little harder to pick up on the nuances that indicate whether someone is genuine or more interested in their own agenda, possibly at the cost of yours.

Intuition helps us gauge whether something does or does not seem right.

When I established Active Property Investing, I made a promise to myself that I would always follow my intuition, and it has never let me down.

Partnerships in business can require a delicate balance. When you have a distinct sense of purpose, values and direction for your business, it's easier to make clear decisions that support this. I recall meeting with a new builder. He sounded like a good operator, had a good reputation, and worked in locations our clients liked. Yet his credibility came tumbling down when he said, 'Well, if they don't have the deposit, just tell them to put it on their credit card.' I shut that down there and then. No matter how profitable or appealing these offers might be, I would still walk away because the quick buck is never worth sacrificing the brand you've worked so hard to build.

On the flip side, when you find business partners who align with you, you'll be able to build *powerful partnerships.* These are the alliances where there's mutual respect and benefit. Where you add value to each other's businesses, and where you can collaborate, create and innovate together. These relationships are valuable and will strengthen your business immensely.

If you're hesitating, you may need to do further investigation into a matter or opportunity. Don't make a rushed decision, take your time to do the due diligence. Time to digest an opportunity gives your intuition the chance to assess it. With enough information and clarity your intuition may just say go for it. When things align with your values and business direction, the courage will be there to take the plunge.

Our intuition provides a valuable radar for our businesses. Stay connected with your staff, clients, partners and the environment that you are operating in, so you can pre-empt hurdles and navigate your way safely along your path. Likewise, when you sense opportunity, have the courage to follow your instinct and *go for it.*

PAVING A WAY FOR OTHERS TO SUCCEED

'Being successful isn't about being impressive, it's about being inspired.'
MICHELLE OBAMA

After the birth of our daughter, I left a global company to step into the property industry. A few years later, I was nine months pregnant with our son when I launched Active Property Investing (API). Having children seems to be a catalyst for propelling my career in wondrous directions, or perhaps it magnifies my determination towards shaping the life we desire. No matter how crazy the pursuit, I am forever cheered on by my biggest supporter, my husband Tony.

Carving your own pathway is a journey shared with the people around you. From a personal perspective, making business and motherhood co-exist has a deep-rooted purpose that drives me to constantly find ways to make it work. By juggling all these balls, I'll inevitably drop some, but I'm open to showing my children the full spectrum of emotions from triumphs to failures, so they can see that our journeys entail many shades of colour. We're all human, and we're incredibly resilient.

As business owners, there will have been many people who played even the smallest role in your success to date, so we have a chance to help them achieve their aspirations too. Share your vision with staff, clients and business partners in a way that inspires them to be the best they can be.

As a leader, I'm intrigued to understand the journey that each team member has embarked on and how I can help them succeed. I'm happy to invest the time to coach and accelerate their skill development, because if I can create an environment for them to thrive and feel valued, they will become the competitive edge that propels the business forward. We are all inter-connected, so the success of one person impacts the success of others. It makes us part of something bigger than ourselves.

Throughout my career, I've believed that if I succeed, then I should be helping others succeed too. As such, API's social responsibility *gives back* to local and international communities. Of all the properties we have built, we are most proud of the homes and schools we helped fund and gift to rural communities in Cambodia through the work of Australian social enterprise Global Village Housing (GVH). The simplest of things like clean drinking water and shelter dramatically changes the pathway for a family and community. Additionally, the gift of education is one we know will help generations of children in those villages and possibly be the catalyst to help many of them out of poverty.

We are passionate supporters of initiatives that empower women and girls like the *Striking Distance* documentary that breaks gender stereotypes. It normalises young girls and women's right to self-defence, self-worth and nurtures that undeniable fighting spirit because we believe that we can truly write our own rules. We also donate to women's shelters helping those escaping domestic violence because sometimes we are so deep in the woods that we need a community to help carve a way out. We need to path the way for our daughters and the next generation of women to value themselves and back themselves no matter what.

Most importantly is that we show people that the pathway we thought we were on is *not* set in stone, but rather that it's within our ability to change direction for a better life.

We are a global community, and these concepts apply wherever you live. Business ownership is not bound to a gender, age or race. It's about the creative minds with a vision taking small steps to deliver something of value. Over time, that chipping away carves a masterpiece that can bring you great business success but make it a journey that lifts others with you. Build more than a business, create your legacy.

'Fight for the things that you care about but do it in a way that will lead others to join you.'
RUTH BADER GINSBERG

CONCLUSION

Carving your own pathway is another way of saying 'act with clarity and direction and you can create the life or business that you desire.' In showing up every day mentally, physically, and emotionally, you will inevitably move forward.

Carving your own pathway will help you emanate on two levels.

As a business owner, it will guide you to build a brand that is true to your values, give you strength to keep going when things get tough and the courage to evolve and explore unchartered waters. The world we live in is saturated with information and imitation. It's fierce with competition and comparison. These are all distractions that can dangerously make you doubt or question yourself. Don't fall for it, stick to your purpose and remind yourself that you are the creator of this journey.

On a personal level, carving your own pathway empowers you to mastermind a way for the most important things in your life to co-exist. It's no longer a choice between family and career, but instead a way for us to thrive in motherhood whilst sharing our gifts and talents for the benefit of our business and the people around us.

Carving your own pathway is about backing yourself and acting on it.

It's not about trying to be perfect or getting everything right. It's the lessons and rewards we get from sticking it out; it's about freeing our creativity and entrepreneurial spirit; and it's the ingenuity that makes us resourceful and inspiring.

***Backing yourself* is the belief that whatever happens, you know you'll be okay. So, go ahead and carve your own story!**

EMMA ALLEN

My parents migrated to Australia with two suitcases, their two-year-old daughter (me) and chased their dreams and aspirations. They literally carved a pathway for themselves and my brother and I, fearless in how they tackled life, prejudice and the way in which they created opportunities to thrive.

Now I'm a mother of two energetic kids and the founder and director of Active Property Investing (API). My family is my greatest inspiration and my most valued achievement. They are the drive when I need it, the reward after a hard day, and in many ways, the catalyst for my business.

After the birth of my daughter, I left a multi-national corporation to follow my passion into the property industry. Years later, when I was nine months pregnant with our son, I took the plunge and designed a business based on my ethics and vision. It was incredibly liberating to create and grow a brand that would challenge the status quo, while striking a balance with the demands of motherhood. I'll be the first to admit the journey has been exhausting, but failure was never an option.

I'm inspired to make financial literacy and money talk less taboo. And I'm incredibly passionate about women and property and helping anyone who genuinely wants to learn about investing. It's so important to do this in an easy-to-understand way that is no nonsense and practical.

API is a service people trust and respect, the type I wish my parents had access to when I was a kid. So, we're sharing this method for everyday Australians to accelerate their wealth and do what many people perceive as unattainable. It's this purpose that drives me to keep carving my own pathway and create environments for everyone around me to continue to thrive and succeed.

API is an award-winning business recognised for outstanding service and finalists for accolades including the AusMumpreneur Awards and the Australian Small Business Awards. Yet some of our proudest moments are the houses we have built and gifted to poverty-stricken families and communities in rural Cambodia, including two schools in collaboration with Global Village Housing (GVH), an Australian social enterprise.

Developing a business in this fast-changing environment needs us to be alert and agile. We have a chance to do this in a way that is meaningful and fulfils our purpose. It's an exciting time to be in business, and I hope this inspires people to make the most of what they have and shape the life and business of their dreams.

Website: www.activepropertyinvesting.com.au
Facebook: https://www.facebook.com/activepropertyinvesting
Instagram: https://www.instagram.com/activepropertyinvesting

What drives you to do what you do

LEANNE MURNER

Here is where my passion to claim the success I now enjoy comes from. Losing everything in one bad decision, I have learnt to find a positive to all my negatives.

- Being told I could not go anywhere without qualifications, changing my mindset of failure, gave me the drive to succeed.
- Having a dream and believing in myself no matter my obstacles, perseverance and overcoming business adversities, and finding my purpose.
- Creating the best scenario for my business to run at its full potential. I keep an open mind and I am now not afraid to fail. Without failure, I fail to grow.
- Self-belief despite the negativity of my past haunting me, personal growth and learning to believe in myself.

- Hunger to follow my dreams, setting myself realistic goals, and after all the hard work and determination, I have learnt to let go of my past to move forward.

1. Humble beginnings

Where did your journey start? Why you are where you are today? The answer is… from life experiences. Starting out in any given industry with no business goal or business plan, trying to get known, standing out from the crowd, it is hard! But do not let these consume your ideas and goals. To get anywhere in life you need to have a purpose, why do you do what you do? What drives you? Where do you want to be in one, five, ten years? These are all the questions we ask ourselves repeatedly. I have for years, and at the age of forty, I have many life experiences under my belt and finally I feel I have found my life purpose. But I would not be where I am today if it were not for the journey I took, goals I had set, mistakes made, and people I have met. Or the risks taken, things I have learnt and most important of all, getting out of my comfort zone.

As a kid, every time I wanted to do something, I always had that negative influence, constantly being asked, 'Why do you want to do that?' or 'Who are you trying to impress?' and being told 'You will never go anywhere in life' and 'You have shit for brains.' I was terrible academically, and always at the bottom of my class throughout my school years. From a young age, I have always wanted to be successful and have people look up to me. Selling Avon at fifteen and being the top seller within eighteen months in ACT gave me the determination to succeed in other aspects of my life. Setting goals at such a young age and achieving them was something I was not brought up on. So, when I could work, I had the drive to prove I could go somewhere in life. In high school I worked three jobs, after school and weekends saving to buy my first home. At twenty, I did just that, purchasing my first home. Over the years I learnt you can't achieve anything if you have not set the intention of having the drive to succeed. It has definitely not been an easy ride. I've had ups and downs and everything taken from me at times, but I always got up and kept going, not letting that voice from my childhood win!

When I first started my business, I had friends snickering and questioning me how I could possibly run a business without a degree or some training. Having a degree does not guarantee you a successful business. Determination and hard work got me where I am today, and I picked up all the skills I needed along the way.

Researching the market, your target audience, branding, suppliers, services offered and standing out from the rest, got me where I am today. I did not follow the trends. I wanted to be different and provide products that were not available in the market. Australian Made has always been something I have been passionate about and hand making everything myself just made my products one of a kind.

2. Hard Lessons

No one ever goes through life without learning some hard lessons, some we seem to experience more than once and others we learn from. These lessons are in our life for a reason. How can we grow and achieve anything without learning from our mistakes? I do not know one person who has not gone through a rough patch, personal or business related that have not learnt a lesson from it. We all work so differently, and we all learn from our mistakes. Shit, I have been making mistakes my whole life, but I would not be where I am today if I didn't learn from them. After all, we are only human.

When I saved my first deposit for a house, my then partner gambled most of it away, so I then saved more and purchased my first home at twenty. I lost it twelve months later to an abusive relationship. It was the hardest time of my life. I was done having someone control me. How did I get myself into this situation? I'd turned into someone made to feel worthless, and it bought back memories of my childhood. And I'd worked so hard for so many years to reach that milestone in life, only to have it all taken away. I needed to learn from this mistake to not let it happen again. My home was only a material item that I could get another of… my life I couldn't! I sat questioning 'why me?' Why did I deserve this? This happened to teach me a lesson. Don't let anyone tell you what to do, make you feel worthless or control you. I came away from this such a strong person.

I experienced a Credit Card scam of $20K in my business, and I learnt don't always try to seal a deal without learning a little more about the customer. (Even if they have purchased from you before.) This man purchased something small and was sent to someone in partnership with him in Melbourne. Do some research, follow your gut. Some experiences seem too good to be true. I was focusing on the $ figure. I feel this was a hurdle I needed to experience, to learn who to trust. Not everyone has your best interest at heart. Some people do not have a conscious.

In life we come across people who like to control us; bosses, work colleagues, business partners. I also experienced this within my business with customers falling into this category with bullying and threats of destroying my business if I did not comply to their demands, regardless of how ridiculous the demands were. You feel guilty if their demands are not met because of the threats of damage, yet angry at yourself for not saying 'no' and standing your ground. Social media is a great tool, but it is used to people's advantage with threats. I felt like it was out of my control. You cannot be a 'yes' man and stand for what you believe in. I was not being appreciated in my business and was at the point I just wanted to go get a job where I wasn't just a number! A job that where when I left for the day, so did the responsibilities.

3. Family

This would have to be one of the biggest struggles everyone goes through finding that parenting / working balance, starting a family, returning to work and not being able to afford day-care and the list goes on! Thank God for grandparents! Family life is hard! Find that working / family routine that works in with your career. This was a struggle we experienced. You hear it so often. 'How can you raise a family and still work?' This was the question I asked myself daily. I did not want to go back to my job. I just flat out didn't want to work for anyone else! I wanted to be my own boss, drop the kids at school and work my own hours. Little did I know that you work so much harder when it is your own business.

Having five kids under six and still running a successful business was a big emotional struggle for me over the years. Our number four was not planned, and he arrived smack bang in peak season! I had him the Friday and was back in to work the Monday. I look back now and just do not know how I did it! It seemed to be such an emotional roller coaster for so many years, I feel like I missed out on so much of my family. I needed to re-evaluate my life when my parents split up after my number three was born. This gave me the opportunity to put myself and my needs first and the ability to let go of the most negative influences in my life.

I felt like I lost my family. It may not have been perfect, but it was all I'd known. I had one parent move on to a new family, which left me feeling a sense of abandonment. And I struggled with a sense of loneliness for so long. I just needed to work through the emotions and find myself, my purpose, and be a mother my boys looked up to. I had the most amazing supportive husband, who was my rock, staying positive and assuring me he was there for me through everything. He has made me the person I am today. Staying positive for the both of us, and I felt a sense of belonging. This is my family, this is my focus, and this is where I need to be.

I realised once you remove the toxicity from your life, things move forward in a positive way. I need to be the role model for my boys and show them that with whatever you go through, you can always pick yourself up and keep going. And I needed to give them the family connection I did not have growing up. I needed to enjoy life, enjoy my family, and put 100% into what I had sitting right in front of me. This was my focus now, moving forward and letting the past be the past. I heard my kids arguing. When I asked what they were fighting about, their reply was, 'I want to be like Mummy and work in the workshop.' 'No, I want to write a book like Mummy.' I just let them go. It was so nice to hear that they wanted to be just like their mumma.

4. Lesson learnt

Over capitalising in business / regrets in being a full control and learning when to let go and what to harness. How to get out of your comfort zone, fear of judgement, rejection, worrying about what people will think, wanting to do it all on your own, needing to learn to block out negative criticism but accept constructive criticism. You know deep down what you are capable of, and do not take people's opinions to heart, learn how to turn the negative into a positive.

In life, I feel like I had so many missed opportunities. I was in full control of my first business and no one would do my job better than me. This is where I fell out of love with what I was doing and lost that drive to grow. I was on the front line each day, doing it all. Doing everything for so many years, but too proud to ask for some help, so many things were starting to slide. Something I learnt was to offload work, to focus on the opportunities crossing our path I was too busy to see. Once I did, it was just too late. This business missed the boat, and I had lost my drive. I have learnt how you do anything is how you do everything. It was not my time. I needed to move forward to receive new opportunities.

I have learnt so much from this experience and with my new business, and I am doing the complete opposite. Now I take all feedback on board, take all opportunities in my stride, hire staff in the fields I need help with to focus on the growth, so we can take on bigger opportunities. Getting out of my comfort zone and being interviewed, talking about my story and being proud to tell it, not being embarrassed of where I ended up, I learnt from those mistakes and I was not making them again. The past was not going to determine my future.

Most of all, I have learnt how to love and trust myself, something I have never done before. I am in love with what I am doing and the love in return is just mind-blowing. Getting all the positive feedback at my amazing products; all my hard work was getting so well received and all this from learning what I did wrong with my past business. Find the right people to have in your life and learn to trust others. Do what you love where you are appreciated and not taken for granted. We also need to love what we do and do what really excites us, and gives us those belly butterflies, leaving us wanting more. There are no accidents in life, only missed opportunities, and it is up to us to make those connections.

5. Who would have thought?

When you remove the toxicity and negative thoughts from your life, things move forward in a positive way. Always being terrible academically, low in confidence and hating where I was in life, I can now say, 'Look at what I have achieved?' This is where I have embraced my drive. Learning to love myself, and who I have become. I did this. I am now where I am because of decisions I have made, lessons I have learnt, and removing people with negative influences on my life. This has given me the confidence to get where I am in life and is my why.

I experienced a life-changing opportunity being nominated for an award with AusMumpreneur. Reading the email, I then deleted it, thinking I was not smart enough for that. About a week later I looked again and thought, *What I have got to lose?* Then I applied. This was the turn in my life I needed to take a chance on. I ended up a finalist for sustainability. Wow! What the heck? So exciting and nervous. I went to Melbourne and sat with a room filled with hundreds of women, hearing their stories and thinking, *What am I doing here? Someone will listen to my story and think to themselves, 'You are just a mother with a little business that is going nowhere.'*

I was so out of my comfort zone. I felt I could not talk to anyone. Anytime I spoke, I just talked nervously and quickly ended so I could walk away. I pretty much set myself up for failure in every conversation I entered. I felt threatened by all these powerful women, wondered why they were all so supportive of each other, and thinking, *Who does that?* Learning quickly this is what that community was all about! By the next day, I then realised most of the women there were first timers too, some as nervous as me, and some more confident than others. Listening to the speakers, I was feeling so inspired and felt I needed a change. I came to realise how much I was not enjoying what I was doing, unappreciated, and from what I was hearing at the conference, this is not what business was about. You cannot move forward if you are hating what you are doing! I was so inspired by one woman's story - Karen McDermott. Her story gave me butterflies, her energy and passion for her business was so inspiring. I wanted to feel like that!

Coming home, I said to my husband, 'I want to do something new.' I did not realise how much I was hating what I was doing. I needed to feel that energy and passion as all those other women did. So, I created 5 Little Bears and started making Educational Resources. I feel I am now giving back, helping educate kids about Australia, and providing Australian-themed resources to the world. I have been working with two connections from the conference and have just published my first of a series of children's books, teaching kids about Australian Fauna and Flora.

This has really been a dream come true. I got out of my comfort zone, built confidence, and have proven you can still succeed in life if you put your mind to it. If I did not have that opportunity to open my eyes to all the possibilities and help that was out there, I am not sure where I would currently be in life. I now have an amazing community around me when needed, hearing their struggles, having a chat on those hard days, or just feeling lonely and know there will be someone I can call on. I did not have this among my friends. None had a business, and I just could not connect to any of them on a business level. They just did not understand. Surround yourself with positive people in similar vibrations as you. Their stories inspire yours. This community has been life changing for me. It is only up from here on in.

Do your research, who are you targeting, the trends, find that difference in what you do, look at what is missing in your market, to stand out, what makes you unique, set realistic goals to achieve. Anything you do in life, you need drive, passion, hunger to tackle it each day. No two days are the same and no business is sunshine and rainbows. There are some hard days and sometimes you just want to give up. You need to find your why. I questioned my 'why' for forty years, and every scenario I was thrown in to, I found the positive out of it to help me move forward to make me the person I am today. Hurdles are there to test us. All these hurdles I have experienced have led me to share my story with you. Do not have a victim's mindset. Things happen for you, not to you. You can always turn a negative into a positive, or at least get something positive out of it. Find your drive, do what you love. How does it make you feel? Bring those feelings into your passion.

My name is **LEANNE MURNER.** I am a wife to an amazing, supportive husband and mother to five inspiring young men. Since having my boys, I have always worked for myself. I am the owner of 5 Little Bears Pty Ltd. My business is an Australian-owned and operated business hand making Australian-themed sensory products, games, puzzles, and educational products.

My business came about after extensive research into trying to source Australian-themed educational resources. I found there was an obvious void in the market. With focusing on teaching Australian kids about their own backyard, 5 Little Bears was born. All my products are skilfully handmade in New South Wales, Australia and all our products are proudly Licenced Australian Made. My focus is to employ other mothers with flexible working hours to get them back into the workforce and work around school hours.

Having a business heavily focused on Australiana, I have written the first of a series of children's books teaching children about Australian Native Flora and Fauna called *Franki and the Banksia.*

I love getting inspired by nature on camping adventures with my boys. This is where I get most of my ideas and motivation to teach kids about the wonderful world we live in.

www.5littlebears.com.au

Daring to be different

HEIDI JONSSON

Daring Differently: How the courage to try new and unconventional things can build your resilience, self-belief, and empire. I've had such an amazing life and done so many things it's hard to put into one chapter, but there are some things that were absolutely necessary for all of them to occur; curiosity and a desire to learn something new, some self-belief and the courage to ask for help, a lot of resilience and perseverance to see it through, and someone willing to give me a go. Owning a business is hard, and in order for it to succeed and stand out from the rest, you need to get really clear on your point of difference. The following is a story of how I have 'dared to do things differently' and how doing that has benefitted so many people's lives.

The beginning

Growing up on a potato farm, we learnt early how to work hard. We learnt that in order to have nice things, and have memorable experiences, you had to go through great extremes. Farming is hard. You are constantly fighting something, be it, the weather, pests, diseases, mechanical breakdowns, emotional breakdowns, the bank, merchants. Everything is a struggle. I guess farmers are just ingrained with an internal grit, an inbuilt resilience that they pass on to their children. This upbringing is what I attribute to my own personal resilience and determination. As kids we hated working every weekend and school holidays, but as an adult, I'm thankful for the lessons I learned about never giving up. You just can't. There are too many things relying on you. So, you push on. And this is the attitude I've carried my whole life.

When I was thirteen and away at boarding school, I got a call from home one night to tell me that my five-year-old stepbrother, Simon, had been run over and killed on the farm. This was a tragedy that affected our family and the community in the deepest way. That was thirty-four years ago and still impacts our family. I think of Simon frequently, and his death is the driver for me to keep going and protect other families from unnecessary heartache.

PART 1

What do you mean girls can't do that?

When I was growing up, I didn't even know that gender was a thing that supposedly defines what you can and can't do. Until one day I got a rude shock when I wrote my mother's occupation as 'housewife' on a school form. She got really mad. My mother was a full-on feminist who kept telling me I could do anything, and to Dad I was another capable pair of hands on the farm. So the concept that girls 'don't do that' was never ingrained. Apparently being labelled just a housewife was offensive to Mother. She was a qualified draftsperson and a capable woman.

When Dad sold the farm where I was leading hand, and had a hands-on role in all aspects, I moved to the city to be with my boyfriend. I found myself in a situation where I had no town skills. I had to reinvent myself, but never felt comfortable. In 2002, our boy Brodie was born. All of a sudden, the handbrake came on and life as we knew it was changed. When our money was dwindling, Scott and I moved to Port Hedland, where he got a job in his trade as a diesel fitter. I got a job delivering parts and each day I'd have to go to the salt mine. On the wall of the salt mine office was a picture of the harvester. It was a big articulated Steiger Tractor, and the harvester it pulled was a mix between a potato and cane harvester. Right up my alley. Every day, I'd say to the guy, 'I'm going to drive that one day.'

Now everyone knew, to get a job at the mine, you had to wait for someone to die! It was one of the most sought-after jobs in Hedland. To my surprise one day, the fellow said, 'You know, I hear they're hiring.' I was so excited. I got the number for the supervisor, Bruce, and pestered him, until one day he said, 'Look, it's unlikely you'll get a start, but meet me here Tuesday night at 6pm for a trial.' BAM! Here was my opportunity. I showed up, Bruce met me and took me to where they were harvesting. He showed me the controls and how to operate the harvester, then got back in his Ute and parked out of the way. I loaded three trucks, then, when I got back in the Ute he asked, 'So how did you go?'

'I loved it!' I said. 'That was awesome!'

His next words were, 'So when can you start?'

I could have kissed him. I gave my other job four days' notice, then started my dream job at the salt mine as the first female plant operator in the thirty-year history of the mine.

It was tough. Not only did I have a whole crew of men who didn't like me for various reasons, I was also inexperienced on all the other plant procedures and not many of the guys would help me learn. 'You'll be right, girly,' is about all I'd get. But I was most certainly not 'right.' I'd go home in tears most days from frustration of doing a crap job, or from feeling alone. I'm sure they all, bar a few, wanted me to fail, but it just made me determined to do better tomorrow. Eventually it got easier, and I got better, and the good days outweighed the bad.

I was also mother to a beautiful son, and twelve-hour shifts are not conducive to great motherhood. The internal guilt of driving off for night shift with your baby crying on the veranda and being too tired to play, so you just put the TV on, is overwhelming. These are things that all working mothers struggle with, so you just have to do the best you can.

Most of the jobs I've had in my life have been 'Boys Jobs.' Roles I've had include farming roles, cane haul out operator, I've driven potato, cane, wheat and salt harvesters; dozer, loader, grader, forklifts, 20Tonne Franna crane and dump trucks. I've been the first female to do many things. Blazing the way, such as being the first female in FNQ to race a Sprintcar at speedway, and the first female cane haul out operator for Mareeba Mill. I was also the first female plant operator at Dampier Salt Mine, and one of the first female crane operators in Mackay. In fact, I got so sick of the words, 'So how long have you been a crane operator?' I used to joke around and say, 'Oh, I started yesterday, yours is my third lift.' You could see the blood drain from their faces' as I was about to unload their multi-million-dollar asset from the truck. It was quite amusing.

Yes, I have had to step out and be uncomfortable, and Scott and I had to get creative with shift changes and day care and dinner and sick babies. But we both wanted it really bad, so we made it happen. The men in leadership roles who gave me a go took a risk too! But I worked three times as hard to prove to them they made a good choice in employing me. They dared to try something different, and I'll always remember that.

Humans are ridiculously fearful of change and therefore it takes many open minds, some faith and patience to modify the way things have been done forever, but there has never been a better time in history to try your hand at just about any occupation you can dream of, regardless of your gender!

PART 2

Take the biggest bite you can and chew like buggery!

These precursors led me to creating Norsafe. One night on the steps of the Sugar Mill, the electrician on shift told me about Testing and Tagging. He said, 'Heidi, if you learn how to do test and tag, I'll give you all my clients.' I was interested. I wanted to be a better mother and be home more for my boy, to be able to make dinner every night, attend the school play and sports days. Until that point, my life was not my own and my baby was missing out. I also had a strong passion for workplace safety, mainly because of Simon's death and the impact it had on our family, so creating a safety business seemed like the perfect thing. Except, I had no spare money, no spare time and no background knowledge in electrical or the licences required. I set about finding out what it was about, and how I could make it happen. I did two TAFE courses online and a basic bookkeeping course in my spare time and during the night, which qualified my Restricted Electrical Licence. With the help of our accountant, I started a company and did all the artwork and logos myself to save money. I picked up a set of farming discs for my mate, Les, out of a paddock and delivered them to his farm and in exchange, he created me a website.

I considered purchasing a franchise. That sounded really easy, someone helping you every step of the way, but I couldn't get past the thought, 'why would I give away my profit?' If I just work a bit harder, I can keep the profit.

PART 3

How to eat an elephant

Reaching your target requires a series of what I like to call 'Little Victories.' Richard Branson has a famous quote, 'Say yes - and then learn how to do it later.' The elephants I'm referring to are the Yes's. How do you eat an Elephant? One little victory at a time.

When I think back on the moments that defined my growth, it's the times when I said YES to the things that scared me the most. I had absolutely no idea how to do these things, or execute these feats, but I did them anyway. I did some research, stepped it all out in my head, thought of everything that could go wrong and prepared for those things too. Some things are out of your hands, and instead of thinking of them as failures, you must use them as learning tools. My son's favourite quote: 'I never lose, I either win or learn.' – Nelson Mandela

In the beginning, I did training jobs in between working fulltime for friends and family. Then the hardest thing had to occur, the thing I dreaded most – getting customers. How could I possibly go out and pretend like I knew what I was talking about, then expect people to give me their money? It was so hard; I was green as grass in the Electrical safety industry, but the thing that saved me was the handful of electricians, my phone-a-friends who would answer my silly questions. These guys I will be forever grateful to. Eventually, I grasped the concepts and the phone calls were less frequent. Nowadays we are so lucky. There are Facebook groups, YouTube video tutorials, and many platforms for sharing information. Use them!

As time went on, Scott helped me submit some government tenders, and one day we won one. It was for a large government agency and the work was in remote Cape York, Far North Queensland. Long story short, this tender led to being awarded another big job, then another, then another.

I recall one of these times. The Estate Supervisor at the University had taken a gamble on me. We won the job of testing all the Safety Switches at the local campus. 2500 RCD's to trip. It was my second 'Biggest Job.' I remember standing there in the car park with three team members all looking at me waiting for direction. I'm just standing there looking up at this big building thinking, 'What the actual F### was I thinking? I can't do this!' After several deep breaths, I looked at my team and said, 'Right, we are going to tackle this the same way you would eat an elephant. One piece at a time!'

PART 4

Growing pains - Realising the business owned me

Some close friends and family members were worried about me. They said I loved the business more than my own family, and I had to change something. Not only that, I had trouble retaining staff, which was a big issue because it takes so much time and effort to train someone. For once, I listened. I did some research. I enrolled in a business mentor course in Sydney, packed my bag and flew off to the big smoke for a week. I went there thinking I had to learn how to be a better boss, and I left there thinking, 'Holy crap! I have to become a better me before I can do that!'

It was a rude awakening and the turning point for my business. I completed several other self-improvement things like getting a mentor, joining a gym, and engaging a psychologist. I asked many questions to all the new people I'd met about how ego works, how to control emotions and reactions, and trying to remove the old 'Stories' I'd been telling myself. I started learning about me! It was the best thing ever because throughout the process I met so many knowledgeable people and my networking skills and confidence improved.

After this, I started learning about how to put processes in place. My next goal was to remove me by 50%. E.g., have someone else doing half the roles required to generate an invoice. After two years of implementing different systems, I felt like I'd succeeded. For the first time, I left the business in the hands of my team and we flew to Victoria for a family holiday! It was amazing. I'd done it! We still haven't mastered it, but we are getting there. I rarely go out on actual jobs anymore and my team members know how to troubleshoot and do a lot more of the tasks, We also outsource certain parts. My roles have changed significantly, and I find a lot of my time is now taken up with regulatory duties and growth strategies. I am so thankful I listened to those who love me because I wouldn't be the person I am today without stopping to find me.

PART 5

Daringly different work processes

Who said you have to work 9-to-5, Monday to Friday, drop the kids at daycare on your way to work and rush home for dinner on the table at 6pm?

If recent events have taught us anything, it's that we can all work well from home! Modified work practices, pivoting, unconventional, unprecedented; all these trendy buzz words we are sick of hearing, are the best way for us to move forward. But let's take that thought to the next level.

Our team comprises mostly of women who are mothers. We are tradies helping other tradies and businesses, so we have to go to site. We can't work from home, so we have modified the way we book in work. We book in our jobs around our kids. Some team members can work early, some team members can work late. One of our team has a newborn, so she has been retrained to do scheduling and more office roles. We base everything we do around our availability, with a focus on our children. Sometimes it can be frustrating and sometimes it doesn't work, but luckily, we all have a support network at home that can assist if plans don't fall into place. The main point I'm getting at, is that as an employer, I have built our own community and support network, because these ladies have skills! They are valuable members of our team and support our clients, just as I did in the beginning. They are giving me their all, and in return I give them a lifestyle job and an opportunity to support their children. I'd be lost without them! I've grown this business from scratch and I'm so proud that it has grown into a living, breathing thing on its own. If I had been a conventional person, well, first, it would never have got off the ground, and second, I would still be unhappily grinding away on my own. I love what we have created and I challenge any of the business owners reading this to dare to think about how you could also change your work processes. That way, more of our ladies and most valuable resource, the 51% of the population, can also add value and be a part of the workforce. If we can do it, so can you!

Now let's take that thought to the next level again! There is a small percentage of female representation in the trades and contracting industries. There is an even smaller percentage of female business OWNERS in these industries. What if you dared to consider OWNING your own trade or contracting business? It's different. It's possible. I'm doing it and you can do it too!

Conclusion

Give it wings. 'If nothing ever changed, there'd be no butterflies.'
UNKNOWN.

To me, gender has no bearing on your aspirations. There is no gender at work. I don't typically speak about gender at all, and it doesn't come into my thought process or decision making. However, I am told by others I am an inspiration, which is quite a humbling comment. If that means someone has a go because they can see it's doable, then I'm ok with that. If I want something, I go get it! And yes, that IS inspiring. My team and I are proof that no matter your age or gender, you can have a go!

I am unconventional apparently, described as an 'Extraordinary Contradiction.' Steel caps to stilettos, amp meters to clutch bag, mother to boss lady, city girl to country, compassionate to tenacious; blazing the trail, and at all times thinking outside of every box ever created. I chose to be independently successful without compromising my role as mother and partner, and I am not held back by what society says girls should or should not do. I have been fortunate to have grown up in a community that is supportive, visionary and relentless. My opinion; if you have a dream, go and get it! It is so true that the magic is waiting for you outside that comfort zone.

In summary, I don't know how many times I've said to myself, 'What the f### were you thinking? You shouldn't be here!' But if I'd listened to that derogatory inner voice, I'd have not done any of those big and scary things, and you honestly wouldn't be reading my story right now. I wouldn't have had the opportunities, the guts, or thought I was worthy. I took a deep breath and said, 'Ok, you're here now, let's see what happens.' I am worthy of being in this book, in this moment, sharing my story, because it took guts to make the dream a reality, seek help, and say YES to opportunities that presented. All I can say is WOW, what a feeling when you achieve something seemingly impossible!

Things I've learned along the way:

- Find your purpose. Google 'How do I find my purpose?' That question will take you on a journey of getting to know yourself.
- Ask for help. There are so many people who are way better at things than you are.
- Automate as much as possible. There are many programs and apps to make your life easy.
- Find an accountant who sees your vision.
- Work hard on balance. This is the KEY to happiness. Work/ life.
- Think outside of the box. Who wants to be in a box? F That! Make your own God damn box!
- You don't need to know everything to do everything. Outsource as much as possible, get creative, swap services.
- Don't take 'no' for an answer. Find someone who will help get a 'yes' answer.
- Learn to say 'no.' Work out what your boundaries are and protect them. People need rules. If you value your time, sometimes you'll have to say 'no.'
- Surround yourself with positive people.
- Back yourself! NO ONE deserves this more than you.

The benefit of stepping out of your comfort zone and daring to do something different is that you grow tremendously! You get to enjoy things you've never done and go places you've never been, meet people you'd never have met, and THAT is called LIVING!

HEIDI JONSSON

Based in Cairns, Far North Queensland, Australia, I am sole director of an Electrical Safety business called Norsafe. Never did I ever think someone would ask me to write my story for inclusion in a book about inspiring others. But here I am. My story, in a nutshell, is about a girl, born into a Far North Queensland potato farming family, who was chastised for being a dreamer by her teachers, and had a desire to do all the things girls don't usually do. It's a story of adventure; daring to step out of conventional boxes and realising along the way I had many traits ingrained that were holding me back. To be free, I had to do some soul searching and improving. It's a story of accepting opportunities, overcoming adversity, dreaming big and learning along the way that the safety business I created from the ground up was inadvertently aligned with my life purpose - To Protect.

Ten years on, Norsafe has evolved. We now service all regions in FNQ. I have a dedicated team who are just as passionate as me in protecting our clients. And I'm so proud of their evolution too. I've witnessed my staff grow into confident people with a whole new skill set and can adapt to varied scenarios.

Norsafe has provided my family with many opportunities and has taken me to the farthest reaches of remote FNQ to provide a safety service to many who would usually miss out. I've crossed swollen croc-infested creeks, driven on bulldust back roads, raced cyclones across the cape and slept in my car all for the benefit of our loyal clients. I'm proud to have educated our clients in the dangers of electricity and removed around 4000 unsafe electrical items from service. And I know without a doubt that we have saved someone's life. I'm proud of my achievements and I hope to continue to inspire others that, no matter their age or gender, to have a go!

I now sit on the board of the National Electrical and Communications Association and recently won Regional Queensland Ausmumpreneur. This year my son finishes school, and I am thrilled he has played a part in the business' success and witnessed what's possible if you put your mind to something.

www.norsafe.com.au

'You can only fly, if you are willing to give up the safety of your cocoon.'

UNKNOWN.

Part Two

Thinking Outside the Square - Focusing on what you can do rather than what you can't.

LAURA ELIZABETH

The only thing we know for certain is change.

A poignant reminder, courtesy of Confucianism philosophy, is that we need to be fluid and adaptable in life; to meet unforeseen challenges and continue with our personal growth.

But here's a little Laura-ism philosophy. Business is no different.

Personally, my business has morphed, expanded, adapted and changed trajectory more times than I can count, and continues to do so. But each stepping stone along the way serves a valuable purpose and allows me to focus on the things I am capable of, one. step. at. a. time.

And in case you thought having one's ducks all neatly lined up in a row might grant you top-secret immunity against having challenges, you'd be thinking… optimistically.

So often I witness others focusing on the problem. They fall into a *Victim Trap,* wasting so much time in a place of low vibration, stagnancy and stuckness. Instead, we can adjust our gaze to open up to all the opportunities in our periphery that can be achieved.

The key to moving beyond the Victim Trap?

Become a maven of adaptability and let go of the control and the attachment to how we think things should be. The universe does not work on our time, but divine time. And trust me, it's always perfect.

Every 'problem' we have is a leverage point to create more opportunities, and for us to focus on what we can do right now rather than what we can't.

So you want to start a business?

Back in 2016, I questioned life choices and was desperately trying to *find myself* again. A recently single mother of three and living at my parents'. What a catch! Feeling a little hopeless, with only one child in full time schooling, I needed an income solution that was flexible for the needs of my young family, and would allow my sparkle to shine through. Good luck to any employer trying to tell me what to do. It had been several years since I'd had a *real* job, and the days of slotting neatly into the *good girl* mould were well and truly over. This was my time to shine.

I was determined with the ultimate rebirth goal. I started a business! Simple. Or not so much. Previously stumbling upon Clinical Reflexology, my new foot fetish naturally served as my inspiration and paved the way towards a solid business foundation.

I developed a five-year plan that would move me from surviving to thriving in a role I'd a passion for!

There was nothing romantic about establishing a business whilst navigating the upheaval of finding a new place to call home. I was eating stress for breakfast. Exhausted and overwhelmed, I lay awake most nights wondering how I would make it all work.

I was focusing on the problem! Trapped in my own story, feeling alone and pushing all the shit uphill... a tedious victim cycle.

Amidst the chaos one evening, tired of the same old loop, I felt inspired to find a quiet space for myself to meditate and journal. I asked myself a simple question. 'What *can* you do right now?'

Bringing awareness into this moment, time and space eliminated all the *what if's* and inspired immediate and deliberate action of *what now?* I set up the spare room as a consultation room and began advertising reflexology and reiki consultations the next day. Being responsible and conscious of your thoughts and taking continuous simple (and I mean simple) action, promotes forward movement and keeps inspiration flowing. We all have the same twenty-four hours in a day, seven days a week. Ten minutes here, one hour there, is enough to stir momentum, is enough to create change. Just do... something.

Before long, I had a steady flow of at least three clients per week. I could afford to hire a consultation room at local wellness centres to build, network and execute fresh ways of showing up; expanding my client reach and alleviating the pressure of maintaining the Suzy Housewife facade, now that I no longer worked from home.

Upskilling is another valuable action to take when it comes to business too. From the moment I qualified as a Clinical Reflexologist, my mind grew hungry for learning. I have continued to invest in renewing and developing my skills, and diving headfirst into new ones. In three short years, several payment plans and many late nights, I have dedicated time to a range of other certified courses, ensuring and affirming my ability to provide a high-level standard to my beautiful clients.

These bite-sized opportunities have eventually led me to my niche. I always knew I wanted to be of service to women, to facilitate transformation and healing, but it wasn't always clear exactly *how* I would manifest this. Who would've thought I'd be serving and empowering women as a leading yoni massage therapist in Perth? Back then, certainly not me, but this period of continuous growth and exploration has allowed me to explore the most perfect, passionate and purpose filled role for me in business. I discovered and rediscovered things I love over and over again, by allowing myself to take action and never giving up, even when that big picture seemed impossible.

Her Centre - A safe space for women to remember, reconnect and reclaim.

Fast forward two years beyond that struggling single mother mask, the kids are all in full time school, and I have a little more space to level up. Hiring a consultation room definitely felt more professional than working from home, but it wasn't always using my time efficiently. By the time I'd loaded and unloaded the car of various trinkets, towels and a bulky massage table, I was losing ninety minutes a day.

An opportunity arose with two rooms available for hire at what was once previously a birthing centre, just a few kilometres from my home. This was definitely a step in the right direction to reach my goal of one day having my own bustling wellness centre, and meant I could decorate and infuse my energy into the space permanently. With a leap of faith, I signed a year's lease, and believed every single day that I would make it work.

With two beautiful permanent healing rooms sufficiently covered with rainbows and positive affirmations allegedly cited by Budda, that extra space meant I could expand a little further and begin facilitating group sessions and courses. Changing up the energy of my business and inviting new opportunities in.

There were great days, there were average days, and there were the days I wanted to gouge out my eyeballs and tear out my heart. Client cancellations and no shows felt like a personal attack. Had I got it all wrong?

Anxiety had always been a close friend of mine, but still determined to find success, I continued bringing my focus into what I could adapt and change in the moment to invite my soul mate clients to me.

The truth is, we are never really in control, and once I grasped and accepted this, the inspiration and ideas began free flowing.

In that first year of leasing the healing rooms, my determination paid off and the business made a profit! Albeit a small one. But it was enough to keep me inspired and thriving and hungry to reach new goals. After only twelve months in the new space, I'd increased my client base from 45 to 156 and was offered the opportunity to lease the entire building! And so, HER Centre was born!

It's now a flourishing wellness centre with four consultation rooms, a large studio space and fully-equipped kitchen. I have fourteen incredible subcontractors sharing space at HER Centre to co-create a safe space for clients to remember, reconnect and reclaim their truth and power.

By focusing on what I can do in the moment, and taking continued action towards my goals, I've created a space for myself to continue serving women in their transformation. Not only that, I have also created a beautiful workspace for like-minded business owners sharing in the philosophy to serve those who are called to their services.

Thinking outside the square

Just eight months into the birth of HER Centre here in Perth, businesses were instructed to close and families were sent into isolation for several months.

No one has a freaking clue what the future holds, and everything felt topsy-turvy.

This was one of those periods where I could have easily fallen into the victim trap and chosen to focus on the problem. Not a chance! I had not come this far only to be told to lay down my sword and shield and surrender back into being small. I am a magical motherfu**er and now more than ever, I choose to focus on what I do best; finding new ways of supporting women to step into their power! Can I get a 'Hell Yes'?!

I created online sessions for my beautiful clients. The results were incredible, and not only did it allow me to continue seeing my current clients, it also opened me up to a whole new world, inviting national and international bookings. It wasn't enough though; I needed inspiration to make it all juicier. How could I support a group of women and lead them through a journey of self-discovery online? Enough of the fluff, I wanted to transform souls.

How can I open them up to the deepest and juiciest parts of their truth and sensuality?

Like magic, the universe heard my call and within weeks TK Byron, a magnificent launch coach in QLD, would extract and unravel the threads of inspiration in my head, and provided the tools to help me weave them into a tangible online signature program for women. Ten weeks later I'd created the most delicious content that would hold women through six months into owning their erotic truth and embodying self-love and power. In a world filled and fuelled by fear, I adapted and used the restrictions as leverage. I dared to be wrong.

In my first launch, I had twenty-one incredible women sign up to this six-month program; twenty-one women, from four states in Australia and two international students. I have since relaunched with another tribe of amazing beings!

TK and I have established a wonderful business relationship. She keeps me grounded and yet encourages my quirkiness to bleed through into my work. We continue to work together, manifesting ideas and launching them into packages that dreams are made of. HER Centre reopened after three months closure and continues to expand and flourish into a dynamic wellness centre. I have maintained a balance between online offers and face-to-face consultations - working smarter, not harder!

Products and merchandise

Having a range of super juicy digital and physical offers and products available for your clients will help to establish solid relationships and keep the communication lines open between you and your ideal humans.

What tools can you offer clients that will support or scaffold their journey while they work with you? Devising creative new ways of generating a trickle income can be fun and takes the pressure off when running a service-based business. Often these offers can double as free marketing tools to broaden your reach. For example, a range of t-shirts, water bottles or stickers that are worn or displayed by your clients when they venture out into the big wide world.

You are literally limited only by your own imagination and creativity. The world needs your magic, so what are you prepared to do to be seen? What action can you take right now?

Delegating and asking for help

What is with that belief system that tells us we have to do it all?

Trust me, you don't!

Drop into your heart and figure out where your magic best flows. That is what you *should* focus on. Then send out the intention to find other incredible humans just like you who are aligned with their magic and skilled in areas you aren't. Magic happens when we work together.

And even though it's challenging to budget for in the beginning, trust me, your time is worth so much more than trying to design your own logo, print your own product labels, or be the good housewife. You may as well stick a broom up your bum and hope for the best.

Make yourself feel better by calling on the services of local business women and sharing the load amongst your community. Use sustainable products and packaging, and schedule in the time for that walk to the park with the kids. You are already doing an amazing job. You do not need to break yourself on the pathway to success.

It is so important to set clear boundaries between work and play. Know when to invest in specialised services. It could even be as simple as hiring a cleaner once a fortnight to lift the load for you and free up some time to flow, or chill, or whatever your heart calls for.

Having *offline* time is another really useful boundary to put in place. If you are sitting flicking through your phone at 10pm, I can almost guarantee you're answering a work email or social media post for business. Do you have the willpower to set and adhere to specific working hours?

Learn to say 'no.' Your ideal humans will be happy to wait for you, and if not then do you really want that energy in your business?

I am one of those people, by 5pm every night, where the thought of preparing a meal feels overwhelming. Not only that, but a meal that is both nutritious and will be eaten by three kids. I've been a mother for nearly eleven years, and the responsibility of cooking dinner still creeps up on me. Meal planning has been a Godsend. Trust me, it's a giant pain in my arse setting aside a Sunday to plan and prep meals, but it makes such a difference in my world to simply select something that *last week Laura* prepared from the freezer. Also, if your budget allows, there are some incredible healthy frozen meal delivery options, even just to get you started for those low energy days you need a helping hand.

Have the wisdom to know the difference between when to be the superwoman and when to delegate!

Asking for help is not a weakness and creates more opportunity for you to focus on things you can do that align with your expertise. Read that again!

The phrase *self-care* gets thrown around a lot, and with good reason. This has been a challenging lesson for me. You see, I believed that getting a massage once a week was going to cover the self-care quota. Nope. As I got busier, I learned that the self-care input has to match the output. What do I mean by this?

In the beginning, I would see 3-5 clients per week for a standard 60-minute reiki or reflexology session. My self-care input was a massage, or an eyebrow wax, or something similar each week. As time went on and my business flourished, I was seeing up to fifteen clients per week, but still only taking that one-hour massage for me to self-care. Hello burn out!

The input did not match the output. I needed to up my self-care quota to reflect the hours and energy I was putting into my business. I'd recommend revisiting your self-care plan every few months, or any time you implement changes in your business. Does the input match the output? If not, do yourself a favour and change it up until it does. Love yourself enough to be the best version of you that you can be, and therefore one kick-ass girl/boss.

If it's not a 9 or a 10 out of 10, let it go!

Being brave enough to say no to opportunities when they don't fully align with your passion, purpose, and drive, is a superpower. I remember a profound moment when chatting with a mentor of mine, Amy Towle. Amy took me through six months of intensive and transformative Yoni Massage Practitioner training, and is a huge advocate for women remembering and standing strong in their power. I had just completed my yoni massage training and was reviewing my business plan. She asked me to write down every service I was providing. As the list grew to over fifteen services, I could feel the anxiety stirring in my belly. In true Amy style she said to me, 'Just because you *can* offer all of these things does not mean that you have to. I want you now to go through this list and cross off anything that doesn't light up your soul. If it's not a nine or a ten out of ten, cross it off.'

And that's exactly what I did.

I allowed myself to review that list and trusted it was safe to let go of the things that didn't make my heart beat a little harder. In doing so, I became aware of what I am truly passionate about on a deeper level. I discovered my niche and business has blossomed and flowed with ease and grace ever since.

My ideal soul mate clients know exactly where to find me since I took this leap of faith.

So, I want to give you permission right now. List all the things you offer within your business. Allow yourself to drop into the energy of your intention and heart space and cross off anything that doesn't ignite that passion and purpose within your soul.

Where is that fire in your belly?

This is how we manifest the life of our dreams!

Hi, I'm **LAURA ELIZABETH**, a trailblazing change maker and advocate for women's empowerment. Author of *Loving Herself Whole,* founder of HER Centre in the rolling hills of Perth, and owner of Laura Elizabeth Wellness/Erotic Maven Medicine.

I am dedicated to creating intimate experiences for conscious women ready to step into a deeper layer of understanding of self, to embrace and embody their sensuality, reclaim their voices, and own their power. I offer Womb and Yoni Massage Therapy, Reiki Attunements, my signature online program Portal to QueenDom, and a catalogue of workshops, education and training online and in person.

A naturally gifted psychic medium born on the East Coast of Scotland, I moved to Perth, Western Australia, as a pre-teen in 1999. With over seventeen years' experience cultivating my skills as an energy worker and holding space for women, I offer the safest and most profoundly intimate containers for women to experience deep transformation.

A boundary pusher and taboo smasher, I am best known for my real, quirky and honest guidance, ensuring the deepest empathy, understanding and non-judgement.

My service to women is most definitely a niche, which I believe is the real missing link in human connection and healing for women. We are programmed to think, feel, and do based on the needs of others, but we unleash our real magic when we set aside time to explore honouring, nurturing, and loving ourselves back into a belief of radical acceptance and remembering our magnificence.

A passionate mother of three, leading by example, smashing goals and living with purpose, I hope to be a positive influence for my own children to reach their full potential and inspire others to do the same.

I hold your hand and love you, while you remember how to love yourself.

www.lauraelizabeth.com.au
facebook.com/eroticmavenmedicine
facebook.com/hercentre
instagram.com/eroticmaven_medicine
instagram.com/her.centre

How to work beyond your passion to have a healthy business

LOUISE LUGG

Imagine a pair of scales, with your passion on one side and a healthy business on the other.

What a delicate balance this truly is. One without the other, and there is no balance at all.

Most people start their business based on their passion for what they love to do, with a big idea for a successful business. How many people know how to have a healthy business? Is it something you learned at school or from your parents whilst you were growing up?

I would like to share a few honest stories from my own journey in business over the past thirty years, whilst being a mother of a large family. I hope this will give an insight to help anyone passionate about starting their very own business.

What is your passion?

Some people know this from a young age, but many spend much time searching for this one thing. If you can work within your true passions, you will surely succeed; to make money doing something you absolutely love. Making a difference is such an empowering feeling. While money keeps the engine running and pays the bills, it is the feeling of true contentment to know that your work has a positive impact on other people's lives.

I would say after many years in the beauty and spa industry that the true success of the business is the special care and nurturing we give to our clients every day. It is all in the detail, creating a welcoming and safe, beautiful environment for our guests to enjoy their personalised services.

Recently, I received a call from a young mother from Perth, on the other side of Australia. She and her family had relocated to a remote area for work. She called me to order some of the lovely skincare products (Subtle Energies) we used on her skin when she had a holistic facial with us last Christmas. Then she mentioned she cried when she walked out the door after her facial as she felt so amazing. She admitted she called because she was not coping with her baby and young children, feeling quite alone, stressed and exhausted. She said she remembered how good she felt after her facial and wanted to feel like that again, so that is why she called to organise her skincare pack.

I had lots of time to chat with her. We cried and laughed together as I am a mother of six children myself and totally understood. I validated how she felt and delivered some words of comfort and positive encouragement, telling her she is an amazing mother. At the end, she admitted she reached out to me instead of Lifeline!

I was so shocked, but glad that after our hour-long chat, she said she felt so much better.

When I hung up, I cried my eyes out and reminded myself that, 'This is why I do what I do.'

I packed her package with an extra little gift to surprise her. Many months later, I received a message from her stating, 'Do you remember me?' and to thank me for helping her so much that day and that all was well.

Sometimes it is the little things you do within your work that can have the most powerful impact on other people. This is far better than money any day.

Am I good enough? Servitude.

Stop running a charity. Charge your worth!

So many of us never value what we do, constantly having self-doubt, which leads to negative feelings.

I personally have suffered from Imposter syndrome for many years. The only positive with this was that I kept educating myself by attending courses and conferences, always striving to better myself. How do we measure ourselves? Who decides the standards?

As I did not really value or have faith in myself, this led to me running a charity. Not charging my true worth. This is the worst crime in running your own business as bills need to be paid. I gave my all above and beyond to my clients, plus being a giver, I gave lots away with my time and goods.

When it came to asking for payment, I would go weak in the knees and fumble about giving discounts out left, right and centre. The problem with this is that the customers loved it, great service and cheap price. They all booked in each month expecting me to keep charging the discounted rate.

What had I started? And how then can I then ask for the full price? I went on like this for so many years. The balance of working hard and giving away all I had, I became, 'Louise to please.' I needed to have the courage to say 'No.' It was my own fault for allowing people to take advantage of my kindness. I allowed it!

My accountant sat me down and said, 'Just look at your figures. Please stop running a charity.'

So that day I did my research on what other people in my industry were charging, and put my prices up the next day. Yes, it was scary, but like my accountant said, 'You will have quality customers who are happy to pay for a quality experience.' We only lost one client.

Well, that was 2010, and now over ten years later, it was the most important decision I have ever made in business. My confidence with charging my worth is restored and now I have a healthy business based on respect, confidence and self-worth. It is important to raise your standards to constantly keep your business current, fresh and always deliver a wonderful, memorable experience every time.

My motto is 'Fake it till you make it!' You must show you are confident even if on the inside you're melting. If people see you are not confident, then they will not have any faith in you either.

From beautician to businesswoman

Time versus money. Who will rescue me, or do I save myself?

Starting my own business with my raw and natural talents in the beauty industry many years ago, I realised how naive I was. But guess what, it worked because I was caring and nurturing to all my clients. Providing a lovely service using my hands and heart. This side of the business was easy for me as I loved what I did and loved people. The problem was, I never realised how to run a business and did not really understand how to manage the finances and legal obligations.

If I could send a message back in time to myself, the most important message would be to put your GST into another account daily, or at least weekly. Once I got behind, I was constantly chasing my own tail financially. I felt bogged down with no cash flow, and a business growing fast in demand. As I was already not charging enough, this got me on my back foot when it came to paying taxes.

If you do not understand your true running cost, then how will you know how much to charge for your services? There are so many costs associated with running a business. This can bring so many sleepless nights, as the stress of learning all of this can be overwhelming.

Thank goodness for Google and Zoom with so much information readily available. Fair work Australia has a wonderful, easy-to-use site to navigate through providing lots of education and support. **www.fairwork.com.au**

The best decision I made was to hire a bookkeeper within my first year. I fumbled along with the help of my bookkeeper and accountant. As I mentioned earlier, the biggest problem was not charging enough.

One of the most important things to consider is your TIME. We tend to easily give this away.

I was yelling out to the world that I did not have enough time. But no one was rescuing me.

I clearly remember attending my first spa conference back in 2006. It was a huge stadium of other women in the spa world who shared their journeys in business. I put my hand up to ask how to get the time to do everything and taking care of my family and myself. I could not see how these other women seem to have worked it all out. And I wanted someone to give me an easy answer and tell me how to get more work-life balance.

It took me a few years, but my tips for achieving a healthy work-life balance are:

1. Give yourself permission to say 'NO.'
2. Put aside your GST, PAYG and Super daily or weekly.
3. Swap time for money. It is equally valuable.
4. Use forward planning by booking a date with yourself on a regular basis.
5. Stick to your plan unless there is a police officer or firefighter at your door.
6. Do not feel guilty for taking time out for yourself.
7. Make yourself and your family a high priority.
8. Maintain standards for yourself.
9. Book time to work ON your business, not just IN your business.
10. Only sell things you love yourself.

'Boss or Mother' - what is the difference?

Stop treating your staff like you are their mother. Create a healthy, happy work culture to grow and empower your staff. Being a mother of six children and five grandchildren, I am truly blessed. It was totally natural for me to open my heart to my staff as if I were their mother. I was totally qualified, as this is who I am, but over the years I looked back and realised this is not a healthy approach to being a boss.

I am not sure if there is a course for 'How to be the best boss,' so I just made it up as I went along. After only a few months of opening my first beauty salon in town, I needed to employ staff as the demand was too much for me alone. I employed qualified therapists who delivered a wonderful service to our clients. And I always felt I owed them my heart and soul and was always kind with time and money. I did not realise I was not always respected, and sometimes taken advantage of in so many ways.

One young lady, after she had moved on, left me with a large phone bill as I found she was spending hours on the work phone on the late shift talking to her boyfriend. I called her family to find her to send the bill. Her mother chatted with me and said she was surprised her daughter even got the job with the overseas holiday she had booked in advance. I was so shocked as she'd come to work one day excited and told me she'd won first prize in an overseas holiday, and had to take the prize. I was pregnant with my fourth child at this time and needed her for work, but I was excited and happy for her win, and told her she could go and I would manage ok without her.

Little did I know she'd concocted this lie so she could go on her holiday. I was so disappointed!

When I sold the shop, I organised the girls to meet me after hours to say goodbye.

I purchased flowers, chocolates and gifts, and to my disappointment, no one turned up.

I felt so sad the girls did not have enough respect for me to show up to say goodbye.

Over the years I allowed so many silly things to happen, but eventually, I realised I needed to find a healthy line between myself and my staff.

I have learnt to empower my team, leading by example, allowing space and time to talk about any issues, problem solving together and not getting too involved in their personal lives. I am truly blessed to now have an amazing spa team who run my business with trust and respect, even when I am not there.

Stuck in the corner of my world - How do I share my passions nationally & globally?

Networking, charity, community, and feeling connected to like-minded people. I am sure I am not alone in saying that, like my own story, I was inventing it all, fuelled by my passion in the spa and beauty industry. I felt like I was in the corner of my world in a small coastal town on the east coast of Australia, and I was putting on a brave face, running my business from my heart alone. I craved to meet other like-minded people, to observe, listen, and learn how others were running their businesses. I was reading spa and beauty magazines, and dreaming of developing a beautiful destination day spa on our stunning south coast.

I discovered the Australasian Spa Association and signed up to become a member, excited to attend my first ever Spa conference.

My husband, Barry, said, 'You don't need to join an association to be successful. You already are.'

I said I needed to feel connected, to learn and grow in this industry. That was in 2006, and it changed my whole life. I met some amazing empowering spa mentors and speakers who took me under their wings.

Kirien Withers (Spa Guru) told me after showcasing a seven-page glossy profile of my business in the Spa Life magazine said, 'Louise, you put the spirit into spa. It is not the building, but what you do there.'

How honoured and humbled I felt. This is when I started to have more faith in myself.

During another ASPA conference, I was blessed to meet the amazing Farida Irani from Subtle Energies. Farida is a recognised practitioner, international speaker and educator in Ayurveda Aromatherapy and Bowen.

I was so empowered by her speaking that I signed up for her short courses. After a couple of years, I spent many years completing their in-depth Diploma of Ayurveda Aromatherapy.

I now work for Subtle Energies as an International spa trainer, personally trained by Farida's daughter Khursheed, a recognised practitioner and therapist herself.

I feel so grateful to have the opportunity to train at the most luxury iconic destination spas in the world, such as Mandarin Oriental, Peninsula hotels & Six Senses resorts. How blessed I am to be paid to travel the world to teach my true passions. So many people ask me, 'How did you get that job?'

I would never have dreamed that this opportunity would come my way. I stepped up and took new challenges guided by my inspiring teachers and mentors. My message to you, is to reach out to join associations and networks, to be recognised and inspired by other like-minded people. Do not stop educating yourself. Reach for the stars with your dreams and desires.

Embrace your local community being involved in committees and charities. It's good for your heart and your business.

I do hope by baring my soul and sharing a few stories from my own personal journey in business, will help you to also feel confident with venturing the changing seas of your life's passion in business. I hope to be a lighthouse and shine my light of experience over the past thirty years, to help guide you through the tides of your business journey, making sure your ship stays on course. I found much comfort and support with finding my own lighthouse women, who embraced and supported me in business after reaching out from the corner of my world to connect and grow.

It is such a delicate balance between passion for your work and having a healthy business.

One without the other and your ship will truly falter. So please spend time in educating yourself with the knowledge and understanding of running a successful business so you can gift the world with your passions in business.

SHINE BRIGHTLY LIKE A LIGHTHOUSE

LOUISE LUGG is a passionate beauty and spa therapist working in the beauty industry for over thirty years.

Louise owns the Multi-Award-Winning Goddess Health & Wellness Day Spa on the south coast of NSW, Australia.

She's a graduate of Ayurveda Aromatherapy, Beauty & Spa Therapy, Advanced massage & spa management.

Louise has worked as an international spa trainer at luxury iconic spa destinations around the world for Subtle Energies, teaching product knowledge and treatment training.

Louise has a passion for supporting her local community coordinating many charity events.

She is a mother of six lovely children and five grandchildren. Her husband, Barry, is a constant support, with family time a high priority.

Louise loves diving and water-skiing with her family, reading books and being in the sunshine.

Her passion is to inspire and empower other amazing woman through her many years of experience owning her own business, to help guide them to reach their goals and true potential and success, maintaining a healthy work life balance.

www.goddessdayspa.com.au
goddessdayspaburrill@gmail.com

Time well spent

DAVINA BORROW-JONES

When we, as women, value ourselves, when we step into our own beauty and accept imperfection, when we start to really value our time and energy, we see we are far more than our current situation. We see hope, opportunity; we see possibility. And then, when we look out with wonder and curiosity, when we listen closely to the people we want to serve, we can educate and upgrade ourselves to help them in the best way. There is no time better spent than embarking on your own business journey, and there is no better time to start that journey than now.

1. Value yourself and your time and everything will follow.

She cried in front of the psychiatrist.

'Please, please, just let me take her home,' she said. She knew too well that the bush and the Pacific, the long walks and salty air would heal my mind, but he wasn't interested.

'Just a few more days.'

It was 2005, and I'd been working in a top US corporate law firm in their London city office. I worked high up on one of the top floors, and lived with other high-flying girlfriends, jetting off to New York and to European cities for the weekend to work and party. I was high on life… until, over a series of weeks,

I broke up with my boyfriend.

I was date raped in Spain.

I got trapped in the 7 July bombings, and…

I lost my mind.

The delicate jigsaw of my brain unravelled. It was horrible. I lost my friends, my fabulous London room, my career. They even took my phone off me. I had the clothes on my back, and everything that hinted at my success dissipated. But there was my mother, her love as consistent as the returning tide, and there was my steadfast sister, and there were a few of my closest, longest, dearest friends.

It took me a long time to start valuing myself again, to back myself.

It took long walks on Australian beaches and hundreds of jigsaw puzzles. And it took a strong family network of support that may not have adhered to any faith but had humility, compassion, and belief far greater than many of the faithful.

The statistics today say that almost half of all Australians will experience mental illness in their lifetime. * If you are in a relationship, then that means one of you will either have it or be the primary carer. And if you are a lawyer, the rates are much higher.

I ended up taking ten months off from my career.

Some ambitious friends laughed under their breath, 'career suicide.' But I came close to suicide of a different kind, and suddenly 'career suicide' didn't warrant the gravity of the words. Since that convalescence, I've taken many breaks from my career. I've spent time being a yoga teacher, mountaineering around the world, living in France, doing human rights pro bono work. And I don't regret a moment of that time spent away from a career.

Once you realise your intrinsic value doesn't depend upon the 'Right Job' or the 'Right Neighbourhood,' you free yourself up to diverse and wonderful opportunities. The world is full of them. The biggest thing of value you have in your life is your *time.*

Once I really started to value myself and my time, other people started valuing me and my time too. So, what is time well spent for you? Do you want to wake up in ten years having spent your time the same way that you are spending it now?

1. You have an intrinsic value unique to you. It is far more than your current skills, what you own, or where you live.
2. Your value as a person is not dependent on whether you make an extraordinary amount of money.
3. Value yourself and your contribution.
4. Value your time, and then others will value your time too.
5. Back yourself.

**Beyond Blue, The Department of Health, and The Black Dog institute all currently state these statistics.*

2. What are you waiting for?

There is a phrase often used in legal letters to let people know when they'll hear back from their lawyer. It is 'in due course.' It is a most arrogant expression and has to be most frustrating to read as a client. Is in due course a week? A month? A year? When the lawyer feels like letting you know?

I was always going to start my business 'in due course.' I was waiting until I got more experience, until I bought a house, until I was in a stable relationship, until I had children… But I'd forgotten about my artful procrastination until I was lying in my son's bed one night reading to him. Reading a book about a waiting place – the most useless place - where everyone is just waiting. 'Waiting for a train to go, a bus to come, or plane to go. Waiting for a pair of pants… or Another Chance!' * And that night, lying next to my son in bed, I realised that finally I'd escaped. I'd escaped that most useless place, the waiting place.

It takes vulnerability to escape. To start a business is to be vulnerable and to allow for the possibility that it might 'fail.' But what is failure but a powerful lesson on how to do things differently. And failure is not often a spectacular fall, but rather a spiral staircase that could easily wind back up again. People say you need *courage* to start a business. You don't need courage, and you certainly don't need a pair of pants, you need vulnerability. Being vulnerable allows you to try new things, to open yourself up to others, to allow them to listen to your problems and mistakes, and to give them the opportunity to help. Vulnerability enables you to learn and be challenged, which is absolutely what you need to run a successful business.

For years I lingered, working for others in frustration. Frustration at the bullying that seemed to go unnoticed, at the mountains of wasted paper, at 6-minute increment billing, and later frustration with the way they treated pregnant friends and parents in the workplace. But perhaps most of all, my biggest frustration was that we weren't serving clients properly, or at all.

Things needed to change, but I never thought it was my responsibility. It wasn't until I looked at all the law firms and said, 'No Way!' that I got beyond the waiting place. When I decided I would take responsibility for the change I wanted in the world, it was an easy next step to start my own business with my own values. There is another legal phrase; 'time is of the essence,' which means acting within a particular time is vital to a contractual agreement. Now *my* time was of the essence.

So, what are you waiting for? If you're frustrated at work or in your industry, ask what needs to change? If you know of a product or service that could improve the world, get started.

1. Time will not stop for you. If you don't start or grow your business now, then when?
2. Ask yourself what's the worst that could happen?
3. There is no failure, it is all learning, and nothing is ever perfect.
4. Find what frustrates you and work out solutions to these frustrations.
5. These solutions are your business ideas.

**Oh, the places you'll go! by Dr Seuss.*

3. Slow down and start listening.

My heart was beating so loudly I could hardly hear her.

'You need to get some sleep,' she said.

'No, I'm fine, I'm ok.'

'No, you're not.'

It went on for a while this dance, the pleasing game… but eventually, she won.

'I promise,' she said. 'I promise that even when you're asleep, his cry will wake you, I promise.'

From a sister who'd been the most loyal, honest best friend, I had little option but to believe her.

'Ok,' I said.

That night, for the first time in five days, I let myself sleep. And he did wake me up, easily, and regularly. And after each feed or change, I slept again, and it was ok, and the next morning I felt alive and invigorated.

Having a baby was my dream. It was my dream for almost ten years. After failed relationships, multiple miscarriages and mental health challenges, there we were. My loving partner, my baby, and me.

My 40th birthday present! A miracle. My miracle baby!

A baby I'd no idea what to do with.

So, the day after the elation of having a healthy baby with two arms and two legs and a firecracker of hair, I downloaded every app I could to be the 'Perfect Mother' and do everything the 'Right Way.' I downloaded an app that told me when he should be sleeping, when to breastfeed, when he was supposed to poo, what each cry meant, how he was meant to grow.

Ping went my phone. Ping, ping, ping, ping!

After five days of incessant notifications of all my newfound motherly duties, I was a right mess.

'And by the way,' she said, 'turn off your phone and listen to him. He'll tell you everything he needs.'

Initially, my hand kept darting, anxious for the next instruction, or perhaps for the next distraction, a tweet, like, comment or the unicorn share to take me away from this incredulous new reality.

But turning off worked.

And it worked like magic. We connected with love and understanding, the love of a mother so deep and so raw, and the love of a baby so innocent, perfect and in need. Of course, he was communicating from day one, I just hadn't been listening.

Technology is incredible. But when it interferes with the most basic of connections; that between a mother and a child, something has gone wrong. When all you listen to is pings and when all you focus on is perfection, you miss a lot of what is going on in the real world.

When I practiced the same art of listening and the same focus as I did with my newborn baby with potential clients, it was a game changer. Listening is a dying art, but we need to switch off and start now. Some of the best insights I've had into clients and their worlds have been after we've finished a consultation, when I've become curious about them and when I've dropped all urgency. Understanding comes naturally and trust grows, we create deeper connections. If you really want prospects to become clients, you need to develop the art of listening and focus. And you should never, ever stop listening.

1. Put your phone away and start listening. First, listen to yourself, what are your beliefs and values?
2. Are you spending your time living these values?
3. Start listening to your potential clients and customers. What are they saying between the lines?
4. Use technology in a deliberate way. Switch off your notifications and check your phone (emails, messages, etc) at organised times.
5. Listen with wonder and curiosity to the world around you.

4. You may have many and abundant skills, but time is wasted until you develop a niche and value your time.

When I started my business, I wanted to create a rhythm of work around family. Initially, I thought I could set up a law firm doing some wills and conveyancing, just enough to contribute my legal skills to the community and help out financially at home. When word got out, a friend asked if I could draft her will. She'd been a delightful but struggling friend for years so I couldn't bring myself to charge. Then another friend asked me to help her brother in a business dispute. I didn't charge him either. Then my family asked me to do work here and there.

I was sliding down the spiral staircase and found myself again in a most useless place. My business was not just costing me in time, it was costing me money.

The will I thought I'd do for free cost me over $100; two long lunches and petrol across Sydney and back. The dispute and other work cost me days and days of childcare fees. I then had to pay for my legal insurance, software, practicing certificate and professional development costs which all quickly ran into the thousands.

This was not the life I envisaged.

Advising business owners on their legal risks is different to running a business yourself. Running a business means selling goods and services for profit, but I was running my business at a serious loss. I knew I was a good lawyer, and after tasting the flexibility and freedom that is running your own show, I knew I could not go back to working for a law firm that conflicted with my values.

It wasn't until I allowed myself to be vulnerable, to admit that although I was a good lawyer, I really didn't know how to run a successful business, that doors began to open. Other business owners gave me ideas. I learnt about marketing and sales and operations, and I joined women's business groups, and they couldn't have been more giving or more encouraging.

I focused on profit.

I conceded there was no point in running a business if I wasn't going to make a profit, so I put a price on my time and my efforts and charged properly. I outsourced what I could.

I found my niche.

My ideal clients were the gorgeous women start-ups I had already met and was helping. I had always been frustrated for the mothers who came into my office with their kids in tow. Trying to understand legalese is hard enough. Having kids crying, pulling at your legs, wanting something to eat during a conversation about complex issues is impossible. I wanted to create a solution to that problem, so I did. And what happened when I focussed on my niche was that I started having fun. A whole lot of fun.

1. Look for your weaknesses and upskill or outsource.
2. Join business groups to learn.
3. Learn about financials. Know where your money comes from and where it goes.
4. Find your niche by focussing in on your ideal client so you can really serve them.
5. A business is, by definition, for profit so make some.

5. Be proactive and plan

She came to me when things went wrong; when she had a fight with her landlord, when her employee set up in competition, when a client demanded an unfair refund. *

I had said, many times, 'We need to get proactive, to get you some proper legal documents in place.' Having legal documents in place makes it so much easier to deal with these sorts of issues, but it was an added expense, and she had a lot on her mind. Getting proactive about your business during an all-consuming dispute is a lesson too late for the learning.

You see, disputes and litigation are honestly no fun, and I should know.

Early in my career, I practiced in litigation. After a while, the solemnity of 'All Rise', the black cloaks and strange wigs, the puffy egos and late-night reading eyes became second nature to me. But I could never get used to the eruption of emotions from my clients.

When a matter gets to a court hearing, there has often been a dispute for years. People have been stewing over memories and facts from long ago. It's not good for anyone's mental health.

For over fifteen years I had avoided the court room focussing instead on other legal work until suddenly, I had no choice. I was called as a witness. Knowing that most matters get resolved before the court date, I pushed it to the back of my mind. But as much as I pride myself on being unflappable, it was an itch of a feather that would not go away. I racked my brain about that day. I stewed, I cried. I'm not afraid of the courtroom, I am a lawyer after all, and the matter was a huge win, but rarely is a win worth the emotional turmoil.

I want no businesswoman to have to resolve a commercial dispute in court.

Don't get me wrong, I'm glad we live in a society where we have the institutions and systems in place that mean resolving a dispute doesn't involve killing your neighbour or maiming a stranger. But if people took into account the toll on their emotional and physical health that a court hearing takes, there would be precisely no one rushing to 'have their day in court.' That's including the time it steals from your life and, the more obvious, legal and financial costs.

My law firm is based on encouraging women to be proactive about their legals. The last thing I want is to see is a start-up ending up in a costly, time-consuming dispute that could have easily been avoided. Whilst not everything is predictable, there are ways we can prepare for the future and for things that could go wrong. The mere act of looking at the worst that could happen for your business can help ensure that it doesn't happen, or if it does, it minimises the impact. Planning for your business is the best way to illuminate and direct its future and ensure you are prepared, for anything.

* *For confidentiality reasons, this client is not named.*

1. Be proactive about your business by planning.
2. Ensure your legals are in order before things go wrong.

3. Don't sign an agreement or contract without first getting advice.
4. Protect your intellectual property – your brand, your copy, your photos, your designs. These are your most valuable business assets.
5. Plan to be outrageously successful, and you will be.

One of the best quotes my mother and I love is this; 'Yesterday is history, tomorrow is a mystery, today is a gift; that's why it's called the present.' So, learn from history, prepare and plan for the mystery that is tomorrow so you can create something magical and enduring in the world, and get started in your business today.

DAVINA is the founder of The Mumpreneur Lawyer. Her law firm helps mum start-ups protect their businesses from legal risk with personalised online legal solutions. She specialises in e-commerce and contract drafting, and also intellectual property and trademarks.

Davina has been a lawyer for over fifteen years. She started working for big corporate law firms in outsourcing and intellectual property in 2005, and then developed a broader focus on commercial matters. For the last ten years she has worked predominantly with small businesses.

'The Mumpreneur Lawyer was born out of a frustration with the legal industry matched with personal necessity. I was vexed with the way law firms were billing clients, and the reluctance for change and embracing technology. And I was disappointed that mums had little option other than to take their kids along to legal appointments at inconvenient times with lawyers who spoke to them in another language.'

'Becoming a mum also helped me realise that working to create a certain number of billable hours each day was an unproductive use of my time when I wanted to spend it bonding with my new son. I realised quality work was far more important than a billable hour. By setting up ways to create quality work for clients with fixed costs rather than billing by the hour, and working flexibly with clients in terms of online and evening appointments, I have created a thriving business that works for me and other mums.'

Davina is an advocate for gender equality and women's empowerment, or more particularly a mum's economic empowerment. She has performed international human rights pro bono work, and pro bono work for organisations set up to deal with various crisis situations such as the recent bush fires on the south coast, and Covid-19.

mumlawyer.com.au

Taking Big but Calculated Risks

RACHAEL FERGUSON

Theodore Roosevelt famously stated, '*Nothing worth having comes easy,*' which I can wholeheartedly agree with. I've lost count of the number of times those powerful words got me through the early years of my challenging entrepreneurial journey.

Taking risks is scary. It tests and pushes us to our limits so we can grow and evolve, constantly becoming a better and more successful version of ourselves. The fight for my success is why I'm so grateful for where I am today.

Being wildly successful is being willing to risk what other people won't. Those risks can entail money, reputation, relationships, another business and time. My risks were a combination of these.

My journey wasn't easy, with many failures along the way. I often thought I'd dug myself in so deep the only solution was to just keep moving. I persevered through the tough times, turning my failures into a manifestation of opportunities, then finally successes.

Being destined for success doesn't mean you need to be the

smartest person in the room or the 'best' at something. I was an average student in a public high school, but I enjoyed learning, so I worked hard for all the opportunities in my life. Being driven and passionate to do podiatry, I completed two years in another degree purely so I could transfer to my podiatry degree. Facing obstacles and overcoming them will only make you stronger.

The key is to show up every single day, be consistent, work hard, be kind, surround yourself with inspiring mentors and be true to your values and your purpose. This will ignite your passion and open doors you could have only dreamed of. In essence, it's the secret to a successful business life.

After seven long and gruelling years, my company *SynxBody* appeared to become an overnight success in 2018. But like many overnight success stories, it couldn't be further from the truth, and certainly didn't happen overnight.

Years of hard work, sacrifice, blood, sweat, and tears went into building the foundations of my company. I truly believe it's imperative to your ongoing success to face the challenges head on, own them, and learn so you can grow and evolve to become the best version of yourself.

To guide you on your entrepreneurial journey to navigate the risks, I'll share my experiences, failures, and successes of risks taken and the importance of being true to your values and your purpose

My Story

I managed two struggling businesses for seven years. Despite working harder than I could have ever imagined, success still seemed out of my reach. On reflection, it's impossible to invest your time and energy into two start-up businesses and expect them to be profitable quickly. With fragmented energy between two or more businesses, it becomes harder to focus on goals, let alone achieve them. In hindsight, I should have invested my time and energy into one business. Whilst I knew both would be hugely successful, I didn't have the time and resources to manage both.

I created *SynxBody* with my co-founder in 2011 after we identified a gap in the market for a slim insole that fitted into more shoes. We used our podiatry experience to design, develop, and bring to market an insole, including a system for health professionals to modify them.

We trademarked and patented our insole design globally and in 2015, appeared on the hit TV show Shark Tank, landing a deal with shark Andrew Banks. This successful partnership is ongoing, with Andrew remaining an investor to this day. However, success for *SynxBody* didn't eventuate until 2018, three years after we appeared on Shark Tank because we still had so much to learn!

My co-founder and I sacrificed so much during those early years, with time away from our families and time spent overseas; working late when others were out having fun. My energy was always split between two businesses and being a mother of two young children and a wife. Trying to make everything work was proving impossible.

By 2017, I pushed myself to my limits, working harder than ever, yet with little success to show for it. My work life balance was out of kilter, and I didn't have time to exercise nor spend time reflecting or planning exactly where I wanted my business to go. I was reactive and responding to every urgent crisis that arose. Yet, I couldn't see what was right in front of me. We had a great product, but our branding and packaging was lost on the shelf against our competitors.

During that year, I finally had the realisation that the only person to get me out of the situation was myself. Until that point, I thought if I kept working hard, success would eventually arrive, but boy was I wrong. If you're feeling stuck and not winning in any area of your life, you need to shake things up massively to see huge shifts in your life.

My world changed when I got a business coach, started journaling, meditating, reading, exercising and eating better. Having the discipline to show up at 5am every day and repeat the same routine was the key to unlocking my full potential.

In 2017, my co-founder exited the business, although remaining a minor shareholder. I made the difficult decision to walk away from my clinic and lead *SynxBody* as the CEO, risking everything I had on the success of the company. Looking back, it was a risky decision, but I researched and strategized on what was needed to take it to the next level.

By 2018, after a huge overhaul in packaging, I added another three brands and ten new products, all while securing ranging of our patented insole, *Synxsole,* in Australia's biggest retailer, Chemist Warehouse. This was a turning point with the product suddenly being in four hundred Australian stores overnight.

The next few years saw rapid growth, with more products being ranged in Chemist Warehouse and other pharmacies, opening the doors for great opportunities in the United States, Malaysia, South Africa, and Dubai. We've seen growth rates of an average 200%, year on year. We've also filmed two TV commercials and appeared on Studio Ten, The Morning Show, and Sky Business, with many radio appearances, including publishing many business and health articles.

Taking Big, But Calculated Risks

Being a successful entrepreneur is mastering calculated risks in such a way that if you fail, you can still fight another day. So, what IS the secret to knowing when to risk it all or walk away? I believe being agile and moving quickly in business is imperative to be successful. Being slow to react can be detrimental to your success, so I like to implement a super quick formula that I refer to as **ACCIS.**

Assess & Ask, Calculate, Core Values, Intuition, Systems.

The most important lesson I've learnt is, don't repeat the same thing hoping for a different result. Do things differently if you want to shake it up!

When making new business risks, I review the risk using ACCIS and making adjustments before proceeding, always ensuring I am true to my purpose and my brand, with my customers' best interests in mind.

Here are my top 5 tips:

TIP 1: ASSESS AND ASK.

Break the risk down, making sure you know exactly what's at stake, asking mentors for guidance.

Assessing, measuring, and minimising risk is a vital skill. Here are some examples of a real risk analysis in my business when creating new products, but this can be adapted to taking on any new risk in your business.

When formulating my pain relief cream *Synxeaze®*, I wanted to create, formulate, and bring to market an Australian made organic product.

The Assessment phase involves breaking the risk down into clear and concise points.

- **What is the risk?** Creating a pain relief cream that is natural, organic and effective in reducing painful conditions. The risk is creating a new product in an already established and saturated market, but the opportunity is making it differently to our competitors.
- **What are the key benefits?** Making an Australian made product from organic and premium ingredients. The key

differences will be around the synergistic way the ingredients work together and also how the ingredients are grown and harvested, and a key ingredient with clear differentiation from our competitors.

- **What are the costs?** Costs can be financial, time, and resources. Identify any significant financial costs and assess the time it will take you, and any members of your team, to potentially allocate resources to the project.
- **Who are your competitors?** Review your market. Research your competitors, identifying your point of difference. Ensure you stand out, otherwise you will spend much more in marketing $$ trying to be the same as your competitors.

Ask Your Mentor

I believe it's imperative to consider different perspectives when considering risk taking in business to reach a balanced perspective. I feel fortunate to have three male investors I can count on for advice and guidance. Equally, I have three females and my business coach. As CEO leading my company, I need to make the decisions but, I can't emphasise enough, the importance of surrounding yourself with successful leaders equipped to challenge and advise during the process.

I consider myself fortunate to have Andrew Banks as one of my male mentors. Andrew is charismatic, calm, reassuring, whilst also being highly intelligent and always offering sound advice. I highly recommend finding a mentor who is successful and uplifting, whilst genuinely caring, or has an invested interest in your success.

I run many ideas past Andrew and his amazing personal assistant, Tricia Stevens, who is one of my female mentors. They are a dynamic duo, who listen, consider, and use their worldly experience and knowledge to assist and advise. Having another valued perspective really helps to identify what may not have been considered.

TIP 2: CALCULATE. Measure and Minimise your risk. Identify what type of risk it is. Is it low, high, or a calculated risk and how can you minimise some of the risk?

I detail the types of risks that occur in my business, and I often have concurrent risks occurring, but only have one high risk and calculated risk occurring at the same time.

Low Risk Approach: An example of a low risk might be adding a new product to a current and established range. The branding is already established, you already have buyers interested, and adding a new product to that range is relatively risk free.

High Risk Approach: Adding a new brand and/or product quickly. I hire a formulator, choose ingredients, do market research and design the label. This approach is fast, allows for minimal research or time to review the risk because it is time sensitive, and doesn't allow room to make changes. My advice is to always proceed with any high-risk tasks with caution and reduce the amount of high-risk decisions in your business.

We took a high-risk approach when introducing our sanitising range, *Pure Sanity Co.,* during the Covid-19 Pandemic. We saw the influx of inferior and expensive sanitising products and the huge shortage of packaging materials. So, we created a fun and on the go range of sanitising products, to keep people safe, with buyers waiting for it.

The project was time sensitive, creating the branding and products in record time, but the shipment was delayed. Which meant by the time the products were available, we had missed the biggest opportunity with buyers, as they had over purchased stock and couldn't take on our range. Because of heavy advertising restrictions on social channels, we couldn't advertise our products.

Whilst this project still has immense opportunity, it was a high-risk project that, because of timing, could have been insanely successful in a short space of time.

Calculated Risk Approach: This is my preferred risk approach regularly used in our business. It's measured, considered, and modified as required. An example of a calculated risk approach is our *Synxeaze®* cream we've been working on for over twelve months.

Ingredients are researched, a formulator found, ingredients finalised, and samples created:

1. To reduce risk, assess the market. Identify competitors, finding a minimum of three points of differentiation. If there are no points of difference, reconsider the project, as the risk is too high.
2. Test samples so real people can trial the product. Feedback is collated, consistency tested, changes to formula made and tried again.
3. Test samples again. I've mitigated further risk by trialling the sample and gathering feedback. This process can go on multiple times until ready for manufacturing.
4. Test packaging. Ensure it's eye catching, with solid marketing points talking to your ideal consumer. Request feedback from test groups. Ensure compliance is adhered to with all relevant bodies, with labelling and claims correct.
5. Test Buyer. Approach ideal buyers and obtain feedback. This process occurs before any manufacturing, therefore reducing further risk.

After we have reviewed the risk against the above process, it is much easier to identify ways to reduce risk or pivot from your idea entirely.

TIP 3: CORE VALUES. Know your top 5 core values and make sure you're aligned to them!

We all thrive when we're aligned to our highest values.

When was the last time you assessed your top 5 core values? The priority of our values changes over time, so it's important to check in now and then.

Figuring this out with my business coach in 2017 was a real eye-opener, as prior to this, I'd been working tirelessly, unaware my highest values were not being met. There's no surprise I was exhausted, burnt out, and my businesses weren't thriving.

I discovered my highest values were love, kindness, honesty, being challenged, health and wellness. Once I figured out what mattered most, it was much easier to make decisions. The biggest value not being met was my health, so I focused on my mindset with meditating and journaling, and my physical health by exercising and eating better.

Once I'd energised myself, it was so much clearer to see exactly what risks needed to be taken to get my company on track, and how I was going to achieve it.

When considering any new risks, ensure they align with your highest values. For me, I need to love and feel passionate about a project. It has to align with my honesty and health and wellness values, so it needs to be made from premium ingredients, ethically sourced and manufactured, all at an affordable price.

TIP 4: INTUITION – Trust your gut!

Our incredible bodies are more intuitive than we give them credit for. Practicing daily meditation brings me great clarity during times of new project risks. Trust your first thoughts and don't overthink it.

Then I ask three key questions:

- If money was no object, would you still be doing this?
- Does it give you goosebumps and butterflies at the thought of it?

- Can you imagine being just as happy doing something else?

Don't allow fear of failure to stop you from taking big risks. Some of my biggest learnings have come from failure. Fear means we are challenging ourselves to grow.

In 2017, I made the biggest decision, relying significantly on my intuition. Taking better care of my health, exercising again, and eating better with a great morning routine gave me more confidence and clarity to take on the biggest challenge in my career.

If I were to win lotto, would I still want to be leading my company? 100% YES! I can't ever imagine wanting to do anything more, even if I didn't need to work again. My business still gives me goosebumps and butterflies when making decisions on a daily basis. I can't ever imagine being happy doing anything else. This is how I knew I was absolutely where I was meant to be.

TIP 5: SYSTEMS. Viable systems in business are a necessity for taking on more risk. Ensure you know your position when it comes to your customers and roles within the business. Make sure time is managed well, processes are adhered to and running smoothly.

Ensuring systems are in place to take on the risk and deal with complications is essential. Business is rarely a smooth ride, and one of the most valuable skills I've learnt is not to overreact when things don't go according to plan.

Hurdles in manufacturing will occur. There will be times when packaging is printed incorrectly, and shipments are delayed. To combat this, we allow for more lead-in time. Don't sweat it when shipments are delayed. We communicate with our customers to ensure they're aware of what is happening.

As a company, we've built exceptional customer service. My team all ensure the number one priority is our customer and their experience is a positive one. If we have a customer who may have purchased the wrong size or an unsuitable product, we go above and beyond to turn that experience around for them. Even if it means sending an extra product at our expense or taking the time to give them professional podiatry advice. Every customer is a lifeline to your business, so all people want is to feel heard and understood.

If there are any hurdles with packaging, we wear the cost and re-print it. Your reputation is everything. Delaying shipments a couple of weeks to ensure it meets your expectations far outweighs delivering a product you're not 100% proud of.

Be clear on company policies and where you stand on customer service to ensure you have the systems to cope with increased demand as your company grows.

Delegation is an extremely important task to master and one I wasn't very good at. If I'm honest, it's still a work-in-progress for me delegating more to my amazing team. In 2017, when my business was struggling, we had minimal practical systems in place. I performed every role, finding it difficult to let go as I felt I needed to be involved in everything.

After hiring my amazing executive assistant and sales manager, we overhauled all our processes, and we now have a clear definition of roles within the business. We also use programs to ensure we have a clear snapshot of our business at any given moment, helping us to make decisions on risk more effectively and responsibly.

Some software we use include:

- Xero
- Shopify
- Unleashed
- Klaviyo
- Salesforce

So, the key message is to know your numbers and know your business. If you're not sure, then re-think the risks you're considering until you have solid foundations in place.

I hope you've found some of these tips on 'taking big but calculated risks' helpful. If you only take one thing away, please remember to *back yourself*. If you're aligned to your highest values and purpose, you will thrive with your big risks paying off with consistency and hard work.

RACHAEL FERGUSON

Rachael Ferguson, podiatrist and entrepreneur on a mission to educate the public on the importance of foot health as well as creating products to help keep people on their feet and pain free because your health really starts from the ground up.

I also enjoy sharing my business knowledge and teaching and inspiring women on their own entrepreneurial journeys.

I grew up in a really loving and happy home with my parents and two sisters in Western Australia and from as young as I could remember my father would encourage me to dream big and have my own business and both my parents instilled the values of being kind, honest, loyal, doing the right thing and working hard in life. Those early conversations with my father and watching his business succeed, ignited my own passion for business. I'm a firm believer that entrepreneurs aren't born, they are made.

I graduated as a podiatrist from Curtin University in 2004 and shortly after becoming a mother at 25, I took the plunge and started not one but two businesses at once, my podiatry clinic, Elite Sports Podiatry and SynxBody, an Australian footcare company. I was also pregnant with my second child over that time and my life was very full raising my two children, running two businesses and a household, the struggle was real.

After 7 hard years, SynxBody became successful and has grown rapidly since then. We now manufacture insoles, specialised footcare products for corns, callouses, burning feet, bunions and much more. We also make no-tie shoelaces, compression sleeves and about to release an Australian made pain relief cream.

Some of my biggest achievements have been winning the

prestigious Gold Stevie Award for Entrepreneur of the Year Asia, Australia and New Zealand in New York and becoming a Western Australian Ambassador for Women's Entrepreneurship Day Organization which was founded in New York. I was also a finalist for the Telstra Women's Business Awards and won bronze for the Ausmumpreneur of the Year Award. Last but not least I won the highly coveted First Amongst Equals title for Business News' top 40under40 and that experience just blew my mind.

So please remember that if I can do it…you can too! So, fill up your cup, make sure your aligned with your purpose and take care of your health and your mindset as that is the key to unlocking your full potential.

synxbody.com.au

Profit should be something that is planned, not something that happens by chance.

VANESSA FIDUCIA

In a world where so much happens that is out of our control as mothers and business owners, the things we need to focus on are that within our control. The ability to make a profit in business is something that needs to be planned and not left to chance.

In business, planning for profit is so important for many reasons. I am not talking just tax planning here. Profit has many important uses within a business and without it, do we have a business, or have we just brought ourselves a job?

I am personally so passionate about this topic; I became a certified *Profit First* Professional in Australia. Currently, my accounting firm is only one of three Certified P*rofit Firs*t Accountants in Victoria, Australia.

I was so inspired to be a part of this collaboration with amazing women because I believe you truly need to have confidence in your numbers and business to truly *back yourself.*

When I first started my business journey, I was like many of you. I had two bank accounts, one for everything and one for tax. Sometimes I felt like I was really cash flow positive because I saw the cash in bank growing. Then all of a sudden, the bills would roll in for the month and I would barely have enough money to pay wages, let alone myself. Not only that, I'd just pulled another 80-hour week and had not seen my children. I knew there had to be a better way. That is when I discovered *PROFIT FIRST*. I could not believe what I was seeing. It seemed so bloody logical, but why didn't we do it? I can tell you why. It's because it's not what the standard accounting principles tell us what to do, and we would go against the grain.

Now let's take a deep dive into some of these vital topics we don't talk about often enough.

What is traditional accounting and why is the formula broken?

Traditional accounting is what most of us are used to. We read a Profit and Loss Statement that our Bookkeeper or Accountant gives us. We look at the figure at the bottom to see if we have made a profit or not. The formula to this is Income – Expenses = Profit. Well, I bet you never thought you would be reading this but, this formula is broken. This formula does not allow for the human behaviours we all have.

While we still need to use traditional accounting for our reporting to the taxation office, it does not serve our businesses in our daily operations and cash flow management. When using the traditional method of accounting, we are not allowing for the cash flow trends within our businesses. We are assuming we are robots and we all work in the same way, which we do not.

A perfect example of why the traditional method of accounting is broken is this. We will call the business ABC Hairdressing Pty Ltd. (For privacy reason we can't disclose their real name, but this is a real case study.)

ABC Hairdressing Pty Ltd was going about their day running their business thinking everything was going great. Money was coming in; they were paying their bills. The Profit and Loss said they were making a Profit.

BUT they had no cash flow management system in place. They didn't put money aside to pay their tax obligations, and they also had no idea where their profit had gone. Their profit was just a number on a piece of paper, what we call 'paper profit', but they didn't have money in the bank or any assets or investments to show for it. They did, however, have a great big dirty tax bill for that missing profit.

This went on for about eight years. The business owner got payment plan after payment plan, after payment plan with the Taxation Office. At the end of that eight-year mark, the debt was over $300,000 and the business owner had to declare bankruptcy. The owner of ABC Hairdressing Pty Ltd was determined to never let this happen again.

In 2019-2020 there were 12,450 bankruptcies listed. **https://www.afsa.gov.au/statistics/annual-statistics**

Some cases could have been avoided, including ABC Hairdressing Pty Ltd if they'd had a good cash management system.

Now for the good news, ABC Hairdressing Owner has now finished the bankruptcy and is using The *Profit First* Methodology successfully and does not owe one cent to the tax department. He also has a new amount of CASH profit (not 'paper profit') sitting in his purposeful Profit bank account.

What is *Profit First*, and why does the system work?

The *Profit First* System is a methodology founded by the amazing Mike Michalowicz. It is a cash flow overlay that compliments yet flips traditional accounting on its head. **https://profitfirstaustralia.com.au/profit-first-book-2/**

Instead of using the aged of accounting formula of Sales – Expenses = PROFIT, we use Sale – PROFIT = Expenses.

The method of *Profit First* focuses mostly on the human behaviours we all have.

The one I love the most and I will use as an example here is the Parkinson's Law. Often Parkinson's Law is used to explain time. For example, if you had eight hours to complete a task, you would drag it out over the eight hours. However, if you only had four hours to complete that same task, you find efficient ways to complete that same task. We can apply the same principle with your money. If you have $10,000 to complete a project, you will most likely use the whole $10,000. If you only have $5,000 to complete the same project, then you will find ways to complete the same task on a smaller budget.

With *Profit First*, we use similar principles with bank accounts. Instead of having all your business funds in one bank account, which can feel you have an abundance of funds, it's separated. It's a fact we've already spent a lot of that money on obligations such as materials and subcontractors, taxes, owner's pay, and all-important profit. What's left after all that is operating expenses. But how on earth will you know what is left for expenses if it is all bundled into one account? There is no clarity.

Most of our clients are actively using and loving the *Profit First* System for so many reasons. Below are some real-life stories of clients who have implemented the *Profit First* system in their business and what it has done for them.

'From mini meltdown to buying a home only a short few months later, the *Profit Firs*t Method has been without a doubt the most important thing we could have done during the pandemic. It immediately showed us our true financials and eliminated any guesswork on available funds. Also, allowing us to slow down, honour the reality and work smarter not harder because we knew EXACTLY how much we needed to earn in an already very tiring and stressful time. Meeting Vanessa and having her introduce this simple approach has made money fun again! I am a complete rookie in this area, so it has been very empowering knowing I can genuinely and accurately understand the financials of the business after a quick look into our accounts. Most importantly, it's allowed us to focus on the magic of our business without worrying about money. Thank you so so much, Vanessa! You and the *Profit First* Method have single-handedly kept us in business. We appreciate you and truly can't thank you enough.' - **Kristian Serainidis, Founder PROJECT KICK IT.**

'I started my business about 3 1/2 years ago, and found that the running of a new business, both in the field, and the administration and bookkeeping were quite a juggle. Ensuring I had enough money for things like insurances, loans, vehicle and trailer registrations, business expenses such as fuel and materials, I always found it to be a week to week and month-to-month struggle. Finding my feet and trying to get up and running as quick and as effortless as possible was quite the dilemma. The hands-on was fine, but the bookwork side needed some love. I decided to employ the services of Vanessa and her accounting team to help me with the back of house side of things. And I haven't looked back.' – **Glenn Simester, Owner JIM'S MOWING (SOMERVILLE NORTH)**

'*Profit First* has been a great match for my budgeting system. As we have huge cash flows from week to week, our budgets allow me to see that:

1. We are achieving sales targets.

2. We are not overspending on operating expenses.

This was evaluated monthly. But that is where the budget guidance ends.

The following factors become unknown quickly.

1. How much GST and Company Tax needs to be put aside without guessing.
2. Exactly how much money in the bank is mine? (My Favourite Part.)
3. Is there enough money available to pay suppliers on time?

The benefits of transparency for the *Profit First* Method are:

1. No longer delaying payments to suppliers. Always needed to have excessive funds in the bank to cover the unexpected.
2. Allows myself to increase Owners pay and still be operating inside the budget.
3. Being able to better allocate funds either inside or outside of the Business depending on what is the best rate of return.
4. Reduce time spent planning future cash flow.

Ultimately, the main benefit for us is the certainty of available funds, which in turn allow for smarter decision making, which leads to higher productivity.'

ROB RICHARDS, OWNER TIGHES HILL CELLARS

Why you need to plan for profit during the worst times.

We never know what is just around the corner, and 2020 as a year has been the perfect example of that. We are currently in the middle of a worldwide pandemic where a lot of businesses have either been forced to close, reduce their hours, or totally pivot on how they do business.

While 2020 has been a year of ups and downs, I feel it has also been so exciting for many reasons. Watching businesses grow to levels they never thought they would and innovate like no other.

Planning for profit has never been so important when times are uncertain. Every little cent counts. Changing our business model might mean we are instantly saving on overheads, but it also means having cash reserves. Or what we call a 'vault' account with three months' worth of savings for all aspects of your business. This includes Operating Expenses, Profit and Owner's Pay put aside is vital. This cash reserve 'vault' has saved a lot of our businesses throughout these uncertain times. And I am sure it will help businesses for many years to come. Just imagine what it would do for you knowing you had a cash reserve for a rainy day that could see you and your business through a rough three months. Best of all, it's something you planned for. So, when that rainy day comes, because let's face it, in life these things happen and you were prepared. It can make all the difference.

What you do when you put profit away?

We often get asked the same questions. 'So, what do I do with my Profit?' Or 'I have been putting my Profit away, but now what?' The key to this is again having a plan.

There are three vital key steps we also go into and it would be to ask yourself the following questions:

- Do I have debt?
- Do I have money in an account put away for a rainy day? (The 'vault' or 'cash reserve'.)
- How do I want to celebrate as a business owner?

Once you have answered these questions, you're a step closer to determining where or how your profit will be spent.

One client, an amazing husband and wife duo in the construction industry have adopted the method perfectly. They have paid off debt and used debt elimination perfect within the first twelve months of implementation. They no longer have any debt with the ATO and are going onto extend their family home with celebration money!

Definition of profit beyond the accounting definition

When people think of Profit, they think it is the final figure on the Profit and Loss Statement. Profit is far beyond what the standard accounting definition gives it credit for. Profit enables business owners to pay their team better through reward and recognition systems. Which enables the business to have access to staff they possibly would not have before. Profit provides personal freedom for the business owner. Profit allows the business owner to work fewer hours.

Most importantly, when you hit a level of Profit within your organisation, it allows you to give back to charity and causes that align with your mission and vision.

I interviewed Barry Williame Magliarditi, the Founder

and CEO of *The Game Changers* and Author of The Path to Freedom. He has been using the *Profit First* Methodology for some time now and had some amazing insight on what his thoughts were around profit beyond the standard accounting definition.

What does Profit mean to you beyond the standard accounting term?

> 'First thing that comes to mind is fuel for growth and I mean not just personal ventures but business ventures as well. Without profit and what I mean by profit is CASH profit, not paper profit. We have not got the ability to reinvest to scale companies, which in turn, makes us more profit. We also do not have the ability to invest in stocks and shares or property from a personal perspective.'

What do you believe Profit does for a business?

> 'Well, a few things. It fuels growth and provides a level of certainty for the business, for its staff and for the business owner. It's the purpose we are in business. Yes, our businesses should be making a difference. But if we make the mistake that I did in the early days of just having a business to contribute to the world and make the world a better place, then we are not really contributing to the world at all, because we are not able to hire staff. We are not able to pay suppliers. We run this sub-substantial business that is based out of a cardboard box. Generating consistent and profitable growth mean we can create sustainability in the difference we want to make within both our internal and external environment.'

Profit Provides 'freedom' to business owners. True or false?

> 'True, as long as it's not paper profit. I guess this is the difference with *Profit First.* A lot of people preserve profit as

what they see on their Profit and Loss but tax is still required to come out of that. What I like about the *Profit First* Approach and what they teach in richest man in Babylon is that its actual CASH. It's cash in your bank. Cash you can use to reinvest and make more cash. It's what I see us as. As entrepreneurs, I see us as asset managers. We need to manage assets of profitability, cash flow, people, investments and ultimately we should be receiving more out of it then we are putting in.'

Does having Profit allow you to give back to your team and the community?

'Yes, absolutely. Often, we will do far more to make 1 million dollars then to keep 1 million dollars when we are making money. Again, our job is to make more so we can spend more. Whether that is spending more on stocks, shares, investments, property, etc., that still feeds people, still fuels people. Money is that energy exchange and again, the more we focus on making it sustainable, the more we allow others to do the same to.'

The *Profit First* Method can work for all businesses. Out with the old, and in with the new formula of SALES – PROFIT = EXPENSES and you are on your way to a profitable business starting now.

First, remember to invest in your business to grow it to its full potential. Second, invest in yourself! *BACK YOURSELF* all the way and with clarity around your numbers and a clear plan to make profit, you will have no problem in achieving this.

It's ok to spend money on the right things. When money is allocated in accounts for its purpose, it's much easier for you to make clear decisions and *BACK YOURSELF* on what you are doing. Having a cash reserve 'vault' account will save your bacon on a rainy day during uncertain times.

Once you have put your profit away, do not forget to allocate it quarterly. We want to pay down debt, put money away into the cash reserve 'vault' and treat ourselves to a celebration.

Last, and most importantly, PROFIT = CASH in the bank, not paper profit on a Profit and Loss statement.

If you would like help implementing *Profit Firs*t in your business, then contact a Certified *Profit First* Professional. You can find them all over the world.

If you would like to purchase a copy of *Profit First*, you can do that online or purchase at your local bookstore. Link to book **https://profitfirstaustralia.com.au/profit-first-book-2/**

VANESSA FIDUCIA

Owner and CEO of Profit First Accounting, a wife, mother, sister, aunty, and daughter. Vanessa started her business owner journey in 2013 at age 21 with a focus on Bookkeeping services for mostly Trade based clients with qualifications including Certificate IV in Financial Services, BAS Agent Registration, IPA Fellow, ICB Member in Practice, Profit First Certification, Xero Partner and Fix This Next Fixologist.

In late 2018 she established Profit First Accounting. As a business owner and founder this journey had Vanessa managing the exit of a business partner, the onboarding of a shareholder, the development and growth of her team along with ensuring clients received the unique program deliverables and expertise required of a bespoke financial services firm.

Vanessa, originally establishing this business as a means to getting more life balance as a mum of two young children she really wanted to spend more quality time with her children who are currently aged 5 and 6 and of course create cashflow to support her view of work life balance. As a woman in business Vanessa soon learnt that her dreams of spending more time with her children would take a lot of leadership and effort to get her business to the point that she could step away to be with her family.

Vanessa's greatest achievement to date outside of being the runner up in the Sept 2020 AusMumpreneur awards for Service Business and Business Excellence. Along with this was achieving a four-day work week with Friday being Family Friday Day, a day of no work for herself and her team. Her dream of being able to spend quality time with her children has become a reality.

www.profitfirstaccounting.com.au

How to create a business that brings you more freedom, money and time

EMMA HEUSTON

You can have it all, but you have to be creative about it. I had to have a near death experience to figure that out, but I am living proof it is possible.

As women, we are conditioned to believe that we must choose between family *or* career. To decide between being happy *or* being wealthy. Opting for either financial security *or* career flexibility. Maintaining a certain lifestyle *or* having business growth. But what if there was a way to do all these things on your terms in your own way?

As a young girl of ten, a well-meaning but wizened neighbour sat me down in her kitchen, her stout frame in front of me, hand on hip, stern gaze fixed on my face. She exhaled, blowing her breath upward to dislodge a stray strand of grey hair that had come to rest in her eyes. '*A secretary is a good career for a girl,*' she asserted as she began a lengthy lecture. I sat there staring back at her, not sure what to say. I was a shy girl, but inside I was busting to ask, '*but what if I want to be the boss?*'

In early 2019, I started my own business. The Remote Expert is an online law firm that helps women with online businesses. I assist them to protect and grow their business empires. I took this step into entrepreneurship after eighteen years of being an employee. Eighteen years of having other people hire me to build their dreams. That's right, almost two decades of working my guts out for other people's companies. Finally, thirty years after my neighbour lectured me on suitable jobs for women, I built up the courage to go it alone. I wanted to shout out loud from the rooftops, '*I am the boss!*'

In less than two years, I have built The Remote Expert up to be the sole breadwinner for our family. The business now employs myself, my husband and a small part-time team. Transitioning to owning a family business has created freedom for our family. Freedom that allows us to devote extra time to my son's learning disabilities, to enjoy coastal far northern New South Wales, and to live every moment of a life that was almost taken away from me.

How did I take my business from zero income and no clients to a 6-figure business in under two years? By developing and applying The Supercharge Method™. I designed the method as a systematic way to create more freedom, money and time in my own business. It was so successful for me that I now share it with others, with my clients and now, with you.

PART 1

Business ownership: the ultimate flexibility for family

'Having a baby changes your life.'

Hands up who has heard those words when they were pregnant? While the cliché is older than a pair of Grandma's undies, it still gets thrown around regularly. While I agree with the sentiment, the cliché oversimplifies the role of children in your life. Having children changes life for each of us in different ways, in ways unique to every one of us.

The biggest and most profound change for me after my son was born was that there was no time to muck about. Since becoming a mother, I am more efficient. I am not willing to tolerate time wasters, and I am determined to create an empire for our family. The birth of my son led to the creation of my business.

My pregnancy was traumatic. At thirteen weeks pregnant I had morning sickness so severe, I wound up in hospital. During a routine medical procedure to give me an anti-nausea drug, things went terribly wrong. The anti-nausea drug caused a sudden cardiac arrest. My heart stopped. My clothes were cut from my body and I was resuscitated, defibrillated and pummelled to keep my heart pumping. I remained unconscious and unresponsive in intensive care for three days after this incident, while my husband sat at my bedside wondering if he had lost his wife and his yet to be born baby. Thankfully, my son, (now eight at the time of writing this book) survived. But nothing has ever been the same since that day.

Following the incident, I suffered from post-traumatic stress disorder. Then there was the battery of medical tests I underwent. The fear that something might not be right with my son or I, was with me all the time. I worried things could end during childbirth or at some other time during pregnancy.

Once my son came along, we realised Sydney and big city life was not for our family of three. We wanted affordable real estate without a huge mortgage. We needed accessible daycare. But most of all, we wanted to experience slow living. Our dream was to take things easy. Not run around in pointless circles on the hamster wheel of big city living so we could pay an enormous mortgage.

In late 2013, we had a sea change to far northern New South Wales. After we moved, I took a job as a lawyer at a traditional local law firm, a firm I had dreamed of working at ever since I decided to become a lawyer at thirteen when I attended a local high school. But even though the commute was great, and I had a view of the beach from my office, 9-to-5 corporate life was not for me anymore.

I then tried a stint as a remote worker as a partner in a law firm for some years while my son was young. That was better, but the volume of work compared to the reward did not stack up. The burn out I experienced because of the role was excruciating. Worst of all, I had to put aside my dreams to build another person's dreams.

My dream was to follow my calling. I found my calling when I published my 2018 book, *The Tracksuit Economy – how to work from home productively and effectively.* I wanted to help other mothers work from home in a way that suits them. My plan was to help larger companies put remote work in place to achieve this goal. But it became plain to me after a few months of getting nowhere with that goal that my mission was different. It was to help other mothers forge their own path. A path, as a self-employed business owner with a virtual team and an online business.

At the same time as my move from employee to business owner in 2019, my son was diagnosed with dyspraxia and dyslexia. The flexibility I knew I needed became even more crucial, and The Supercharge Method™ was born.

PART 2

The Supercharge Method™

Once my business' virtual doors were open, I had no idea *how* to get clients or to make a client-focussed offer. I understood what it was like, not knowing where the next client was coming from. And I knew firsthand the sick feeling in my stomach about whether I made the right choice leaving my secure job.

I know what it is like to feel small when you hear other people dismiss your 'at home' business as a hobby. A hobby you can fit in around caring for the kids and carrying the mental load at home. But let me tell you that 'little business' you run from home... that business is important. Please, for the love of all things holy, stop calling it 'little' or a 'side hustle.' It is your business, your big, messy, imperfect yet important business. Never minimise your business or your life.

In building The Remote Expert, I grappled with these issues. In fact, you might say I had more issues than Vogue! But it was time to get real and to stop begging for a seat at the table by building my own.

In building my own table, I not only built a profitable business for myself, but I created The Supercharge Method™. In this chapter, I share this method with you to help you supercharge your business by:

Promoting your business

1. Narrowing your niche
2. Producing prospects
3. Converting clients

Perfecting your offering

1. Bringing your boundaries
2. Setting your scope
3. Perfecting your pricing

Pushing ahead

1. Boosting the breadwinner
2. Scaling your services
3. Pushing your partnerships

I have followed The Supercharge Method™ in my own business and achieved great results. So, grab that pen and paper and let's settle down to see how The Supercharge Method™ works.

PART 3

Promote yourself

The first step toward supercharging your business is visibility. If you don't tell anyone about your business, how can they buy from you? Part of my fear of starting my own business was a fear I would not get clients. That people would not want to buy from me. I realised early on that unless I became visible and developed a brand, I would struggle to get clients. It was scary at times, but worth it to see my business grow. I realised the fear I felt was only a story I'd told myself to keep from striking out on my own.

Narrow that niche

It took a while, but I found my ideal clients to serve in the business. The key to finding those ideal clients was first finding my niche. The narrower my niche got, the stronger my business grew. It wasn't until I could get into the head of my ideal client and ask them what they wanted that I worked out how to sell to them. But by then, I wasn't selling, because I was delivering products and services with my ideal client in mind. I was providing them with something of value they needed, not trying to sell them something they did not need.

Producing prospects

I also found out where my ideal client hung out online. It turns out that 80% of them are on Facebook. How do I know this with such precision? It is because I worked out how to find the business statistics I needed to find. I familiarised myself with Google analytics and my website analytics. I made business decisions based on data, not drama.

Using this strategy, I made decisions that led to more business.

Converting leads to clients

But knowing where your ideal clients are doesn't automatically make them clients. You need an offer. You must have services or products that your ideal clients need. And you need a clear call to action. You also need to express these things on your website, on social media, and during calls.

My favourite way to convert an enquiry to a client is through a discovery call. I have an automatic booking page through on my website. I know if someone takes the step of booking a call with me, it means they generally need my services. Then, during a short call, we unpack their questions and I will explain what it is like working with me

If the client wishes to proceed, I have a process in place for my team to issue a quote. If a client accepts their quote, there is another process to follow to complete the work, and so on.

PART 4

Perfect your offering and protect your boundaries

My niche is to provide legal services to women with online businesses. While that niche may sound narrow, it means I am firm around the boundaries of my offerings and the type of work I take on. It also means other people know what I do and seek me out for my help. It makes me a specialist in my area. And in a noisy online world of business, that is critical.

Boundaries

Being in business, particularly a service-based business like law, is about helping people. But it is impossible to be all things to all people, especially when you have to conserve energy to give your family and yourself.

Be selective and prioritise yourself before your business. Look after yourself before you look after your family. You need the energy and mental bandwidth to help others. If you collapse in a heap, where does that leave your family and your clients?

Boundaries are so important in all aspects of life. Set boundaries around when you will work, when you take calls and what is non-negotiable time. This is how you create and protect the precious family time that we all strive for. It is not an accident that I have Friday afternoons free to take my son to the beach after school. It is not an accident I get a remedial massage once a fortnight. I schedule these items in, and if they don't happen, I am grumpy and not as functional in my business.

When I started my own business, I made a rule that I would only take appointments on Monday to Thursday between 9am - 2pm. The reason for this was to make sure I was available after school. Friday is also my day to work on the business (rather than in the business). I find this routine helps me create a balance between life and work. It also keeps my business fresh and evolving.

How to scope client work

The other thing I had to look at with The Remote Expert was the type of work I accept. I know from twenty years of practising law that there are certain types of work that fit best with a virtual law firm. I also know what I enjoy doing. Early in my business, I decided to focus on that type of client work. I don't take on dispute-based legal work. I refer that to colleagues who enjoy that work and are good at it. The client is happy and so am I, because dispute-based work makes me miserable.

Pricing

As a new business (and a home-based business), I tried to compete on price when I opened my doors. It is easy to do. It is also easy to become obsessive about your competitors. To scope out their websites, check up on their prices and generally stalk them, especially in the online space where your Instagram feed is full of your competitors. But if you keep that up, it is a race to the bottom, and if I am frank, it can do your head in.

My advice around pricing, to perfect it using The Supercharge Method™, is to charge what you are worth. I work from home, but it doesn't change anything else about my professional profile. I am a lawyer with twenty years' experience. Should I charge less because I don't have a fancy water view and big overheads? Challenge the assumption that home-based business cannot charge for their skills. And remember, no matter your location, your business is as legitimate as any other.

PART 5

Push your business ahead

Once you get the foundation parts of the business sorted, it is time to think about the future. How will you build a business that sustains you and your family for the long haul? The answer is to scale the business by growth or changing the way you operate.

Be the Breadwinner

Before I could grow my business, I had to get comfortable with the numbers. I learnt how to read a profit and loss statement. And I knew how much it cost me each month to keep my doors open and so on.

I worked out how much it would take to pay me a regular salary. Then I added a second salary for my husband. Once I had that combined figure, I set incremental monthly targets to reach our goal. I tracked the goal each week and month.

We reached our goal half way through this year. Six months ahead of schedule. In October, my husband joined the Remote Expert as

Chief Operating Officer. The change has been transformational for our family. It has allowed my husband the freedom to spend more time with our son now that he is also self-employed. It has also freed me up on the home and business front to work on the business more. I can focus on scaling the business and creating more passive income.

Scaling up

The Remote Expert is a service-based business. Scaling means either modifying some of our services so they are 1 to many (rather than 1 to 1) or growing the team. With a bigger team, it means I can step back and take on more of a management role rather than an active role.

Without these techniques applied, The Remote Expert will reach a cap on growth. After all, there are only so many hours in each day for me to work with clients and complete the work. Risk of burn out aside, this is not the picture of freedom I had in my mind when I established the business. So, I rolled my sleeves up and applied The Supercharge Method™ to this aspect also, to find that freedom.

How does this work in my business? I have my online courses that are group programs. Plus, I have help with the one-to-one work I do with clients by employing a small remote team to help me in the office.

Partnerships

Partnerships are crucial to business success. That is the final puzzle piece of The Supercharge Method™. When I say partnerships, I don't mean to get a business partner. I mean strategic alliances you can make with other like-minded business people. Alliances that will help you join together for specific projects or promotions.

In my business, this has worked well, running joint webinars or seminars to add value to clients. But if you had a product-based business, it could also be a joint promotion. The sky is the limit. The key is the ability to leverage other businesses to help you grow your own. For example, imagine two business owners teaming up to run a retreat. This would bring together two client lists and two skill sets.

The result would be far more impactful together than one person could create alone.

The business benefits of this type of collaboration can be powerful. But I wouldn't be a lawyer without warning you to make sure you document it. Every partnership you enter should be a win/ win relationship. Otherwise, it isn't a true partnership at all.

Conclusion – Freedom, money and time

Using The Supercharge Method™, I have built a business that has given me money, time, and freedom in my life. The beautiful thing is that these methods continue to apply, no matter how big my business gets. They help me supercharge my business, whatever stage.

5 hot tips

1. Not everyone will experience motherhood in the same way. Stop comparing yourself to others and do what is best for you and your family.
2. No more referring to your business as 'little' or a 'side hustle.' It is a business.
3. Narrow the niche for your ideal client and get an ideal client profile nailed down. It will change your life.
4. Be confident and enforce boundaries. Only do the work you want to do and charge what you are worth.
5. Change your service offering from 1:1 to 1 to many. Moving to a 1 to many model opens up a whole world of possibility to you.

EMMA HEUSTON

I am a lawyer, author and lady boss. I live in far northern New South Wales with my family and a tribe of pets. We try to enjoy the slower pace of life, but it is sometimes hard with a bunch of crazy pets.

Life wasn't always this way. In 2011, I was on the traditional lawyer corporate path. I had an office job in a boutique firm on the North Shore of Sydney. A near death experience changed my views on work/ life balance. It made me realise life is way too short not to do exactly as you please. At thirteen weeks pregnant, I had a common anti-nausea drug administered to help with morning sickness and had a sudden cardiac arrest in reaction to the drug. I collapsed on the floor in front of my husband, who was ushered out of the room, while I was defibrillated so my heart would start again. Thankfully, my baby boy (who is now eight) survived.

Having a baby in Sydney was crap, and house prices were out of reach, so we had a sea change in late 2013. After the sea change, I worked remotely at partner level in a law firm for many years, which was great for a while, but it didn't light that fire in my belly. The fire I had to help other women see what they could do. To help them build their own empire, and let them know it was okay they didn't have to buy into the 9-to-5 corporate life while trying to raise a family.

In 2018, I wrote my work-from-home bible, *The Tracksuit Economy: how to work productively and effectively from home.* Lawyers Weekly at the Women in Law Award named me as 'Thought leader of the Year' in 2018 and in 2019 I won a gold AusMumpreneur Award in the Women's Business School Excellence Award (Ignite).

All of this has helped boost my purpose to help women succeed in business; women who work from home and may not otherwise have the legal and mentoring help they so desperately need and deserve.

www.theremoteexpert.com

Part Three

Scaling Up

KAREN MC DERMOTT

I would not be enjoying the level of success I have today if it were not for some important success strategies that I grew into as my business evolved. Yes, you got it; I am a 'build the plane as I fall from the sky' kind of girl. It takes courage to act on an inspired thought, to take the plunge into the unknown. For me, it wasn't so much the fear of failing; it just wasn't an option not to explore the unwavering knowing that I felt deep in my core. Life is an adventure, after all! Follow that with surrounding myself with amazing people to learn from and grow with, some strategic investing, and learning to be patient when I plant seeds of intention. Most importantly, learn to love the process of evolution by embracing challenges and upgrading my mindset from the hustle, to the 'owning it' stage, without losing the essence of my passion of sharing stories with the world. Well, that is the success recipe for scaling in my book!

I am happy with the advancement I have made in eight years of business. Many people don't reach it in a lifetime. What I am proud of the most is that I haven't compromised my most important value of all, which is being a present, hands-on mum to my six children.

Yes, I live my life by design, my design. It is not a one size fits all. My life would probably be a nightmare for many people, but for me, it is a dream. It fuels my passion to continue to grow and make a bigger impact on the world through the power of story. I hope my story inspires you.

1. Acting on the right inspired thought.

From day one, my business was an adventure. In 2012, I was guided into publishing after a negative self-publishing experience left me disheartened about my first novel. 'It shouldn't be like this,' I thought. 'I have a book in my hand. What should I do next?' Then the inspired thought came that changed everything. Just like the quote at the beginning of my first novel reads, '*From every negative situation is the potential for a positive outcome,*' I acted upon my inspired thought and did some research (thanks Google). The result of which was discovering the print and distribution network, who my US based publisher used, had recently opened a base in Melbourne. I decided if I was accepted as a publisher, I would do my best to make sure authors would have a positive publishing experience and feel guided, not abandoned, when they have their book in their hands. I would dedicate my time to sharing stories with the world, both my own and others.

In 2010, when I had a loud inspired thought to write a book, I committed to the project and writing 1667 words a day for thirty days, and had a 50000-word fictional novel that had my story interwoven through it. Little did I know what a huge catalyst that book would become in my life. Not only did the publishing journey lead me to my calling, but the book itself has reached many people and helped them through their grief. Apparently, there are wisdoms woven throughout the text that bring comfort to those who are experiencingcrippling grief.

There is something wonderful that happens when a story gets told, when it makes its way out into the world. You can change someone's day, life or year with a story that connects. When a child is read a story, there is a connection that turns into a memory. When someone endures a life trauma, they can feel hope and comfort in someone else's journey. A business story will gift a reader insider knowledge, strategies and inspiration.

As you can see, acting on aligned inspired thoughts can lead you to your purpose.

2. Find Your Tribe

Starting a business can be a lonely, all-consuming endeavour, especially for a mum who is salvaging every moment to build a business and serve well. And I can guarantee there is no compromising on quality when you work with a mumpreneur. You will get their all.

In 2015, my business (and personal) life changed when I took the plunge and flew from Perth to Melbourne to attend the Ausmumpreneur conference. I made so many connections with women who got it! In the room there were hugely successful million-dollar business owners and start-ups just like me. I thought I was doing well, but my goodness did I not learn to think bigger in that room. The stories shared were going-for-gold stories and so many of them aligned with my life principles of when time and circumstance align, magic happens. It's not all about setting an intention and sitting there waiting for it to happen. It's about setting a big fat juicy intention and positioning yourself ready to receive it. I learned when we set huge intentions; they are usually beyond us at that point; but they set a ball in motion. One that attracts opportunities to grow into the person and business we need to be, to be ready to reach our goals and go way beyond them!

In 2015, I went to the conference and came home a completely different person. It was as if I was gifted a baton and should I choose to run with it, the race to the finish line was mine. This is what finding your tribe is like. They support you; they cheer you on and they get you! I started to see things bigger and found courage to step up and identify aligned opportunities. But most importantly, I had found my people, fellow mums in business who I could run things past in confidentiality, grow with and give value to. My business grew so much that year I went back in 2016 not only as a speaker, but also as an award-winner. I was so proud and more than that, I felt totally in flow.

3. Strategic investing/back yourself (be brave, there is no fear in knowing)

One of the biggest things I have observed is that many people work really hard to raise equity to grow in their business, which is wonderful for those businesses serving these needs. But for a business growing, it can feel like all you are doing is working your arse off to reinvest. But when do you reach a point where you are earning and not just growing?

I have been through this process and I have my own unique way of strategically investing along the way to make maximum impact, raise my vibration and enjoy the process. In 2015, I booked tickets for me, and my five children, to go back to Ireland. My eldest son was nineteen, and had returned a year previously. I had been in Australia seven years and hadn't seen my sisters in that time or my parents in the past few years. And I had set an intention to be open to an out-of-the-box growth possibility, and then it happened.

I had heard news that the Earl of Crom had passed away. Crom Castle always had a special place in my heart as I grew up visiting the grounds and often brought my first son there. The opportunity came to me that I could visit with the new Earl whilst in Ireland to discuss a potential writers retreat at the castle. I took the plunge and booked the castle not even knowing if I could fill it, but 100% knowing that even if I didn't, it was one of the best marketing moves I could ever make.

It felt so natural and exciting, definitely the next right step for my business and goodbye to playing small. In March 2017, we hosted our first writers' retreat. We filled every room and had the most impactful and wonderful retreat ever.

Magic happens within the walls of that castle.

I had my expectations managed; I priced the experience at an attractive price point and to be honest, I didn't expect to break even like I did. Quite often when you pull something huge off, it costs the first year and then the following years are where the profits happen. I know I was fortunate there.

By investing in this experience, it meant I raised awareness of my brand. There was an epic fifteen months of exposure before it happened. When we went to the castle itself, it was such a next level experience and the people who came together were such a dynamic group. It all flowed beautifully, the experience was positive and memorable, and so we booked again for 2019.

Through this high-level experience, I attracted the attention (and respect) of high-profile people in my arena. This enabled me to build and nurture high profile connections, up-level my prices, and sign high-end clients.

You see, although the castle was never beyond me, it wasn't in my sphere of possibility at first. I just needed to believe it was possible and have the passion to make it happen.

And of course, as I am in the publishing industry, I see first-hand how publishing a book is one of the biggest things you can do for your business to increase visibility. I get extremely excited when I see business owners publishing books. It always expands and enhances their reach in so many ways.

4. The marinate and recharge period

Being both an author and business owner, I have many inspired thoughts that I act upon. Sometimes the inspired thought will return a result quickly, some will not go anywhere and often, they are long-term gains, especially when they are big inspired thoughts.

I have to confess; I am a recovering impatient person. I have seen the light! And the reason being is that when time and circumstance align, magic happens! I have had many occurrences in my lifetime when I have pushed something to existence. But since reflecting on all the many amazing things that happen in my business and life, I know the power of waiting for that magic moment to take action and then leave it to marinate.

My job in the process of achieving my goals is to plant the seed of intention, act upon the opportunity aligned with that intention, and then have faith that I have done everything I need to for it to come to fruition when the time is right. The best results are long-term. The biggest results come when the time is right and when you have evolved enough to do it justice! So, when you have done all you can for now, step back and let it come to fruition. This time of intention marination is a time to replenish your energy. It takes energy to make things happen, and instead of continuing to empty your cup, fill it to the brim again. My thing is to go to the beach and hang out with my kids. What is your thing?

After my cup is full, I get productive. I have a mental check in with my goals and if I don't need to be taking any action at that point, I distract myself with other seeds of intention. My approach to success is to work hard, but I also treasure harmonious downtime that fills my cup. Because when challenges come and you are hanging out a high vibration, you are best equipped to conquer them.

5. Mindset upgrade/ Owning it!

One thing I didn't realise when I started out in business was the importance of checking in with my mindset! As my business grew, it required my mindset to as well. Not in an ego 'look at me' kind of way, but definitely in an upgrade to acknowledge and own the scaling I had accomplished on the way.

I know I am not the only one who has people they look up to when they start out, and you could never imagine being in their league in five- or ten-years' time. Yet it is totally possible when you embrace and honour the process of evolution that comes with scaling yourself and/or your businesses.

Owning your success is an integral part of scaling. Standing proud amongst your peers and daring to be greater, by positioning yourself alongside those you admire, will assist in your scaling trajectory.

Be confident and fearless in your approach. Not in a 'fake it till you make it' kind of way. Do it confident in all that you have achieved. When you learn to be proud for you, owning it within yourself and never needing external validation because you have done all the internal work needed to be where you are right in that moment, it is yours for the taking. All the stars have aligned for you to experience this moment, and no one can take that from you.

In my experience, people with a high profile don't feel any different than you do. They like to have meaningful conversations. If anything, they are at a disadvantage because they have to take additional precautions to protect themselves in certain situations. But when they have the freedom to be themselves, they will and they will be grateful they can feel at ease with you.

So own it, you've earned it, and be sure to check in with your mindset regularly to acknowledge how far you have come. Smell the roses of the present moment and get excited about the adventure you are about to embark on.

Conclusion

My top tips for scaling your business are what I prioritised as the main areas to focus on when planning huge growth, and you will have yours too. One thing I did not mention was to not set such a concrete goal in place that you cannot see past it. Had I not had more of an organic approach to growth, I would not have achieved as much. I could never have imagined the possibilities available to me as I began scaling. If I'd limited myself to a goal and filled every moment in the pursuit of that goal, I would not have had any room for the magic that happens in the space in between.

I highly recommend that when you are scaling, declutter at least every six months and shed the things that no longer serve you. It is ok that things are there for that season of evolution and then you move on from it. From my experience, once it is done with grace, gratitude and loving intention, there is never any ill will.

Gratitude and giving are super accelerators in scaling. Being grateful for everything you receive will ensure you stay in a high vibrational energy, and that always makes good business sense! I am a giver by nature. It's in my DNA. I get as much out of giving as the person receives. When someone invests in my services or books, I always over deliver. It's important to me that people know I treasure them, and I always see huge potential in others, and that excites me. My calling is to share stories with the world, and I want a positive narrative when people think of their experience of working with me. Of course, I don't get it right all the time, but I do give it my best.

There is one thing I know for certain, there is no limit to what you can achieve in this lifetime. It is up to you how you find that perfect spot for you that will be a perfect space between ambition, values and your dream life. You deserve it, and you can have it now with a little shift in perspective. You might already be closer than you think.

And if you are truly ready to scale, publish a book!

KAREN MC DERMOTT

Multi-award-winning publisher, TEDx Speaker, author, and advanced Law of Attraction practitioner, Karen McDermott, is a sought-after speaker who shares her knowledge and wisdom on building publishing empires, establishing yourself as a successful author-publisher and book writing.

Having built numerous highly successful publishing businesses from scratch, signing major authors, writing over 30 books and establishing her own credible brand in the market, Karen has developed strategies and techniques based on tapping into the power of knowing to create your dreams. Karen is a gifted teacher who inspires others to make magic happen in their lives through utilising her power of knowing strategies. She mentors multiple new authors through her Everything Publishing Academy.

After working with Karen, you'll walk away with essential tools and know-how to write and sell your book, get published or build your own successful publishing business, all in your own way.

kmdbooks.com

The Power of Delegation

KATRINA WURM

'If something can be done 80% as well by someone else, delegate.'
JOHN C. MAXWELL

Before we start a conversation about the *gift* of delegation, what does it actually mean?

My favourite definition comes from Merriam-Webster – *the act of empowering to act for another* (www.merriam-webster.com>dictionary>delegation).

Delegating is a concept widely used in leadership courses, books on personal development, effectiveness and even my favourite, self-care. I like the conversation to start at home. Think of it as cutting your teeth before you use this powerful tool in your business.

The Eisenhower Principle, made popular by *The 7 Habits of Highly Effective People* (1989, Simon and Schuster, New York), was my first exposure to the *gift* of delegation. The Urgent/Important Matrix is the tool I still use now to organise tasks based on priorities, not only at home but also for business. This helps prioritise important tasks instead of being distracted by what seems urgent and running around putting out fires.

Delegation is a gift, not only for you to free up your time to do other things, but it's also a gift for whoever you delegate to, whether someone in your team or in your household.

When we decide what to delegate or even to whom, we need to firstly have a conversation around time management.

What is your time worth? Do you know your accurate hourly rate?

Think of it this way. If your hourly rate is $100 an hour and you can delegate a task to someone else for $30 an hour, is it not worth delegating it? Especially when it's a task they can perform up to a standard of around 80% of how you would do it.

Yes, I just heard you:

But they won't love my business like I do?

But they won't do it as well as me?

But they won't do it the way I like it done?

Yes, I get it, but once again, how much is your time worth?

Let's break it down now and see where you can delegate.

Delegating Enterprise: Structure

When I started my coaching business, I knew I needed help in setting up the financial side of it. I also knew I needed help and coaching in this area.

The onus is on you to realise you don't know everything and don't need to. It's about delegating to people you trust, people you look up to, people you admire and handing over that responsibility to help you. Even though I have studied economics and accounting, do I want to do it every day? No. Does it light me up? No. Is it my passion, No? But for the people I delegate this to, it is their passion.

Delegating Enterprise: Knowledge

In 2020, I was awarded Gold at the 17th Annual International Business Awards in the Company of the Year – Consumer Services – Small category. Considering there were over 3800 nominations from 63 nations and over 250 professionals worldwide who participated in the judging for the awards, you can imagine my utter disbelief and total shock to receive Gold in my category.

The reason I share this with you is because my company is me, just me. Working in my home study, coaching mothers via Skype or phone, it's pretty amazing to be internationally recognised for what I do.

The reason they recognised me, besides the fact I have totally gorgeous clients who refer me to everyone, is because I have a marketing agency who help to make me sound great. They do my copywriting; they take my words, ideas and concepts and present them in such a way that magazines publish my thoughts, publications profile me and what I do, and I win awards.

Although everything they write about me is true, they know how to package and present it in a way I never could. They have years of experience and this is their passion. Yes, I could learn it and spend time doing it, but going back to what my time is worth, I would much rather be spending my time on a call to a client than coming up with copy.

Winning awards is an affirmation you're on the right track, but for me, the biggest benefit of being an international award-winning coach is that my message of neurodiversity acceptance and that all mothers deserve to have time to work on their own passion, gets out to a wider audience.

Knowledge to me is a gift and I love learning, but I realised I didn't have the time to learn everything about every detail of business. I sat down and worked out what I wanted to achieve in my business, where my knowledge gaps were, and found people who could fill them.

When you start your business, it may be just you, and you may not have the finances to hire staff, or even pay for an expert to assist you. Fortunately, there are many cost-effective options for outsourcing and delegating work. Any task you need done can be delegated.

At the start, delegation can feel like a bit of a hassle. You may have to train, teach or explain how you want tasks done, but by delegating, you hugely expand the amount of work you can do. There are programs where you can record your screen to share with someone how you want tasks done, or record a video of you doing the task, or write a standard operating procedure. Technology has made delegation so streamlined and efficient.

If you have your own team, delegation helps them to grow and reach their full potential. Delegate tasks that take too much of your time and are a low responsibility and ones that provide an opportunity for growth of that person's skills. We always want it to be a win-win situation for all involved. Think about who can grow from taking on the responsibility; what experience, knowledge, skills, and attitude that person already has, what training/assistance they may need, and what their long-term goals/interests are, and then if this new responsibility fits with those, It's worth a try.

When you first delegate, once again, remember they might not do it the same way you do, to the standard you do it, and it might take them longer. At least initially, but always remember why you delegated in the first place, to give you more time and to build the skills of the other person.

Delegating Self

As an entrepreneur, if you don't take care of your 'self-care', you may find that eventually you will be the one needing care from others. Self-care is not all about having bubble baths and massages. It's looking after your physical, emotional, and mental wellbeing. It's actually hard to do, and many women I know feel guilty that they're being selfish.

As mothers, if we don't have the physical and mental energy to wear all the different hats we need to, something will fall through the gaps. When I first started my business, I wasn't the healthiest I could be. Multiple surgeries over several years had taken their toll. Not stopping and taking time for myself resulted in me being diagnosed with an autoimmune disease.

Luckily, I had many friends and colleagues at the time who I could go to and ask for help in setting up what self-care meant to me. This is what I use and share with my clients.

1. If it feels wrong, DON'T do it.
2. Say exactly what YOU mean.
3. DON'T be a People Pleaser.
4. Trust YOUR instincts.
5. Never speak bad about YOURSELF.
6. Never give up on YOUR Dreams.
7. Don't be afraid to say NO.
8. Don't be afraid to say YES.
9. Be kind to YOURSELF.
10. Let go of what YOU can't control.
11. Stay away from drama and negativity.
12. LOVE.

As a huge fan of planning, organisation and structure, which is really the cornerstone of my coaching, if it's not in your diary/planner, it's not going to happen. My first delegation recommendation for your SELF is to delegate it to your diary. You put other appointments in your diary, work commitments, deadlines. From today I want you to schedule in YOU time. Whether it's for meditation, taking a walk, reading a chapter of a book, painting, sewing, whatever your passion is, delegate it to your diary.

Delegate your Self-Care not only to your diary but to someone else who will hold you accountable. I delegate a lot of my self-care to girlfriends. Girlfriends I go to Pilates with, girlfriends I have regular dinner dates with, girlfriends I try out new recipes with, girlfriends I can call at any time to talk with and share what's going on with me. I have girlfriends with who I have a sort of code. When one of us says, 'I need to talk,' the other will say, 'Ok, what do you need from me? To fix it, to provide a solution or just to listen?' Try it with a friend and see how it works for you.

I call them my Spark Team. People I surround myself with who lift me up, no matter what. This is about my emotional self-care.

Another person I have delegated my self-care to is my husband. He knows when I haven't eaten or had enough water, I supposedly get 'grumpy'. He knows when I need alone time, or if I need to be saying 'No' more often. Trust me, I do not take being told what to do well, but I have learnt to accept his opinion when I can't see it for myself.

In your life, right now, if you have roadblocks around taking time for self-care, who can you delegate too, who will hold you accountable?

Delegating Childcare

New Year's Eve 2007, I was done. I'd failed big time, and I'd decided my son needed a new mother. A few days later I was admitted to a mother-baby unit at a private hospital and diagnosed with severe Post Natal Depression. I spent months locked in that unit. Yes, you read that correctly. Months and LOCKED IN. I wasn't a danger to anyone else but myself. I am an organised, in control sort of person. My life was planned, I'd achieved and achieved and achieved - multiple degrees, postgraduate work, a management position, but the one thing I couldn't control was 'mothering' and my life crashed down around me.

Our son was my fourth pregnancy. For the first three, the words, 'I'm sorry, there is no heartbeat,' were becoming a recurring theme. So, with my fourth pregnancy I kept waiting for something to go wrong. At twenty-six weeks I was hospitalised for a few weeks because of complications with Placenta Previa, but our son arrived safely.

Then, for the next two months, he screamed and screamed. Breastfeeding was akin to water torture, and the lactation specialists just made me feel more inadequate. I had limited support; my family were all hours away and my husband had to travel for work leaving us at home alone. I was not coping. Years later, we discovered our son had major bowel issues resulting in being unable to feed and associated pain, but we didn't know that then.

After finally discovering a medication, while in the mother-baby unit, that appeared to be working, the plans were put in place for me to return home. The main criteria were that I had support and childcare. This was the start of my mother's guilt journey. After all, how can every other mother on the planet look after their own child, but I couldn't? You can see how I was blowing it all out of proportion. Childcare was organised, one day a week at a childcare centre and one day a week at family day care.

When our son was almost three in 2010, I fell pregnant again, this time with triplets. The hunt for a nanny started. Unfortunately, the pregnancy was high risk and resulted in the loss of the first two in utero, and then our beautiful baby was born on Father's Day and passed away thirty minutes later. During this time I'd been hospitalised, and with my husband away more than he was home, I needed someone to look after our son. He was still attending childcare and family day care, but I needed someone twenty-four hours to be there for him. My generous sister made the journey from overseas to take care of our son while I was in hospital, trying to hold on to first, the triplets then the remaining surviving baby.

For me, mothering was a challenge and the only way I got to where I am today, not only in my business but also in my home life, was to learn how to ask for help and delegate child care. When our son started school, we began inviting au pairs to be part of our family. What a journey that has been. We've now had ten young people live with us, who are part of our family and have shared so many experiences and lessons with our son.

Being a working mother is hard. Being a mother is hard. I have always thought we need to update the African Proverb, 'it takes a village to raise a child,' to say, 'it takes a village to raise a mother.' New mothers are expected to know it all and do it all, many living far from family support and not knowing their neighbours.

Our son has some physical limitations and a neurodiverse diagnosis. I knew early on, if I wanted to work, I needed to build a team of people around me who I could confidently delegate the care of our son to.

Delegating the Household

If delegating is new for you, in the home is where you can try it out first.

In our household we have personal chores, pocket money gets paid on these, and family chores, which we do as a part of the family.

When you delegate chores to your children, they're not going to do it as well as you. You need to get over this because delegation is about giving you time back and providing a learning opportunity for the other person.

Having had au pairs living with us for many years now, I was surprised at how inadequate some of their skills were. Being able to see the different ability and understanding levels of these young adults to common household tasks gave me the ideal starting point to practice delegation.

Having clear processes in the house, from simple tasks of how to turn on the washing machine to daily cleaning schedules and meal plans, meant I could delegate whenever and whatever I wanted.

I am going to let you in on a secret. I haven't made a school lunch or touched a child's laundry in years. Yes, years, because I delegated that. Our son makes his own lunch and does his own laundry. I never have the question of, 'Mum, where are my … (insert numerous clothing items),' because I do not touch them. The same with lunch.

You should have already worked out your hourly rate. If not, I'd love you to have a go, then time how long it takes for you to do certain household activities, e.g., the laundry, the ironing, the cleaning, the cooking, etc. Now figure out whether your time is best served doing those things, or if it is more productive if you delegated them.

If you had all the money in the world, what household tasks would you delegate? Look at those and work out whether you can start delegating some of them right now?

Delegating in the household is teaching your children life skills. I want my son to look after himself when he leaves home; to cook, to clean, to understand what a budget means and to perform routine household maintenance. All the things he can do here and now, learning through trial and error, before he has to do it for himself.

I want you to think about all the tasks you do that your children or partner could be doing?

Being a mother does not mean you have to put your life on hold while you are raising children. You just need to realise you cannot be everything to everybody. Learning to love delegating is the first step to reclaiming you.

- Delegate your Enterprise – whether structure or knowledge.
- Delegate your Self – use a diary/planner, have accountability – your girlfriends, husband/partner, personal trainer.
- Delegate Childcare – family members, childcare centres, nanny, au pair, babysitters.
- Delegate the Household – children, partner, paid services.

Who am I?

Having worked for a worldwide legacy airline for almost thirty years, over half of those in a management role, I was not looking for a business venture for myself. I was happy with work, spending time not only training and facilitating, but also coaching people.

Then I met a Life Coach, a term I hadn't come across, as it was still a fairly new concept then in Australia. He said something that resonated with me. If I had a story to share that could help just one other person, then I was selfish not to be sharing it.

I became that person I needed years ago at the start of my mothering journey. If I could use my experiences and knowledge gained through my journey, then who was I not to help another mother at the start of theirs.

Parenting a child who doesn't fit into the standard box, meant I had to ramp up my organisational and planning skills to a stratosphere level. I soon discovered this was my superpower, and now I have had the benefit of being the cheerleader of many mothers.

I help them implement structure into their own households and businesses, so they, too, can take time to find the space and grace to be truly living their best life.

Anything and everything from meal planning, household schedules, chore charts to routine charts, my clients allow me to broaden my offerings as I come up with solutions for their problems.

Winning International awards for the work I do is because my clients have trusted in themselves to stop and decide they need, and deserve to be, the best sparkly version of themselves, not only for their family, but for themselves. That is why I love what I do, and this is where I am meant to be.

KATRINA WURM

For most of us, living our dream life seems to be a notion doomed to float amongst the stars. Too often we are held back by what we think we should be doing, and what we feel is safe. Katrina has experienced many challenges and much adversity throughout her life. Against the odds and through sheer determination, she has made the impossible, possible. By learning from, rather than being beaten by obstacles, Katrina has navigated her life's path to her dream life. Now an Empowerment coach, she enjoys helping others traverse similar hardships to what she experienced herself. Katrina gives her clients the guidance and tools they need to empower themselves to live their best life.

Katrina uses her life experiences to assist and coach other parents. She believes everyone is put on this earth for a reason. Hers is to steer others in the direction of making their impossible possible.

Katrina says, 'Never let what happens to you define you. Choose how to define yourself.' This is the heart of her story and success. Too many of us hide our true aspirations because of fear: fear of failing, fear of being unsafe, insecure, appearing wrong, or many other reasons. Though it took Katrina a roundabout way, her path led her to where she is today: a life coach with a flexible time schedule to be available to her family. She has a fulfilling job where she empowers others to live their best lives and by doing so, she is living hers.

www.stressfreesupermum.com
www.katrinawurm.com.au
https://facebook.com/KatrinaWurmEmpowermentCoaching/

Resourcefulness

YONA SIGNO

Yona: Good morning, IT Service Desk, Yona speaking, how can I help you?

It's been so long since I've had to say those words, but it remains with me till this day. Imagine, I said this greeting approximately fifty or so times in a day, Monday to Friday, for several years since my undergraduate days. I got a casual role (shared with another student) on the help desk of the university I was studying at. Many years later, and even as I sit here today, I realise many of the skills I've mastered and the strong work ethic I have were established from this phase of my work life. Whilst being in an inbound call centre role got the better of me on some days, for the most part, it was where my solid work foundation was laid. And I harnessed creativity in problem-solving in the workplace, especially in resourcefulness.

According to Oxford Languages, 'resourcefulness is the ability to find quick and clever ways to overcome difficulties.'

'To be resourceful means to be able to create useful and unique solutions in challenging situations. Useful means your solution works, and it's practical. Unique means the solution is interesting, unexpected, or clever,' says Dr. Todd Dewett in his **LinkedIn Learning (previously Lynda.com) course.**

Resourcefulness or being resourceful is a skill, and it is a skill that is critical, especially at the start-up phase of a business. Being resourceful is useful in all phases of business and life in general. This is a skill we all have; we may need to be more mindful to use it, especially when we face obstacles. During these challenging moments, it's human nature for individuals to focus on what they don't have; this is what we need to shift. It is during these moments that we must focus on what we have and then activate our creativity and confidence from within. This way, we are coming from a place of resourcefulness, a place where we make the most of what we have.

Yona: Can I start off with your staff number please?

Here are guiding principles of resourcefulness that have helped me along my business journey and continue to help today:

Your why… and everything that goes with it

'People don't buy what you do; they buy why you do it. And what you do simply proves what you believe.'
SIMON SINEK

I refer to my 'why' as my guide, my compass for my business. Clarity with your 'why' enables you to set your goals and business objectives clearly and easily and ensures the tasks you work on align to the big picture, your big picture. That means all the time and effort you are expending is working towards your mission and vision, which ultimately rolls up to your 'why.' This will help you prioritise what needs to be done (and what doesn't), and will help you determine when it needs to be done, which will stop the feeling of being overwhelmed and help you feel more in control.

I started my outsourcing and virtual assistant business when I was at a crossroad on whether I should go back to a corporate job. Or whether I should start a business that allows me to help people using my expertise and qualifications in project and service management and continuous improvement, particularly in Information Technology. I was certain I wanted to help people who wanted to help themselves. Identify what outcomes I want business owners to achieve, what type of remote work opportunities I can create both locally and globally, and services to offer that would support turning this into reality.

During this time, I discovered *Simon Sinek - Start With Why - TED Talk Short Edited* on YouTube, which is the short version of his *TED Talk How Great Leaders Inspire Action*. When I first started, my firstborn was the centre of my 'why.' And at its core, I wanted to help people with my skills whilst having the freedom to be with my baby girl, so I can watch her grow and enjoy our quality time together. I continue to strive for work-life harmony, where work and life don't have to be exclusive from each other, where there is a strong connection mutually working towards a greater purpose. Especially now I have two little ones.

My businesses, and any activity I am involved in, including tasks I work on, need to work towards my 'why.' It is my guiding compass.

- When you are ready, contemplate these things and feel free to journal if it helps:
- What do I strongly believe in that fuelled the start of my business?
- What is the purpose overall, my 'why'?

- What is my Mission, my goals for my business?
- What is my Vision, where I want to take my business?
- Are the business objectives, goals, and tasks I am working on, working towards the above?

Getting clear about this will help in your business journey and will be a solid foundation for you and your business to build on and grow from. This is an exercise I recommend you do each quarter of the calendar and/or financial year so you can manage your tasks more efficiently and increase productivity.

Yona: Have you restarted your computer?

Start from within

'Be thankful for what you have; you'll end up having more. If you concentrate on what you don't have, you will never, ever have enough.' -

OPRAH WINFREY

Before we continue, I would like you to close your eyes, breathe deeply and slowly at least three times, then open your eyes again. Think about your 'why,' your vision, and your mission. Breathe and observe how you are feeling. I hope you are feeling hopeful and positive now that you have gained clarity in your 'why.' With this in mind, think about what you have already in your existing 'toolkit' that will help you with your mission. Your toolkit is unique to you because it contains all your abilities and capabilities, which you can also share with others.

As I established my businesses, I had many discussions and brainstorming sessions with my husband. I remember the earlier conversations we had, about leveraging what I already have and what I have access to. It was a time where I reflected on myself. I completed a stocktake of my own skills, qualifications, and certifications; my personal and professional experience and areas that needed development. I also thought about who in my network I could speak to, to gain insight and learn from, particularly in the areas I needed to develop. Whilst I listed down a few areas where I needed help, going through this exercise gave me the confidence to create a plan for my next course of action to turn my ideas into reality.

This is a great opportunity for you to journal, list things down, or create a spreadsheet:

- What are your qualifications or certifications?
- What are your strengths and skills?
- What knowledge do you have that you've learned through study and life?
- What personal and professional experience do you have?
- What about your personal and professional network, or community that you can call on?
- What areas/aspects do you need help with?

Now you've established your own 'toolkit,' whether it's full or needs adding to, be confident at the fact you have existing 'tools' for you to use to get you closer to your 'why,' and to help you with the tasks and activities to realise your mission and vision. And for the areas you need help with, don't be disheartened, because the fact is, you knowing this already puts you steps ahead, and there is no other way but to move forward from here.

Yona: Now that we've restarted your computer, can you take me through the process of what you were initially trying to do?

Continuous improvement

'Practice the philosophy of continuous improvement. Get a little bit better every single day.'

BRIAN TRACY

We are in an era where access to information is readily available and is at our fingertips. The power of research and technology allows us to investigate and explore any topic at hand and provides us access to tools to improve efficiency and productivity. Learning something new or learning from past experiences is a choice we make. Continuous improvement is the ongoing effort where we improve our services, products, and processes. It is the technique of identifying the challenges and the opportunities for improvements; planning the implementation of the identified improvements; executing the implementation plan; review the improvements as per the feedback from your team, customers, and other stakeholders. This process is not only critical for the growth of our business, but it is essential to our own development and progress. We can also use this technique in areas that we need to improve both professionally and personally, so we are constantly improving as business owners and as individuals.

When I first started my business, I addressed several (not all) aspects of the business where I could use my knowledge, skills and experience. At first, I felt a little overwhelmed by the parts of the business I wasn't quite knowledgeable about (e.g., which business structure type to choose, tax, etc.). However, I quickly learnt at least the basics of the topic, by doing a quick search online, and then I reached out to a friend who was an accountant to verify a few things I'd just read.

As you are confident and comfortable with your existing 'tools' in your 'toolkit,' for the moment, let's address the areas you need help with:

- List down each area/aspect you need help with (you can refer to the previous list you created).
- Next to each area/aspect, specify what you need to learn/ address next. You can even write down your initial questions that come to mind about that particular topic.
- For each area/aspect, brainstorm your next course of action, the way(s) in which you can learn more about that particular topic, e.g., by online research, directly contacting a government entity, a professional, or an outsourced specialist, or even contacting someone in your personal or professional network, etc.
- Choose two actions you are comfortable learning more about the particular area/aspect.

We all have different ways of fact finding, so go with the way you are comfortable with as some prefer purely research, some like to go straight to the source, e.g., government websites or their hotlines, and some like to speak with their immediate network first. Either way, you are making good use of the resources you have and have access to, which enables you to keep moving forward.

Yona: Let's try this instead and see if the issue still exists.

Seek advice and be open to ideas

'It takes humility to realise we don't know everything, not to rest on our laurels, and to know that we must keep learning and observing.'

CHER WANG

As mothers, we've all received advice (even if unsolicited) and have also been fortunate to provide advice to others when called upon. The curiosity from not knowing something or being unsure about something is not a sign of weakness, but rather an indication of your willingness to learn and grow. We have many sources of inspiration around us: observing and reaching out to your existing personal and professional network; finding someone or even forming your own support group of people, consisting of your friends, associates, previous work colleagues, mentors, coaches; joining a group with people who are in a similar situation as you, like the Women's Business Collective.

All the questions and uncertainties as I was starting and growing my businesses were opportunities for me to constantly observe and connect with others and communicate more, which was great, as my businesses are remote with my teams located locally and overseas. I know many start-ups, small businesses, solopreneurs, alike are working remotely and some feel quite isolated. So, having the option to interact with others (even if virtually) is crucial to ensure we aren't only taking care of the health of our business, but our own mental health too. As a leader, it's also important to seek advice from our teams. This ensures that together we can communicate about and collaborate to reach common goals more effectively and efficiently. This also brings the best out in our team members, as they step up to share their particular expertise, which is something they are quite passionate about.

To date, I have formed my own business support circle of the people who I can consult with for brainstorming, accountability and advice. This helps me grow as an individual and as a leader and helps me evolve my businesses to transition with the times. My support circle is especially helpful when striving for harmony with the many roles I play, particularly as a mother, wife, and daughter. This has truly helped build my confidence, manage my time, and create a space for growth for myself and others.

With the action items you put together for the areas/aspects of the business you want to learn more about, list down:

- Each area/aspect you are curious about and the questions you want to ask or information you want to validate.
- The two actions you are most comfortable in performing next to each area/aspect, i.e., research on Government website, book a meeting with a professional, schedule a call with an outsourcing specialist, etc.
- Specify the date in which you will perform the two actions.

Being open to learning from other's expertise and experiences and being open to ideas not only enriches us as individuals but also on a personal level (human connections) with others. It enables us to see our business from different perspectives, which creates a constant source of opportunity for growth.

Yona: How was it trying the new process I showed you? Great! I'm glad that the issue no longer exists.

Work smarter, live better

'Time is more valuable than money. You can get more money, but you cannot get more time.'

JIM ROHN

Before we go further, take this time to review the simple mini action plan you've created, and then take the time to also reflect on your 'why.' I hope going through the process has provided you with a different way to gain clarity on what's important to you and what needs to be done using a simple action plan. When starting out in business, many business owners feel isolated and overwhelmed. You can live differently. You don't have to be alone on this business journey, even when you are starting out and resources are lean. You can go on a different journey.

You have access to experts who specialise in areas of your business that may not be your particular strength or within your skill set, i.e., accountants and lawyers; businesses that provide specialist services, i.e., advertising and marketing agencies; cost-effective outsourcing solutions, i.e., delegating to a virtual assistant. You have access to people who can assist and take the load off your shoulders so you can focus on the parts of your business you enjoy the most and the parts that need your attention.

With these suggestions in mind, and reviewing the list of areas and aspects of your business you need help with:

Can you contact a professional and/or specialist to support you with tasks related to their expertise?

Which tasks can you outsource and/or delegate to a virtual assistant to make better use of your time?

I truly believe we should be efficient in business so we can maximise the time we have with our family, friends, and anything else that's important to us. There are options out there for those small business owners, solopreneurs and start-ups who are limited in resources (time, energy and money). Just reach out and ask questions. Don't assume your resources aren't enough. Focus on what truly matters most in life and in business, so you are working smarter and living better.

Yona: Is there anything else I can help you with? Feel free to call again if you have any further questions. Have a great day. Bye!

Resourcefulness is your way of being creative when you face challenges and are solving a problem. Be creative with what you have and what you have access to, and use it to your advantage. Be patient as you implement all the above and continually focus on your 'why,' which will help you realise your mission, vision, goals and objectives.

Being resourceful does not only mean you can work your way through scarcity or limited resources. It also means you can open yourself to new opportunities despite problems, redefine yourself even if you lack the skills and talents, and empower yourself amidst challenges. Believing in yourself and allowing yourself to stand up and do something great out of the ordinary is what will help you navigate the rollercoaster of motherhood and entrepreneurship.

Whilst some days at the IT Service Desk were crazy to say the least, I am grateful for the experience, as it helped shape the business owner I am today; with a strong work ethic and solid professional foundation, whose resourcefulness will trump any challenges to move forward with hope and abundance.

'Your potential is limitless. You are unique, valuable, capable, and worthy of the dreams in your heart. Most of all, you have what it takes to transform and transcend whatever challenges you face.'

MARIE FORLEO

YONA SIGNO is a proud mum of two little ones with a supportive unit around her consisting of her husband, parents, family and friends. Born in the Philippines and raised in Australia, she holds both countries close to her heart. Yona combined her passion for empowering people who are passionate about helping others, with her tertiary qualifications, certifications and work experience in information technology, project and service management, in the tertiary education sector and Founded *Kaya Services* (Australia) and *Empowered Virtual Service*s (Philippines).

Kaya Services is responsible for employing a highly skilled and remote workforce that helps businesses in Australia and beyond achieve operational efficiency so they can focus on growth objectives tied to revenue and expansion. *Empowered Virtual Services* is a virtual learning academy for Filipino freelancers and virtual assistants that empowers them with the tools for self-worth and skill-enhancement, so they can live a life of freedom and prosperity while supporting a global clientele.

Yona is backed by a team that operates on the notion of doing good for others, ensuring the highest level of service and accountability that resonates with her client base today. Those who have had the privilege of working with her, know and understand she lives with integrity. She attracts clients and employs people who believe in what she believes. And she strives daily to make a local and global impact, demonstrating the collective strength of cultural diversity.

Yona is an AusMumpreneur 2020 Bronze Award Winner for Multicultural Business Excellence, a published author, program creator, host, speaker, and outsourcing and business strategist consultant. She enjoys bringing ideas to life with a particular interest in helping start-ups get off the ground.

kaya.services

Culture in business: The sleeping giant of success

RACHEL NEATE

Why is culture important in business? The relationship between culture, productivity and profit.

A negative business culture slowly crept up on me years ago. I didn't see it coming and everything seemed fine, until all of a sudden, it wasn't.

Over the years of working for a variety of businesses and now running my own successful company, I have learnt there is nothing more vital to generating productivity and profit than having a great culture. This is underpinned by promoting staff wellbeing, customer satisfaction and overall happiness within a workplace. Culture affects every aspect of a business from management decisions to the behaviour and motivation of staff. The culture of a business is a continuously evolving set of mutual values, beliefs. and goals within a workplace.

For a business to achieve success, regardless of how you define it, the culture of the business is at the core of determining the potential for said success. Whether it be profit, staff and customer satisfaction or any other key performance indicator, they are all affected and reliant on a good culture within a business, no matter how small or large that business may be. A good and clearly defined culture breeds satisfied staff members, makes it easier to attract the right staff members to your growing business, and attracts more customers to your business; all of which increase the productivity and profit margins.

The culture of a business is a complex topic and requires extensive development over time. However, this chapter will give guidance on how to implement the necessary stepping stones to developing a great culture within your business, regardless of the business you are looking to create or change. Think about the business you are invested in as you read ahead, and you will find useful tips to create a culture your competitors will be envious of.

What is your business culture? It starts with you.

Culture is often not defined, but more so implied and engrained in all aspects of a business. It is the 'feel' a business emits. Regardless of the type of business you are building, whether it be a local shop, an online store or an international brand, the culture is the heart of the business, no matter how big or small that business may be. Once a culture is well-established, like-minded people will gravitate towards your business without you even trying. Without a clear culture, staff will pull in different directions, which leads to a lack of cohesiveness, teamwork and clarity.

A business culture should always start with you, so it's important to play to your strengths and lead by example. Studies have shown women, in general, are naturally predisposed to a nurturing, tender-minded and altruistic personality type when compared to men (1 to 2). Using your natural strengths is key to developing a great and unique culture within your business that supersedes those of your competitors. You MUST believe 100% in your culture; it must represent who you are and what your values are. If you don't believe in it, no one else will.

The business you are creating will affect the culture you create to a degree, but we can all agree that most, if not all businesses have a few common core values in place. Good organisations strive to have an inclusive, motivating and strong team environment. What will make your organisation unique? For me, I sat down and thought of all the things I felt were missing from my previous workplaces and all things I enjoyed about my previous workplaces. Personal experience is the best place to start. Ask yourself the question, 'What would I want to make my job more enjoyable?' This is an excellent starting point to define what culture you will strive to create.

It is also important to recognise that a business's culture is an evolving concept with multiple moving parts. No team member will have identical core values to you. It is important to be flexible and open to change as each team member brings their own unique personality and professional approach to your existing culture. Building on the foundations you created is a good thing, providing those values are not in direct conflict with the core principles you envision.

Self-reflection is a vital attribute that business owners need to have. In hindsight, I was too rigid in the initial stages of my business, which led to team members not feeling heard, a topic we will cover later in this chapter. Learning to listen to your team and allowing their voice to resonate through the business will help your culture become louder, clearer and more united.

Tip one: List five values you think are vital to your business. This will form the solid foundation of your culture. I would recommend one of your five values relate to consistently delivering excellent customer service, and closely monitoring feedback (both positive and constructive).

Understanding and empowering staff: Listen, and learn their driving factors.

Every member of your team will have different aspirations, goals, values and beliefs. It is important to empower your team to ensure they are on a path to achieving their own goals in line with their beliefs. Understanding your team's motivations and aspirations also helps to ensure your rewards and bonuses will be personally targeted at that particular employee to encourage further growth, progress, and development. Staff members who do not feel heard will not perform to their potential, will not encourage growth, and may move on from your business or become despondent in their current role.

A research report conducted in 2016 identified that organisations that score in the top 25% on employee experience report almost three times the return on assets. These organisations also double the return on sales when compared to those in the bottom 25% (3). This is an astounding statistic and shouldn't be taken lightly. Understanding and empowering staff plays a vital role in increasing an organisation's productivity and profits. A separate research project developed an 'Employee Experience Index' which identified five dimensions to an employee's positive work experience. It found that staff want to have a sense of belonging, purpose, achievement, happiness and vigour, or sense of energy and enthusiasm within the workplace (4).

Knowing this, it is important to sit down with each team member and discuss what motivates them. Being able to target your rewards, set clear goals, and create a sense of belonging and purpose within a workplace will require individual input from the team. Regular meetings with your team can help to identify areas that your business can improve and reinforce to the employee they are being heard and their thoughts, opinions, and beliefs are being taken into consideration.

From personal experience, I recommend meetings with each team member once a month, in a small local business. Obviously, this will depend on the size of your team. For larger organisations, creating a standard survey that can be emailed to your entire team will be beneficial. At a minimum, annually, is an efficient way to learn your team's driving factors and ascertain their current level of overall job satisfaction.

Since implementing these one-to-one meetings in my business, I have noticed a more satisfied workforce. I have found the 'power of being heard' is second to none, and my team have expressed it is one of the things they love about working for me. Feeling like you are contributing and feeling valued at work is important for every team member.

Tip two: Create a standard template for you to fill out in the individual meetings with team members that asks what drives and motivates them. And what gives them a sense of achievement or pride in their professional endeavours.

Goal setting: Creating a sense of meaning and purpose.

Goal setting is vital to ensuring your team have a purpose and a clear direction. Regular refinement of these goals will continue to encourage progression and a forward momentum within your business. Both short-term and long-term goals need to be set, along with macro and micro goals. Macro goals are larger, more general goals a business aims to achieve as a whole, and micro goals are smaller, individual or team-based goals that all work towards one or more of the macro goals. Using the SMART goal formula is a simple process to ensure you can accurately measure the achievement of goals (5).

SMART goals by definition are Specific, Measurable, Achievable, Relevant and Timely. A business should have both short-term and long-term goals for itself, and a team member's goals should contribute to the general forward projection of the business as a whole. For example, with respect to a Physiotherapy business, if a team member's goal is to upskill to a higher qualification. This could align with a business goal of providing a better and more qualified service to its clients. It is also important to think outside of the box when listening to your team members' goals. If a team member has a goal to achieve a greater work-life balance, it would be naive to think this doesn't help to grow a business. If a team member has a better work-life balance, it has been proven that they are more productive at work, which therefore increases the business's output. It is important to ensure that the goals do align in some way with the business's growth and direction, and form a more cohesive culture within the workplace.

A business or a team leader actively engaged with assisting its employees with achieving their goals demonstrates a nurturing environment. Their team feels more valued and again more empowered, which gives the employee a reason to strive for greatness. A way in which you, as a business owner, can demonstrate your support is by creating a tiered rewards program to assist them in achieving their goal(s). Using my previous example of your team member wanting to upskill their qualification, if your team member hits a certain target you have set. For example, sales, a small financial bonus can go into the 'kitty' to contribute towards their desired course fee, or the creation of additional annual leave hours above the standard to add to their paid time off to study.

Clear and measurable goals are essential to any business and its team. Clear goals help to motivate staff to keep on target, help the business grow in a desirable direction, and most importantly, encourage staff engagement in their own growth process, which lends itself to career satisfaction. Having all members of your team working towards a common macro goal is vital to encourage a cohesive, clear and unified culture.

Tip three: create three to four macro goals for your organisation, then sit down with each of your team members and find out what they want to achieve while working with you. Spend some time working out how to use their micro goals to work towards the macro goals, while devising ways in which to assist with them achieving those goals. Coming up with these rewards together is a great way to encourage your team members' voices being heard and creating a sense of empowerment, allowing them to carve their own path.

Embedding the team: encouraging social connection and creating a 'family' environment.

There are numerous studies that have shown shared social activities play an important role in employee wellbeing and team building (6). Staff, and people in general, need a sense of belonging, and this can be enhanced by ensuring a positive social environment is maintained within a workplace. Feelings of isolation and separation are not desirable and also make it more likely an individual will leave their place of work indefinitely. Social activities need to be targeted, keeping in mind your teams' values and beliefs, to make it clear to all members that the activities have been specifically designed for them. This sense of belonging will decrease staff turnover and increase job satisfaction and overall wellbeing, which, as discussed above, will increase productivity and work output.

We can encourage social interaction via a variety of different mediums, platforms, and environments. One of the major advantages of the development of technology is that it has opened up ways in which businesses can utilise online programs to enhance social interaction. It has meant that no matter how large a company, team members can still interact with each other regardless of their location.

The types of social interaction that can be utilised range from things as simple as arranging lunch breaks at the same time, ensuring crossover in the staff rooms, to large-scale Christmas gatherings or functions provided by the company. The type of business you run will influence the social interactions you may want to encourage and facilitate.

Sitting down with your team and brainstorming things they want to participate in is essential to ensure the activities you implement are relatable and beneficial to the team as a whole. It is also beneficial to foster an environment where your team takes the initiative to create their own social interactions and team activities. For example, one of my staff recently created an online 'trivia night' session, via Zoom every six weeks or so, to spend some time together outside of the work environment.

When your team *wants* to spend time together, it enhances their experiences at work and ensures the continual development of a positive culture. Wanting to be at work also embeds a team member into the business. This encourages the team member to feel as if they are an important contributing factor to the overall culture of a business, giving rise to a sense of importance and value, which everyone deserves.

Trial and error is one of the most effective processes to test different ways in which you and your team can interact. Trying new things is fun and keeps things interesting for all involved. Think outside the box and find what works best for you and your team. Some examples are staff gatherings on a semi-regular basis with food and drinks provided, staff dinners, joint birthday presents where everyone contributes, and team building days (e.g., paintball or surfing lessons). The possibilities are endless.

Tip four: get your team to fill out a survey that asks what their five favourite activities outside of work are. Once you have compiled your list, you can start brainstorming ways in which you can incorporate some of these into the business' social activities.

Being a reflective boss.

Self-reflection is the ability to look internally at your beliefs, values, and actions; and the reasons that may lie behind them (7). Self-reflection as a boss is important to ensure you are accountable for things that may not be going well. This gives you the power and ability to change them, even if you don't naturally behave or work that particular way. The culture in a business is a unified set of values, and everyone, including the boss, has to make adjustments over time to ensure a positive environment for all involved. Admitting you can be incorrect or realising the processes you have implemented were not appropriate or beneficial after reflecting on its efficacy, is one of the most powerful tools a boss can have.

I started as a sole trader; therefore, every decision was made by me, and the impact of those decisions only affected me and my customers. I did not have to consider any other team member's feelings, beliefs or values. One of the biggest self-improvements I have worked on in my career as an employer, and continue to work on every day, is to learn the art of self-reflection and ownership of fault and failure, whether small or large. This allows me to cultivate a culture within our company where staff feel they can approach me with questions, suggestions or concerns. Approachability is key to ensuring the employer is aware of what is happening within their company and allowing staff to feel supported and heard.

It is also important to regularly reflect on each aspect and process of the business itself. Reflecting on what works and what does not is a constant process that should occur in the background all the time. Depending on the stage of your organisation, you can delegate some or all of these monitoring processes to specific employees, or you can do the reflecting yourself. Regardless, to ensure the business continues to project forwards and upwards, and to ensure the culture is improving and evolving, reflection is key.

Learning to identify a threat to your culture is also important and often doesn't come naturally. It is something you will learn over time. It is usually obvious if there is a major issue, as this is relatively easy to identify. It's the smaller issues and problems that arise over time that will slowly damage a business's culture, which often gets noticed too late. For example, hiring an employee who is clearly the wrong fit, is easy to identify in a relatively timely manner. But hiring an employee who almost fits, but is rigid in their beliefs and therefore not open to change, will slowly taint the good culture you and your team have created. Reflecting on hiring processes and screening processes once we identify these issues is vital to preventing poor hiring choices in the future.

Tip five: Sit down and choose three decisions you have made for your business in the last three months and reflect on how those decisions have affected your business. Then sit with your team or a select few members and ask them whether they feel those decisions were good choices.

Hopefully, after reading this chapter, you can see the vital role that culture has in the success of a business and its working environment. Culture is forever changing, and it is impacted by every aspect of your business. For me personally, learning to work with my team just as much as I lead them has been an amazing growth experience for me thus far. It will benefit my business and my staff in both the short term and the long term. Having a great business culture is the most rewarding aspect of running a business.

Don't get me wrong, it's nice that a good culture leads to increased productivity and profit. But learning not to focus on profit alone, and focus on the business processes and joys of being a part of something great, is far more rewarding. Business profit is a great consequence of an excellent culture, not the other way around. Building from the inside out is a sure-fire way to ensure the multifaceted success of your business, and your staff will thank you for it. Feeling valued and heard at work is something that everyone wants and desires. Being a nurturing, tender-minded and altruistic leader is a strength, not a weakness. Build on your natural instincts as a mother, daughter, wife and grandmother to enhance the culture of your business and individualise it in a way that your competitors will be envious of.

References:

- https://www.ncbi.nlm.nih.gov/pmc/articles/PMC3149680/
- https://hbr.org/2012/03/a-study-in-leadership-women-do
- https://www.ibm.com/downloads/cas/XEY1K26O
- https://www.ibm.com/downloads/cas/JDMXPMBM
- https://www.mindtools.com/pages/article/smart-goals.htm
- https://www.ncbi.nlm.nih.gov/pmc/articles/PMC5580621/
- https://dictionary.cambridge.org/dictionary/english/self-reflection

RACHEL NEATE

Rachel is the founder and sole director of Preston Physiotherapy Pty. Ltd. Rachel started her boutique clinic in June 2016 as a sole trader. She rented a small room inside a massage clinic whilst still working part-time at her previous Physiotherapy role to support herself financially. The business started with only one client in the first week of trading. In only four years, it's grown into a successful multi-service clinic with two locations, employing nine staff, who provide care to over two-hundred clients per week.

Rachel started Preston Physiotherapy because she felt there was a need for longer consultations at a reasonable price that championed patient wellbeing and care. Yes, it meant less money in the short term, but the business has grown so quickly because of the patient care provided, it was well worth the initial financial sacrifice. Rachel spends large amounts of her time continuously working on the business's culture to strive for the best workplace environment possible. She takes a lot of pride in knowing her staff enjoy coming to work every day.

In her downtime, Rachel enjoys hanging out with her amazing little family of four. She and her husband, Rhys, share the joy of raising their two wonderful daughters, Lily, two, and Harper, only one week old. Rachel hopes her example of being a mother and a business owner teaches her children and all other women that if you put your mind to it, you can do both, and you can do both successfully.

Rachel has won multiple business awards in wellness and wellbeing and, more recently, an international award for best female entrepreneur in small business. Rachel looks forward to embarking on a new journey into education and mentorship over the coming years. Rachel plans to grow Preston Physiotherapy into a larger single location clinic that will forever remain 'the local physio' of Preston 3072.

www.prestonphysio.com.au

Community over Competition

NICOLA LE LIEVRE

I think we all are wonder women, strong, and creators of life. I believe collectively; we are powerful and unstoppable. Real queens should be fixing each other's crowns when nobody is watching.

At times we are all guilty, intentionally or not, of putting another woman down and on the flipside, having another break us down even from a really young age. I sadly see this with my young daughter and my elderly mother.

We must stand together and help and support each other genuinely, instead of continually trying to be in competition, being 'better' whatever that looks like to you. Stop judging and making assumptions; this serves you no purpose.

My passion is to make as many women as possible look and feel beautiful. I strive to be different, and like being known within my community as the girl with the big red smile.

I hope you find this chapter helpful and have a few lightbulb moments. Everybody is struggling with something challenging in their lives. Let us be kind, compassionate, and support female empowerment.

No matter what challenges we face, we dust ourselves off and fight harder. You have all the power you need inside. You are enough. Believe you can achieve anything you put your mind to and back yourself.

PART 1

Proximity = Power – Find Your Tribe

'Surround yourself with people who are going to take you higher.'

OPRAH WINFREY

You can be more productive and save time by seeking somebody successful who is doing something you want to do and asking them how they did it. Sounds simple, but what are we so afraid of? Fear of judgement we are not good enough? Is it rejection or fear of being labelled as a copycat? You do not have to figure it out on your own. I love spending time with people who are more successful and learning about their entrepreneurial journey.

Being a business owner can be quite lonely at times. I have found during my business journey that finding support and giving support to like-minded women with similar goals and visions, has been extremely powerful and inspirational. Reaching out and making the connection has been the start to some of my most valuable friendships.

When entering my tribe, we make a pact to look after each other through good and bad times. It takes time to work out who really has your back, but once you find your people, it is a game-changer. I have a small group of incredible friends, all salon owners, 'The Spice Girls.' Their support and encouragement were invaluable during the most challenging times of being a leader and owning a small business. These women have seen me vulnerable, stressed, anxious and ugly cry, everything is welcomed. I love using valuable time forming connections and having meaningful conversations, the ones you walk away from feeling inspired and knowing you are not alone.

I follow many inspirational women online, famous and local small business owners. This is a really great place to start. Seek out the ones who resonate with your beliefs and have successful businesses themselves. I have found the more successful the company is, the owner generally will offer the most support, valuable feedback and share ideas. Interesting, isn't it?

Join supportive business and industry groups who can offer constructive advice and support during your journey. I belong to industry groups, which I resonate with and find valuable tips and ideas. Some you join will not be as supportive or genuine. That is all part of finding your tribe. Do not involve yourself with negativity, simply remove yourself.

I have really enjoyed forming connections with businesswomen in other industries, which I have mainly sourced through my AusMumpreneur network. It is inspirational hearing other industries' success stories and journeys, and how they overcame challenges.

Having a Mentor has been so valuable for me and I believe everyone should have one. Many of the most successful women in business have a mentor to keep them on course and accountable for reaching their goals. You may have a few different mentors during different times of your business journey. Find one that makes you a better version of yourself.

PART 2

Be Uniquely You – The Power of Being Different

'In order to be irreplaceable,
one must always be different.'
COCO CHANEL

What makes you stand out in your community? What makes your business unique? Are you shaping decisions around your core brand values?

Brand values are the foundations of your business, and being crystal clear on how you want your brand to make people feel is vital. The experience or journey is what will set you apart. Stay true to your vision and mission, trust your gut instinct, and remember why you started in the business. When you speak to everybody, you talk to nobody, and knowing your ideal customer is what will propel your business forward.

You are responsible for everything that happens in your life. Owning your mistakes and learning from them, stepping up and making better choices will help you grow as a business owner and an individual.

Fixing someone else's crown is terrific, but when was the last time you straightened yours? Playing full out, trusting my gut and taking a chance is really what helped me pivot my business. You see, nobody can do what you do. Nobody can get inside your mind. When I purchased my beauty salon in 2014, although already with a solid reputation, I felt it was just a successful boutique beauty salon. Once I worked out what I wanted my business to be known for and how we could stand out in a noisy industry, the magic started to happen.

I spent the early years of owning my salon with FOMO - Fear of missing out. This was before I cemented my core values: ethical, sustainable and supporting Australian made and owned brands. These values resonate with me personally and therefore, into my business. Most decisions are based around them. Before I found my brand 'identity,' I was unsure about what was the best way of doing business and therefore tried to do everything. It is so essential to navigate your 'why' and if unsure, grab a notebook, pen, and do some critical thinking. I schedule a time for critical thinking every week and put everything in my head down on paper.

Think about the customers you want to attract? What is their demographic? What are the needs and concerns they have? How can your business support them? This is valuable information to have when you want to do target marketing, and the more specific you can be, the better the outcome.

Putting my head down and not concerning myself with what others around me are doing, has been so much less stressful. I strive to be known not as the best in my industry, but as different and original.

One of the most significant assets you can have is being unique. Your business is unique and different because of you.

PART 3

Staying in Your Lane – Avoiding Distraction

'Distractions destroy action. If it's not moving you towards your purpose, leave it alone.'

JERMAINE RILEY

When first purchasing my salon, I was so guilty of falling victim to bright shiny object syndrome. You know the latest new best thing, product, equipment, or just something pretty to look at.

Everything you do is moving you closer or further away from your goal. Being distracted by what others are doing does not serve you. Over the years, this has contributed to my anxiety and left me feeling I am not doing enough. You do you, and let them do them, and never compare as you do not know what is going on in their business or lives.

It is so easy to get distracted from your course, I feel especially in my industry, as it is ever growing and changing. There are always new, fun, beautiful things available. You can be distracted by people, offers, or just by your own overthinking and overanalysing. Staying focused is vital and finding what anchors you. I like writing job lists; they keep me focused. I plan the most challenging or tedious tasks first; this gives me the momentum to keep going once completed. Job lists also assist me in deciding what needs to be outsourced or delegated to a team member.

There is always a new offer, buy 5 get 1 free, spend $500 and get free shipping, etc. It is endless. These are effective strategies; until you purchase stock you don't really need or something you like but does not resonate with your core audience.

When first purchasing my business, I worked with a fantastic coach. She taught me the value of analysing your Costs of goods sold and not to overspend. This changed my mindset to think if I really need that product now, or is it something that could potentially sit on your shelf? We all love a good deal, do not get me wrong, but are you buying up because you have FOMO or the scarcity mindset that you are going to miss out?

Social Media is a perfect example of being flooded by so many similar businesses. I recommend occasionally having a social media 'detox' if you feel overwhelmed with what your competitors are doing, and you are not. If businesses like yours keep coming up on your feed, stop and think if that is something you really need to be spending your money on right now?

PART 4

Analysis Paralysis – Overthinking Decisions

'Get out of your own way... stop the paralysis by analysis... decide what you want, create a simple plan, and get moving!'
STEVE MARABOLI

Have you experienced so many ideas floating in your head that you felt immobilised by having to make a decision? Therefore, you get overwhelmed and start overanalysing? Perhaps you are wasting more time in no action because you fear doing the wrong thing?

We have more choices and options than ever before; therefore, information overload can quickly leave us feeling overwhelmed, and inaction and procrastination take over.

When overwhelmed and confronted by a difficult choice, our instinct is often not to choose anything at all. We often walk away from a decision empty-handed because of the responsibility and potential regret of choosing the wrong option, even when all options are good.

Do you get overwhelmed when presented with too many options? This often happens to me and got me thinking it is more than likely happening to our customers too. Less is more and too much choice is stressful.

I like to use the example of my husband getting overwhelmed when going to Subway. He feels there are so many options and the staff ask so many questions. 'What bread, what topping, salad dressing.' etc. He is happy just with a plain cheese and salami sandwich. Although lots of options sound like a great idea, streamlining offerings can sometimes be more effective.

At *intherapy* we sell a beautiful range of candles. I liked to have one of each scent in the collection, which was usually over ten candles. I noticed our guests were taking so long to decide or would not take any. Therefore, I now have 4-6 of our top sellers and have an increase in units sold.

When you cannot decide, delegate another person to assist you in the process and to lend decision support. For example, when unsure what to order from a menu, we often ask the server to tell us what they think, or order the same thing as the person dining with us.

As a business owner, there are always lots of decisions to be made. You need to be clear about where you are going or what you want to achieve to make the right decision in the first place. However, fear of failure often holds us back. Get started and trust in the process. Once you gain momentum, you will find it so much easier to keep going. Not overthinking what needs to be done, and starting at the top of my to-do list, has helped me gain momentum to keep pushing through.

Progress over perfection has been vital to me. Procrastinating over a task to make it 'perfect' can cause delay and therefore you miss out on the result you originally wanted to achieve.

Sometimes the most significant thing holding me back is myself getting into my own way. Do not get overwhelmed, just get started. Small steps consistently are the key. Where focus goes, energy flows.

PART 5

Celebrate Wins – The Impact of Awards & Recognition

'Remember to celebrate milestones as you prepare for the road ahead.'
NELSON MANDELA

Success begins at the end of your comfort zone. Making the conscious decision to enter an award is an excellent step for your business, becoming a finalist is a giant leap and winning is fantastic!

An awards application process is a valuable way to reflect on your business. It reflects what you are doing well, where you can improve, and a reminder of how far you have come. Becoming a finalist is such validation you are on the right track, and recognition from your peers and community is such a fantastic feeling. I love the excitement it brings amongst my team, knowing they are part of the success and how the perception of being a finalist or winning an award is received by customers.

It is more than just winning; I love the comradery of awards events and the sense of community they bring. Being in a room with so many of your peers and mentors clapping for you gives you that validation of 'Yes, I did it.' Holding that bright, shiny award and giving an acceptance speech (although nerve-racking) is such an accomplishment.

Children have a rewards chart and receive a gold star or sticker to show them how well they are tracking towards their goal. This is how we are conditioned to receiving recognition when we are doing well. Receiving an award is the same concept on a larger scale.

I believe with that recognition comes responsibility. Your peers will look up to you and watch what you are doing. You need to shine in their light positively. If you win awards and your peers ask you how you compiled your award, or what you did to make it a standout, is an incredible compliment. You see, you are uniquely you and your business, so even if they did what you did, it would never be the same. I encourage other beauty salon owners to enter awards because of the great validation it brings. I encouraged another salon owner to enter the Australian Beauty Industry Awards. We were both announced finalists in the same category. So what? She is such a beautiful person and kick-ass salon owner; it makes being next to her in the same award category so much more powerful.

You cannot always receive the shiny award, and this is ok. It is nice to clap for someone else too and let them experience the excitement. Part of winning is also sharing your knowledge, positive energy, and for me, this is part of the awards circle.

Feeling afraid of failure is normal; however, many do not try because they let this feeling paralyse them. My advice is to just go for it, enjoy the process, and do not give up if you don't become a finalist first time. Keep going, learning and growing.

Conclusion

I would like to pay tribute to the beautiful and unique lotus flower, an element incorporated in my business branding. The lotus flower holds meaning to me, one which I am sure you can resonate with: compassion, beauty, grace, and persistence to keep going even through struggles.

A lotus flower blooms most beautifully through the deepest and thickest mud.

Be like a lotus: trust the light, grow through the dirt and believe in new beginnings.

We have all had obstacles in our entrepreneurial journey. Still, the key is to not let these bring you down, but like the lotus, struggle through the mud to emerge beautiful and whole.

All the power you need is inside you. Sometimes you might need support and encouragement; lean on your circle of trust. Your circle could include a friend, mentor, or family member you trust to have an open and honest conversation with.

Now strap yourself in and put on a red lip (just try it), to transform you into wonder woman mode. You are in for a fantastic journey; you need to believe that. You do not have to travel alone; the power of the sisterhood is surrounding you. Start with small steps, make a connection, ask for help and always stay in your lane. Ignore the outside noise, which is not serving you or your vision, and keep up the momentum of moving forward.

Wishing you all the success and happiness you deserve.

ox Nic

NICOLA LE LIEVRE

From the moment six-year-old Nicola saw a perfectly polished Estée Lauder woman proudly donning a red lip, she knew she had found her people. From her elegance, attention to detail to exceptional customer service, little did that Estée Lauder woman know she was inspiring the idea of a future business owner. Nicola is known for her signature red lip. 'I believe putting on a Red Lipstick is like putting on a superhero cape,' says Nicola.

Fast forward to today, and she is proudly surpassing twenty-two years in the beauty industry. Nicola has crafted her passion into becoming a multi-award-winning industry leader featured on Channel 7, The Courier-Mail, 9News and Professional Beauty Magazine.

Born and raised in Johannesburg, South Africa, she completed her International Beauty Therapy Diploma. Nicola packed her bags, and off she went to travel the world working in Spas onboard cruise ships. She met her Dutch officer husband eleven years later working onboard Holland America Line.

Nicola had a dream backed up with a business plan to open a Balinese Style Spa on the Garden Route. Sadly, this dream was shattered when Nicola and her family were victims of an armed robbery which ultimately changed her life course to immigrate to Brisbane, Australia.

Nicola managed various beauty salons, including *intherapy*, which she later purchased in 2014 and since has been *intherapy's* Chief *Glow-Getter* for her Red Hill community. Creating unique client relationships, her community inspires her to deliver the industry's absolute best each day.

Nicola's commitment to the environment has seen *intherapy* transform into Queensland's leading sustainable salon, a network that strives towards zero waste within a salon environment. Proudly stocking Australian beauty brands, *intherapy* passionately practices clean beauty for treatments that are kind to our skin, furry friends and the world around us.

Mother of Chloe, who has a dream of following in Nicola's footsteps. The 2020 Mumpreneur Silver Winner says, 'I believe in finding support and giving support to like-minded women.'

Founder of *Tender Loving Beauties*, a volunteer beauty therapy group who launched in 2009. A collaboration with Hummingbird House, Queensland's only children's hospice, offering relaxation treatments for families of very sick children who need some time out. Nicola has a vision of reaching more woman in the community who need support in the future.

https://intherapy.com.au/

Networking is Key

KRISTY MOORE

No matter what your goals are in business, who you know is as important as what you know. But it's not just who you know, it's what you do once you know them. That's where networking comes into play.

Networking is a combination of sales marketing and relationship building. It's the difference between those who get by and those who are getting ahead.

We network to build long-lasting business relationships, as people do business with people. Success comes from constantly making new contacts, following up and keeping in touch.

I fell in love with networking as an activity about four years ago because it offers so much more than most people realise. I've seen people's business and lives changed, including my own, though networking.

Through networking, I meet Kylie King. She gave me the courage to chase my dreams and make them a reality. Now I am running my own travel agency, a dream I have had since completing year 12, twenty years ago. Kylie was my first client, even though we have never met in person. Networking is key.

Networking in Business and finding the right fit.

Networking is about interacting with people. It's the process of establishing a mutually beneficial relationship with other business people and potential clients or customers.

Networking itself is a skill; it's building circles of people around you and assembling your crowd.

You can network face-to-face at networking group events, social events, conferences and through industry associations. You can also network online, through zoom events and sites such as LinkedIn and in Facebook groups.

There are so many networking groups out there, and they all run their events and groups differently. So, it doesn't matter if you are networking online or you're attending an event in person; you need to find the right fit for you.

I would've attended over 200 different networking events and been a member in several groups over the last four years. It took time to find the right ones for me and my business, but it was worth it.

There were so many events I couldn't attend, like a 7am or 6pm, as first I am a mother and need to be there for my daughter. I had to keep looking for events that fitted into my schedule and that worked for me.

I finally found an event I could attend, so I registered and paid my fee. But I found after attending, the group that ran this event wasn't for me. I couldn't commit to what they were expecting, so back to the drawing board and off I went to find a new event to attend.

I attended quite a few events with different groups, and all of them didn't seem like they were right for me. They had expectations

I couldn't commit to. I couldn't build any business relationships and wasn't seeing any return or growth for all my invested time, effort, and money and thought 'networking isn't for me. It's not working like everyone had told me and I just plain suck at it. Might as well go back to doing what I was doing before and counting to run my business like I had previously done.' Until I received a reminder email for an event in two days' time. I had a ticket for it I'd forgotten about so decided as I had already paid, 'might as well give it one last shot,' and I am so glad I did.

It was at that event I finally found the right fit for me; I found a group I felt comfortable with, a group where I belonged. This is where my love for networking grew. I loved attending networking events, as that's where I got to make new business connections that lead to support and business growth.

I loved attending this group so much I decided I wanted to build a group just like that one but for my local community, for all the Mothers and women in my area. So I became the coordinator for my region, and for the past two years have been running and hosting my own networking events.

Not all the events or groups are a right fit for you. It will take time to find the right events for you to attend and which networking groups you should be a part of that work for you.

Getting the most out of networking

Once you begin networking, it's likely you'll receive invitations to more events from people you meet. Before you know it, your networking group will grow. One of the biggest benefits is that networking can be an inexpensive way to promote your business.

Building a successful business takes a lot of time and drive. It's good to have a network of friends and associates to surround yourself with, to draw energy from, and keep you going. By surrounding yourself with people who share a similar drive and ambition, you are more likely to move forward as a group. But that's not the only benefit of networking. Through networking, you can share knowledge, discover new opportunities, make new connections, build your customer base, find new suppliers, increase your confidence and raise your profile.

It's natural that networking will result in opportunities. The thing you will not know is when or how they will materialise. Whether it's a referral, partnership offer or request for your service or product, it is important to be ready to seize opportunities when they come along. Remember, you are not just gaining exposure to the people in the room at the event; you are building connections with their network too. If someone they know has a need that matches your business, if you have made an impression, you will likely get a referral.

Most importantly, remember networking is not just a one-way street. You need to give to receive. If someone in your network matches a business you encounter at an event, don't hesitate to share his or her details. It will only strengthen your relationship.

People are always asking for recommendations, and I love being able to offer a recommendation from someone in my network, as I know and trust them and their business. I don't hesitate and I don't do it just so they can return the favour and recommend me when they know someone looking for my services. I do it as I love being able to recommend someone I know to help them gain new business.

To get the most out of networking, you must be able to give, even if there is no instant gain for you. You need to be the biggest advocate for what you do. Networking can build you a crowd of contacts who will be passionate on your behalf, but that has to flow from you. Be proud of your business and get yourself out there networking, building new relationships and making new connections.

It's not what you know but who you know.

It seems like all our parents and teachers focus on when we are growing up is the importance of building 'what we know,' but they never once touch on the importance of building 'who we know.' Why did they put so much emphasis on us learning, rather than building connections and a network? In fact, it's the popular catchphrase, 'it's who you know, not what you know,' that rings true in daily life. Who you know might matter more, or at least be just as important as what you know, in getting business opportunities.

The meaning of the catchphrase saying it's 'who you know, not what you know' is that people get ahead in life based on their connections, not on their skills or their knowledge.

Anyone can build 'who they know' as long as you can communicate with other people in one way or another. But it's not just who you know, it's what you do once you know them.

Don't be afraid to ask your connections to introduce you to theirs. This is how you build your network and make new connections. Every opportunity I get, I try to make new connections and build on the people I know, as the more people you know, the more opportunities will come your way.

You've already been networking without realising it!

Before you decide networking isn't for you, before you tell me you're not the sort of person who goes networking, remember, you're already networking and telling people about your business. You already have a brief introduction, which you tell people when asked what you do. At the school gates, at the swimming pool, at the gym, at work if you're building your business on the side, on Facebook and wherever else, you talk to people. You talk to people about what you do and you talk to people about what your partner does too, so you already know how to introduce other people's businesses too.

And you build networks within networks and circles within circles of people who like the same football club, the same rock band, and the same reality TV programme. You form alliances with other parents at pre-school and with other people who go to the gym at the same time as you. You know the people at your church and what they do for a living. And you know the other scout leaders and regularly go out for meals with them. You still keep in touch with all the people who were on the same course as you. And you still keep in touch with your old school friends on Facebook and know what each of them, and their partner, does for a living. You network already because that's what humans do. We're interested in what the other guy is up to and want to find out what 'so and so's' husband does because 'in computers' doesn't cut it. Networking is nothing new, scary or complicated and is an extension and a refining of what you already do, every single day.

You can always be networking, no matter where you go, even when you least expect it.

I wanted to get some branding photos taken. I looked into it and realised all the photographers I knew from my network didn't do branding shoots, so I added it to my ever-growing to-do list. A few days later, I spoke to Cassandra, my hairdresser, who is also part of my networking group, like you do when you get your hair cut. I mentioned I wanted to get some branding shots done and will need to book my hair in for when I find someone to take them for me. Well, my amazing hairdresser then tells me to, 'Wait a minute, I got something for you,' and hands me a flyer. Not any old flyer, but a flyer for a photographer that specialises in branding photo shoots. She knew the photographer from another networking group she is part of, and she often does a lot of the photographer's clients' hair for their photo shoots.

Don't fear networking

One issue around networking is that it goes against everything you were told as a child. Something I was repeatedly told by parents and teachers was that I shouldn't talk to strangers. Thirty-odd years later, and I was walking into a room full of people who I didn't know, all of whom were strangers and all of whom I was expected to talk to.

This talking to strangers filled me with dread for a lot of reasons. First, it went against those teachings from cleverer and bigger people than me when I was little. Second, I convinced myself that everyone else in the room was somehow 'better' than me. I convinced myself that everyone else would have a better business, would be much more confident in what they were doing. Who was I, just starting out in the self-employed arena, to have anything in common with these giants of the local business world? I learned a valuable lesson in those early days, which I have had to learn and re-learn pretty much every day since. If I wanted to be any sort of success, I had to learn to get over myself and my little fears and insecurities.

Ultimately, networking boils down to introducing yourself to people you don't already know. But how do you introduce yourself to someone you don't know, someone who may end up being your best ever prospect, referrer or supplier if you can only get to know them? You'll get more from an event by setting yourself the goal of getting to know some people who you might follow up with, rather than feeling you have to achieve anything more tangible while you're there. Put any thoughts of selling to the back of your mind and just go with the intention of making a few more relationships.

When I walked into my first networking event, I convinced myself of several things. First, I convinced myself that everyone else in the room was more confident than me and somehow better at handling these events than me. I knew, deep inside me, that all these people would somehow be better business people, even though

I didn't know what 'better' meant, and certainly had no evidence to support that belief at all. One of the biggest discoveries for me, which took me a while to realise, is that most people in the room feel exactly the same as me and have butterflies in their stomach.

It's common to feel nervous about networking, but the process doesn't need to be complicated or daunting. Networking can be as simple as introducing yourself to someone who has a similar business to yours, or who might know someone who can help your business. Try to relax and be yourself. This will help you enjoy networking. People will appreciate talking to someone genuine, and this can help you earn their trust and develop good relationships. Talk casually about yourself and make sure you ask other people about themselves and their business. You don't need to be overly formal with people, just be polite and avoid being too overbearing and doing the hard sell. Actively listen to the people around you. Networking is about both receiving and giving information.

Networking is an investment in your business. It's an ongoing process not just a one-off event, and most of all, it takes time. With up to 80% of opportunities coming from people you already know, take the time to network, as the more people you know, the more chance you've got at winning new business.

It doesn't matter if you are networking online or you're attending an event in person, treat them in the same way. You get to make a great first impression, get to practice your pitch and build rapport, which will lead to generating strong business relationships. By networking you have a place to grow yourself, an opportunity to build your business, develop friendships, find support, share your passion, be visible and you get to be yourself. One of THE best things about networking is that it enables you to accomplish the goals most important to you.

We network to build long-lasting business relationships, as people do business with people; people they know, like and trust.

When you're in business, it can be a lonely journey. It can feel like a crazy rollercoaster ride with lots of highs and lows. But having the right support and people around you can make all the difference to your success. Networking is what you make of it. You get to build relationships and make connections that can help support you both personally and in your business.

I know I am always networking at every chance I get. I want to add to and build my existing network, so I surround myself with people on a similar journey, people who have been where I am and people who have done what I want to achieve.

Success comes from constantly making new contacts following up and keeping in touch. Networking Is Key.

KRISTY MOORE is no stranger to business or networking. She has owned and operated different businesses during the last twelve years, and in that time, she hasn't let anything stop her from achieving her goals and dreams.

She has overcome many obstacles to get to where she is today. She is a Cancer survivor, grew up in a domestic violence household, lives with Crohn's Disease, suffered eight miscarriages and is raising a child on the autism spectrum.

She runs her own travel agency, which is part of Travel Counsellors, is one of three certified autism travel professionals in Australia, founder of Adventures with Kayla the Koala, and manages Macedon Ranges Cabinets, which is the family business she owns with her husband.

Kristy loves what she does, is passionate about her business, and she loves supporting other women in business too. She is proud to be an ambassador for Australian Ladies in Business Initiative and runs Mums in Business Australia, where she is the networking event coordinator for the Macedon Ranges and Hume regions in Victoria. When she is not running or attending a networking event or working in her businesses, you will find her helping and supporting the local community. She is the president of the Parents and Friends association at her daughter's school, a coach and on the committee of the local little aths club, and supports many local businesses through sponsorship. She also runs fundraising events to bring awareness to Autism, Crohn's Disease and ovarian cancer.

travelcounsellors.com.au/kristy.moore

Part Four

Sales & Marketing

KATY GARNER

You can have an amazing product, beautiful website and great packaging, but if you don't have customers, you won't have a business.

Marketing starts by knowing who your customers are, what they want and need and where to find them.

A LOT of money, time and energy is wasted when businesses don't know WHO their people (customers) are and the best ways to find their people. For example, there's no point paying for advertising in a television commercial if your people are spending time online instead of watching TV, or paying for a billboard if your people don't drive.

The same goes for social media. If your people are on Instagram, and you're spending all your time focusing on LinkedIn, you're just wasting your time. Getting to know who your ideal customer is, is where all marketing should begin. Knowing who they are can hold the clues to how to reach them, and even the kind of words and images to use in your campaign to engage with them. The more specific you are in knowing who you're trying to reach, the more successful your marketing efforts will be.

So how do we 'find' our people?

First, it's important not to get bogged down on every potential customer you could have. Remember, this is about your ideal customer. To really find out who they are, start by asking yourself these questions. Are they male or female? Where do they live? What age are they? What clothing do they wear? Do they have children? How many? What would their average day look like? What do they do for fun? What social media do they use? How much money do they make? What events do they go to? How do they relax? What are their favourite colours? What level of education did they achieve? Do they have kids? Renting or own a home? What are they interested in? Hobbies? Interests? Online use? What do they read – newspapers, magazines and which kind CLEO or BRW? Do they watch TV? What sort of shows are they watching?

Once you have the answers to the questions, close your eyes and imagine what they look like. Get a clear picture in your head of what your ideal customer looks like and give them a name. You can even create a mood board for this person. Be creative. You can draw and use colours to give you a clear vision of your ideal customer. Now you've identified who they are, what they're interested in, their age, their gender, where they live, how they spend their time and who is important to them. These things give you little clues about how you can market to them and what sorts of places they go to find information. The big question you should be asking is, online or offline, or both.

Online marketing is typically more cost effective than traditional marketing, however, it's not the only way to reach your audience, so it's a good idea to analyse all of your options. If your business consists of selling online, and most of your customers are Australian, targeted online promotion might be your best option. If you have a local cupcake business, targeted local advertising with a combination of online and offline might be your best option.

So, let's stop now and think about your people. Focus on that one person you identified. Let's think about offline (even if you're not going to go that way). What magazines do they read? What TV shows do they watch? Which radio stations are they listening to and at what time of day? Which newspapers are they reading? Are they driving past billboards or are they travelling on trams, trains or buses? Do they attend markets, go to trade shows, what sort of events would they be at?

Online marketing can be overwhelming because there are so many places you could find your people, so the easiest thing to do is to start by making a list. Start with the major social media sites – Facebook, Twitter, Pinterest, LinkedIn, Instagram and Google. These sites will continue to change and even be replaced over time, but currently Facebook is the most universal site, LinkedIn, Google and Twitter are for professionals, and can be good for service businesses. Instagram and Pinterest work well for visual products such as clothing, food and homewares. Do you know which ones your people are using? Often, it's more than one, but think about where they are the MOST, rather than trying to cover all channels.

Once you've thought about social media, think about the kinds of blogs and websites they're visiting to find their information. Are they reading reviews, visiting comparison sites, influenced by articles and opinion pieces? The magazines you identified in your offline marketing can also give you an insight into the sites they'd be likely to visit online too. Make a list of the kinds of blogs and websites they might be reading or visiting regularly. Next, think about distribution. Which businesses are your people using that you could possibly get your message out to them through?

Reaching your people. How can you reach your niche?

Social, face to face, PR, online, newsletter. We know WHO your people are, we know WHERE they are, and now it's all about HOW to reach them. Strategies for reaching your people include PR and publicity, social media, Google search, Newsletters, Face to Face, Advertising, Signage Flyers, brochures, catalogues, Affiliate referrals, Word of mouth.

There are more, but these are the main ways to reach your people. PR and publicity are some of the most valuable strategies a business can use. You can gain thousands of dollars' worth of advertising for your business for free from a clever PR campaign, enabling your business to be seen on television during prime time, featured in national magazines and talked about on radio.

The best thing about PR is that it isn't even that hard to do. All you need is an interesting story about your business written as a press release and the right contact details for the media you'd like to appear in. You can do it yourself if you have the time and are a confident writer, or you can hire a PR company to work with you. Social media is an important marketing channel for most businesses. It is one of the few ways that allows you to talk 'with' your people instead of just talking 'at' them. You can create real conversations where they ask questions and you reply, where they speak and you listen. It's about creating a real connection between brands and their tribe. In the fast-paced world we live in, having a brand that will take the time to listen to their people is a refreshing change. And it's something that small business can do a lot more effectively than big business can.

Google search is so important for small business. People are looking for what you offer every day, but if you're not coming up on the first page of Google search, they won't find you. Don't panic! There are ways to improve your Google ranking without paying a lot of money. Invest in a good book or do some research online into what you need to do. Newsletters are one of the most powerful ways for you to reach your people. People subscribe to your newsletter because they want to hear from you. Newsletters give you the opportunity to really speak to your community and tell them about what's happening in your business.

There are many techniques for encouraging people to sign up to your newsletter, including:

- Offering a free download of an eBook or a checklist.
- Holding a free webinar that they need to sign up to for access.
- Holding a giveaway or competition of some kind. (Keep it relevant to your people.)
- Displaying a sign-up form on your website.
- Giving the option to sign up at checkout when they order from you.

Even if you're just sending to four or five people to begin with, be consistent with your newsletter. Once a month is just about right for most small businesses. Ensure your content is interesting and relevant to your readers. Special offers and exclusive packages work well to keep these people, (your most devoted people) interested.

Face to Face - Face to Face marketing is one of the best ways to make a true connection with your people. This can be through public speaking, giving a presentation to a room full of people, talking to people at tradeshows or market stands or networking at business events. Whenever you're networking or having a conversation one-on-one with people, remember to listen more than you speak, but when you speak, be confident in yourself. Don't be afraid to tell them about your business and what you do. Enthusiasm is contagious.

Trade shows can be expensive, so invest in some time to plan what your objectives are and how you will achieve them.

Advertising is a minefield for start-ups and small business owners. I've heard of people spending thousands on poorly chosen advertising and getting just a handful of orders in return, and others who've spent only a small amount and had significant returns on their investment. The key is always to know who your people are and where you will reach them. You also need to do your research and understand what you're paying for and what you're hoping to achieve from the exercise. Start small, be strategic, and always measure your results, otherwise how will you know what works and what doesn't?

Signage is important if you have a brick-and-mortar business. Make sure it's easy to read and visible from the street. The same goes for signage for market stands or trade shows. If you're using signage, keep the text brief and to the point. Flyers, brochures, and catalogues are an inexpensive way to get the word out. Include them in your orders if you're sending products out. Hand them out at tradeshows and markets and take them with you to business events, networking and conferences you're attending or presenting at.

Affiliate referrals are an excellent way to get the word out to more people. Affiliate works by sharing a percentage of sales with your affiliate partners, these are usually fellow business owners, and is easy to set up if you have a WordPress site. We've used this strategy and seen great results. You can also offer affiliate commission through websites like commission factory and clixgalore, where businesses you don't know will promote you. In the early days in our business, we also used affiliate banners from big brands to create some extra income.

Word of mouth is the best kind of promotion there is. This is where your people tell other people how wonderful you are! A personal recommendation from a friend is far more likely to be trusted than any other kind of promotion. Some businesses encourage word-of-mouth referrals by sending a little gift or a thank you note when they receive a referral.

Research each of the options. What will they cost you (in time & in money) and what will you get in return? Will you reach 100 people or 1000 or 10 000 people? Pay attention to this because it makes a big difference. If you're doing paid advertising and the information isn't visible on their advertising page, contact them by email and request a media kit or advertising package. With the information you find, create a spreadsheet so you can compare the pricing and the number of people you'll reach. It's always important to know and understand this information, even if paid advertising isn't something you want or need to do right now. This knowledge will help you with determining where you want to be focusing your time, energy, and efforts for your unpaid promotions too. Which strategies will you use to reach your people?

Creating Your Marketing Plan

Now you know WHO your ideal customer is, WHERE to find them, and you have decided on some strategies to REACH them, we can now start creating your marketing action plan! First, think about what you want to achieve for the next twelve months through marketing.

1. How much income do you want to bring in?
2. How many new followers or newsletter subscribers do you want?
3. What events do you want to hold or attend?
4. Which campaigns will you focus in for the year?

The next step is to think about how you are going to achieve this. I love to brainstorm as many ideas for activities, campaigns and events

I could potentially hold during the year on a big piece of Butchers paper. I think about the seasonal events I could explore, e.g., New Year Goals, End of Financial Year, plus the timing of our activities. Women's Business School intake is always at the beginning of the year, the Awards campaign begins in May, and September is for new projects. Once I have everything down on paper, now it's time to edit. Which campaigns can I achieve in one year? For each campaign, I need 6-8 weeks' lead time to make sure I have enough time to market them properly. This is also where I set my targets and what I want to achieve from each campaign. i.e., $ or new clients, etc.

How to Create Your Marketing Campaigns

There are four steps we use to create our marketing campaign. This is the one we use ALL the time, and it works for us every time. We tweak it to suit each project and change the wording, the offers and the images and copy, but the structure of our marketing campaigns remains the same each time.

Step 1 THE CAMPAIGN

- What is it you're offering?
- What is the purpose or benefit for customers?
- How long will it go for?
- Who is it for?

For example, we're promoting our online program - the 28-day challenge. It's a defined event that has specific purpose or benefit – to help business owners plan their year ahead. A specific time that it will run for – it goes for 28 days, starting on 16 Nov and finishing on 15 Dec, and a specific audience – mums with young children who've been in business 0 - 5 years.

Step 2 THE STRATEGY

This is the timeline a typical campaign might follow. Ours usually looks something like this.

Week 1 - Launch Phase: The launch phase is the introduction. It tells people what it is you're doing, it's the education and information phase. You might not get any sales straight away, but that doesn't mean people aren't thinking about it.

Week 2 & 3 - Early Bird Phase: The early bird phase creates a sense of urgency and appeals to people who are price sensitive. The early bird offer can be a discounted price or include a bonus reward of some kind or both! It doesn't have to be huge to be attractive.

Week 4 & 5 - Competition Phase: A competition can help customers decide they want what you're offering. We often run a scholarship offer and to enter, we ask people to tell us why they want to be a part of it. Having to think about this question and then put it in writing helps us to get our message across. We know that anyone who has entered that competition is keen to be a part of the project and sometimes has already decided to buy.

Week 6 - Last chance phase: This is the conclusion of your promotion, your last big push to convince potential buyers to join in. Creating a sense of urgency and focusing on FOMO (fear of missing out) can work for some buyers. For others, just the reminder it's time to buy is enough to encourage them to make the purchase.

Step 3 THE PLATFORMS

Where will you reach your audience? This always depends on who your audience is; knowing this is one of the most important things to understand about marketing. Being clear about your ideal customer can help you understand where to promote your message to reach them. Getting these wrong costs businesses LOTS of money, so pay attention.

In the old days, to reach your audience, you had to spend money. You might take out an ad in the local paper or if you could afford it, on TV. Now there are several ways to reach your audience that don't have to cost you a lot of money. They still take your time though, so you have to be clever about it and strategic.

Social media is powerful, but you have to understand your customers and where they will be. - Instagram, Facebook, Twitter, LinkedIn, Pinterest, Google, YouTube.

DIGITAL Paid – Targeted Facebook ads, Google AdWords, online advertising, affiliate marketing. Free – newsletter, blog post, social media posts.

TRADITIONAL Paid – Magazine advertising, newspaper advertising, TV, radio Free – PR, flyers, posters.

Don't get too caught up in all of this, trial and error will help you know what works for you. Be cautious about spending too much money to begin with. It's better to make use of the free tools first and then experiment with small amounts of money to see what works. Always focus on the platforms you know your audience will engage in the most. Our demographic are predominantly all online business owners, so they're using social media on a daily basis. Knowing this helps us know where to focus our energy when it comes to marketing campaign promotions.

Step 4 PUTTING IT ALL TOGETHER

The way you 'market' your campaign in the end really comes down to how compelling your images and copy are. Are people paying attention to what you have to offer?

- Images – Avoid using stock images and use real life

professionally taken images whenever you can, never use clip art!

- Headline: Sum it up in a few words. Invest time in getting this right and researching catchy titles.
- Copy: Get attention and then clearly identify the problem + Give the solution. Outline the benefits. Instead of listing the features, think about how it will make them feel - Social proof.
- Present your credentials. Share testimonials from happy customers to build trust and credibility for your brand.
- Make your offer + Call to action. Always end with a call to action. What do you want the customer to do? How will you entice them to click through to your website and buy? What is it you're offering?

KATY GARNER

Award-winning entrepreneur and author, Katy Garner is the co-founder of The Women's Business School, which supports, educates, and inspires women to create businesses.

With a background in events and community engagement, she's passionate about being a voice for women. She's been active in advocating for more recognition of the work of Australian women in business with State and Federal politicians, to encourage more funding and support for women in business. Katy was on the board of the Queensland Small Business Advisory Council.

For the past ten years, Katy has organised the AusMumpreneur Awards, a national awards program that celebrates mothers in business and recognises the amazing achievements and economic contributions that mumpreneurs make to the Australian economy.

As a mother of three children who runs a successful business, she knows how tough it can be and why it's so important to find the support of others facing the same challenges. She also knows it's important to take time to stop and celebrate the wins along the way.

ausmumpreneur.com

Sharing your story with the world…

CANDICE MEISELS

As a business owner and as a business founder, or even as a potential business founder, you have a secret weapon you can pull out effortlessly when it comes to getting a leg up on bigger brands. This same secret can be used to connect to your customers and the media.

The many hats you wear help create your secret weapon.

You are wearing so many hats on a daily basis; whether the hats you wear consist of the hat you wear as a mother, as a sister, or a daughter, or a friend; or a business owner, a business founder, a business partner, a wife or partner, or any other label you wear as a hat so stylishly.

You may find that on some days those hats feel heavy and you would love nothing more than to take every hat off and just enjoy the feeling of your very own company. That is normal and happens to every one of us, which is why it is so important to include self-care into your frantic schedule.

However, every one of those hats helps to create your story and your businesses story and that is your secret.

Like you, I wear many hats. I am wife to my British-Australian husband, and daughter to my parents in South Africa, where I was raised and lived for twenty-four years. I am a sister to my brother, who still works there as a successful ear, nose and throat, and head and neck surgeon. I am an aunt to four nieces and four nephews. Maybe most important of all, I am mother to five daughters aged 10, 8, 6, 3, and a few days short of 2 whilst writing this chapter. I am currently a foster mother, and at the tail end of the process of open adoption.

I am a pet mother to three rescue cats, two ageing rescue dogs, niece, cousin, friend. And I am founder and owner of Candice Meisels PR, a PR Consultancy that works with start-ups and small to medium-sized businesses. I am a Publicist to my many wonderful past and present clients. I am an author, tertiary educator, foster care and adoption advocate. Currently, I also own a social enterprise that helps small Australian businesses that have been affected by the tragic bushfires, the drought that affected so many businesses in Australia, and the cruel Coronavirus pandemic. Fairy Fun Toys stocks Australian small business educational toys and resources and donates profits to grassroots charities.

Why am I telling you this? To describe to you that the hats you wear, some days with ease and some days with ever present struggle, make up your story.

Your story is your secret weapon.

Your story is your secret when it comes to publicity, connecting to your audience and taking on larger brands and businesses.

How can my story fight against a large brand's budget and resources?

Large brands have a story and a history, however, many of them have changed management teams many times, which waters down the authenticity of their history. Does a story really feel real when it is told by the seventeenth CEO? Can the CEO really share small details? It is hard to relate to a founder that existed twenty, thirty, forty or more years ago.

As a start-up or small to medium-sized business owner, your story is the essence of your business. Your story is in fact your 'why'. It is the reason you get up every day to work in or on your business. Your story is the why you started your business, the how, what, when, where and who.

Your 'why' is what sets you apart from the big brands. And your 'why' is how you can get media coverage, customers and connection.

Your 'why' can build brand awareness, brand loyalty, increase your SEO organically, boost your social media followers, increase your credibility and position you as an industry expert.

The nuts and bolts that make up your story.

Your story starts at the beginning, not at the middle, nor at the present moment. It can include both personal and professional facets that led you to your business idea.

Your story will include when you came up with the big idea, why you came up with the business idea, what you did to implement it, when you officially started the business, how you started the business, how you grew the business, what lessons you learnt, what mistakes you made, what challenges you overcome and tips for others.

Your story will lead your customers, the media, your employees and colleagues on a journey that they will feel they relate to and have a part in somehow when you share your story.

I work with start-ups and small to medium-sized business owners on a daily basis. I get them a lot of media, and that is because of their unique and fascinating stories.

Why would the media care about my business or my story?

The media loves stories and I feed them interesting stories of real people who have started their own businesses and a behind-the-scenes look at their story and the business story. I also include the ups and downs.

People are always intrigued by entrepreneurs. They want to know how they got to where they are today. They want to know their secrets, their failures, their achievements, how they came up with their business idea and how they implemented it.

How to write and flesh out your story?

Before you begin, you need to remember to be yourself. Authenticity builds connection and credibility. Avoid 'salesy' language and just be real.

Step 1:
The first step, and I recommend doing this first, is to set up a quiet area where you will not be disturbed, grab a coffee or tea or water, and get writing.

Step 2:
Start from the beginning explaining to your reader what events, whether they be personal or professional (and they are often both), led you to start the business.

Explain to your reader how you came up with the idea and

take them through the journey of conception through to where you are today. If you have relevant qualifications, then add them in to boost credibility.

When writing, stick to the first person rather than the third person. Aim for 600-800 words. Think of your reader and any questions they may want answered. Add tips, challenges, mistakes and success to your story.

When writing your story, include an introduction, body and conclusion. You can even add a catchy heading and sub-heading.

Step 3:

Once you have written your story, look for photos you can dig up that can illustrate the story to your reader. Perhaps you have an old photo of you working somewhere when you first started? Or perhaps you have photos of your products or service at the very beginning.

If you can source 3-6 photos to illustrate the story, it will make it more authentic and memorable.

Step 4:

Once you have your photos and story ready to go, you can add it to the 'about us' or 'our story' section on your website. You can also send it to your database in an email. You can add it to your blog if you have one and use it for PR and Marketing.

Every start-up and small to medium-sized business has a great story to share. This story sets them apart from multi-nationals which have large resources and budgets. Your story can give you more media coverage than you ever imagined possible as long as you pitch it correctly.

Pitching your story to media.

When pitching your story to the media, ensure you are targeting the media your target audience consumes. Think of your ideal client or customer avatar and allow yourself to flesh out what media they consume. This includes TV, Print, Online, Radio and Podcasts.

Once you have worked out what media they are consuming and when, start researching media outlets and make a media list of their contact details.

The next step is to develop a sharp, concise pitch. The media are extremely busy, and they are inundated with pitches and press releases every day. Your pitch needs to entice them to contact you to interview you or to feature your story.

When I was in Primary School back in South Africa in the 90s, my English Teacher used to pedantically ask us to write exactly one hundred words. I remember counting each blue ink engraved word and adding brackets at the ends with the word count.

We would have to painstakingly edit our work to ensure it was exactly one hundred words. This thorough tool proved to be useful later on in life when I have to create and craft pitches for my clients on a daily basis.

To create the best elevator pitch, go back to your story and summarise it into no longer than two paragraphs. It needs to be concise yet intriguing.

If you are emailing the pitch, don't forget to work on a striking headline and subject for the email too.

After seven years of working with start-ups and small to medium-sized businesses in Australia, I can accurately say your story is one of the most powerful assets you have when it comes to fighting the larger brands who have greater resources and budgets.

Now that you know how powerful your story is, I hope to inspire you with my story.

I was born in Johannesburg, South Africa. I grew up in the golden age of advertising and Marketing. My father ran a Marketing recruitment agency and later worked in trade expos. I loved the excitement of the expositions when I visited him. And I remember looking at the huge brand names, their annual creative stands taking on bigger and better personas and promotions at the event each year.

I visited these events from my early teenage years. I used to look at photos from international events my father attended and loved checking out the different promotions that brands beautified.

Although I didn't know it at the time, slowly my creative juices were awakening. I loved nothing more than to browse through glossy magazines taking in each page of carefully laid out editorial. I'd look at the detailed lifestyle photos and carefully thought-out double-page spreads, inside front covers, front and back covers.

I also loved to write. English was my favourite school subject and one I somehow aced.

I didn't know it, but my love of Marketing was slowly coming together piece by piece. Only now, many years later, can I look back at the jigsaw puzzle and piece it together and see the big picture.

At eighteen, I set up my own Student Research and Marketing agency. I studied a Bachelor of Business Admin Honours Degree in Marketing Management.

I hired students studying Marketing for promotional events and trade expos. One year, a group of student friends worked on a trade expo for *Appletiser*. A couple of us used to conduct face-to-face surveys at trade expos. I would then work out the results and create a Market Research Report for the client.

I also worked for *Procter and Gamble* doing in-store promotions for products such as *Pantene, Head and Shoulders*.

My love of Marketing evolved, and I won an academic award for International Marketing.

I continued to run Student Research and Marketing throughout my studies. I also tutored where I could as I loved to teach, plus the money was good, and as a student very welcome too.

Once I finished my degree, I found a dream job in Marketing for an importer and distributor specialising in video games. This start-up was successful in securing international European and UK Video game publisher deals. The video game industry was also booming and filled with incredible talent and opportunity. It was male-dominated at the time, and I loved being one of the females striving to work in a male industry.

The company scaled quickly, and my career catapulted with it. My role was mainly Marketing, but there was no PR department. We needed to secure previews, reviews, seed announcements to the press and organise giveaways. I started doing this and the results were great.

One day, the MD called me into his office and gave me the opportunity of a lifetime and the gift of what would become my career.

"Candice, we would like you to head up and create a PR department."

I grabbed the opportunity with both hands and created a PR department from scratch. I worked with major movie brands that were turned into video games, with huge video game franchises and well-known brands.

After organising local events, I went to international video game expos and took media international press trips. I also taught Marketing and PR at night at a local media college more to inspire and pass on my love of Marketing and PR. And I marked exams for a Major Marketing institution, which was more of a hobby.

I loved my job, and nothing stood in my way until I met my husband who was from England. After a few long-term relationships, this short whirlwind romance led to engagement and marriage. Within three months, I literally moved across the globe to another hemisphere.

It was easy for me to let my London-based contacts know I was looking for a PR Management role in the video game industry in

London.

I secured a phone interview with The Walt Disney Company's video game arm, Disney Interactive Studios. One interview led to another, and I flew to London for a long weekend and a series of interviews at Disney's London office in Hammersmith.

I got the job, packed up my life in South Africa, and moved to London where I worked in strategic PR at Disney Interactive Studios as Associate European PR Manager. I then worked at another Milton Keynes based Publisher and had my first child. I worked on some great franchises and with an amazing toy brand.

I studied a short course in Journalism whilst pregnant. I wanted to understand what makes a journalist tick, what stories they seek out and how to make a story newsworthy.

As a teenager, I visited Australia a few times, and I fell in love with the country and lifestyle. I found life in England hard as the culture and climate were starkly different from life in South Africa. We started our papers for Australia and one snowy December day, my husband saw a two-year transfer to Sydney, Australia on his company's, at the time, intranet. He applied and six weeks later we were back in the Southern Hemisphere, a little more South East than previously. I freelanced in PR, which would work well for our family, and I fell pregnant with our second daughter soon after.

In 2013, I opened Candice Meisels PR to help give start-ups and small to medium size businesses a voice.

In 2014, whilst pregnant with our third daughter, I also studied a Cert IV in Training and Assessment to teach Marketing and PR in Australia.

The demand for a publicist who helps small businesses grew quicker than I had ever imagined, and seven years later, the business has helped hundreds of start-ups and small to medium-sized businesses.

In 2017, I gave birth to my last biological child and juggled the girls and a growing business. In 2018, we became foster carers after a client who fosters inspired me. Two weeks after becoming official foster carers, our princess was born, and she was placed with us. She is now almost two, and we are almost through the challenging open adoption process which we have been working towards for the last eighteen months.

I am blessed to wear the many hats I carry, some days with grace and others with stress. My heart is full and I am grateful to juggle family life with my business.

I am also and always will be rooting for small businesses, the underdogs, and reaching my hand out to help, uplift, and root for the little brands.

I am handing you the writing hat, so you too, can share your story and receive success, connection and publicity from all you have achieved and from all that makes you… you.

Tips:

- Do share the challenges, mistakes, and how you overcome them.
- Celebrate the highlights, achievements and joys.
- Be authentic and avoid selling yourself.
- Schedule time to write your story in a quiet place with no interruptions and a cup of tea, coffee, water, or any other beverage of your choice.
- Own your story, be proud and confident.
-
- Imposter syndrome and anxiety are real, but overcome yours by reaching out and getting the correct help.
- You can write a longer story and a shorter story. Online media outlets prefer 600-800 words.
- If you get disheartened, then remember you know your story inside out. It is boring to you, but not to others. Your

story can inspire and help others while boosting your brand awareness, credibility, and connection with your customers. Only you can write your story. Now go on and schedule in that time so you can download your story and motivate others.

CANDICE MEISELS is the founder of Candice Meisels PR. Candice used to work for large brands when she realized her heart was really rooting for the little brands. She set up her PR Consultancy to act as a publicist for the start-ups and small to medium-sized businesses in Australia and has been doing so for seven years.

candicepr.com

Building your community

PEACE MITCHELL

I was crying on the floor in my walk-in wardrobe. My first business had ended before it had even begun, and my dreams of ever doing anything meaningful or important with my life had been ripped to pieces.

I'd never felt more alone than in that moment, and these words kept playing over and over in my head, like a broken record.

'If you want to go fast, go alone.
If you want to go far, go together.'
AFRICAN PROVERB.

This quote both inspired me and challenged me.

Not the fast part. The fast part was easy. As a young girl growing up, I would speed around the streets on my bright red bike, and when you're on your own with the wind in your hair you could go really fast. And fast was the hustle that kept me up day and night trying to get it right.

It's the 'far' that was hard. It's far that kept replaying in my mind, over and over.

Far meant that the best university for me was in Townsville, over three hundred kilometres away from where I grew up. Far meant that the best business conferences were in Brisbane, an eighteen-hour drive away. And Far meant that going to China to meet with manufacturers and find the best quality materials seemed impossible. Far meant that the opportunities for me to succeed often seemed just out of reach, especially when my children were young, making it hard to even get to local networking events.

As an entrepreneur in regional Australia, I felt isolated and alone. Where were my people?

No matter who you are, where you live, or what you do, we all need connection.

My first idea was hand-embroidered bikinis. I'd big visions for this business; colourful designs, embellished with luxurious ribbons, sparkling glass beads and golden thread. I'd the creativity, the vision and the ambition, but I lacked the right connections. Without fashion experience or a mentor to guide me, without a warm introduction to retail stores that never returned my calls, without being connected to manufacturers that understood quality, the business was destined to fail.

This story is not unique. Australia has hundreds of thousands of incredible businesswomen. They grow global empires from spare rooms on remote cattle stations. They bounce between school and sport and play dates, all the while bouncing products into international markets and juggling deals. So many of them are doing it by themselves.

But it's not just by themselves. They do it alone.

44% of mothers in business feel guilty they're creating any

business at all. And nearly as many, don't have a single other entrepreneur in their network to talk to.

Although my first business failed, it was a big part of my eventual success, because I realised the lack of connection I'd experienced was something women all over Australia were facing. So, I called Katy, and we started dreaming up plans for an online community to connect women everywhere, called AusMumpreneur.

It would be a place where you would always feel welcome, supported and included. A place where you could share your challenges and your wins.

AND where you could find connections that would be pivotal to your business journey. If you needed an accountant, a graphic designer, the contact for the buying agent at Walmart or Harrods, or to anyone at all, someone would know someone who could help you.

The community grew quickly and is now over six times the population of our hometown.

Every week Katy and I received notes of gratitude. Women sharing how someone they met in our community had shared an insight that transformed their business. And years later, how that same incredible business connection had become a lifelong friend.

As bright as these women shine as individual stars, Katy and I could see how much more they achieved as glorious constellations.

We'd found the magic we'd felt through connecting local women, but now it was happening all around Australia as though someone turned the volume all the way up!

We'd created our own - *Connection Economy*.

The *Connection Economy* is a beautiful discovery with elegant simplicity: The better connected you are, the more value you create and experience. And so do your connections. Everyone grows together, so the collective value grows exponentially.

The *Connection Economy* is the economy of prosperity,

collaboration and infinite possibilities.

As society continues to evolve beyond the industrial economy and the information economy, we are seeing personal connection, trust and authentic relationships become a valuable commodity. This economy is significantly different to all those that came before, such as the industrial economy or the information economy. Because, inherent in this economy, is the connection to a deeper sense of purpose and meaning over production and consumption. This marks a global trend away from the aggressive winner-takes-all approach to the way the world works.

The *Connection Economy* is driven by qualities such as collaboration, cooperation, communication, and sharing and enables us to take a different perspective in solving today's toughest problems in business, education, sustainability, politics and government.

By building relationships, listening, nurturing, collaborating and fostering connections rather than assets, the connection economy provides opportunities for solving problems. It also finds profits, and redefines success in ways that benefit society as a whole and not just the few wealthy individuals at the top.

Our ability to connect has been hyper-accelerated by the internet, but as The Australian Ambassador for Women in Tech, I can tell you, without question, there's a difference between reach and connection.

Connection literally has the power to change the world. When our actions come from a place of genuine desire for collaboration and generosity instead of a drive for profit and individual gains, the outcome is better for everyone. Can you imagine a world with more empathy, more compassion, and more kindness? This is what a world based on the values of the connection economy looks like.

The C*onnection Economy* rewards value created by building relationships and fostering connections, rather than assets, like the industrial economy. The industrial economy values more, better, faster, whereas the connection economy builds on who you know, what you know, and how that knowledge influences your connections.

It used to be 'we're big, you can trust us,' but today the bigger you are, the less trusted you are. Today the most trusted companies are more intimate, they are more authentic. The companies that have the best reputation are smaller, or they have found some way of connecting in a more personal way.

But why do we need connection?

We are social beings. We need each other. We are all interdependent.

Mother Teresa once said, *'If we have no peace, it's because we have forgotten that we belong to each other.'*

When we're connected:

1. We're better able to find solutions for complex problems
2. We're healthier and happier and
3. We have access to more experiences and opportunities

Brene Brown specialises in social connection and says, 'A deep sense of love and belonging is an irresistible need of all people. We are biologically, cognitively, physically, and spiritually wired to love, to be loved, and to belong. When those needs are not met, we don't function as we were meant to. We break. We fall apart. We numb. We ache. We hurt others. We get sick.'

I recently heard a story about a traditional village where all the women washed clothes together down by the river. But little by little they all got washing machines, followed by a sudden outbreak of depression. No one could figure out why. Why on earth was having a washing machine giving the women depression? But you see, it wasn't the washing machines; it had nothing to do with them, really. It was the loss of time spent doing things together. It was the absence of community. And it was the loss of an opportunity to socialise with each other and talk about the things that mattered.

As people, we've become so independent. 'I'm fine' we tell ourselves when in reality we're depressed, we're overwhelmed, we're lonely and we're hurting. 'I'm fine. I'm just really busy right now,' we say when days, weeks, months, and years go by without connecting with friends. 'I'm fine, I'm fine, I'm fine.' It's so easy to say, even when it's not true.

We've become so isolated that it's hard to know how to get back. It's so hard to know how to even begin to build the relationships we need. And in our current culture, it's just not as easy or organic as it once was. It's more work now there's a greater distance. Because now we all have our own washing machines. We don't depend on each other to do laundry, or cook dinner, or raise babies anymore. We don't really depend on each other for much of anything if we're being honest.

Brene Brown believes being isolated can be as damaging to our physical health and the length of our life expectancy as smoking fifteen cigarettes a day. Our longing for connection is real. It isn't a luxury or an extra to fit in when we're not too busy, it's a necessity. We don't want it. We need it.

So why is it so hard to achieve connection?

We are profoundly social creatures. We may think we want money, fame, beauty or a new car, but at the heart of most of these desires is a need to belong, to be accepted and to be loved. Yet despite this, we so often pride ourselves on our independence, on pulling ourselves up by our own bootstraps, being a self-made success and never having to depend on anyone.

The challenge of distance is something all entrepreneurs working from rural, regional and remote areas face, but our research has found that women in cities working from home with young children, often feel just as isolated.

Then there's an emotional distance, and it's taught to every girl from a young age.

Our society doesn't encourage us to collaborate. From a young age fairy tales and Disney movies send the message that women and girls must compete with each other, distrust each other and envy each other. Where are Cinderella's, Snow White's and Ariel's female friends? Disney princesses are more likely to be friends with animals than other girls. They rarely have mothers, and the lead women are evil stepsisters and wicked stepmothers out to betray them and bring them down whatever it takes. Disney films send us a clear message, from a young age, that you can't trust other women.

Then our education system reinforces this message, insisting we must always do our own work, be independent, and that sharing or collaborating is akin to cheating. This teaches us to compete for grades, instead of collaborating with our fellow peers, and striving for individual achievement and the highest mark in the class at all costs.

Then, in business, we're taught to be aggressive. Be first to market, get a good lawyer and make sure everyone you meet signs a non-disclosure agreement because everyone is out to steal your idea.

The voice of our inner critic comes into play here too, telling us we don't deserve to ask for help, that others don't want us to inconvenience or annoy them, or no one would want to help us. If we were smarter, we could figure it out by ourselves. It's the fear of rejection, fear of criticism, fear of failure, fear of imperfection, fear of humiliation, fear of admitting we can't do it alone. That we are in fact an impostor and if we ask for help, everyone will know. We've been conditioned to do it on our own. Asking for help is almost like admitting failure or that you're not clever enough, strong enough, or competent enough to do it on your own. Our own deepest fears and insecurities attempting to keep us safe by keeping us small and self-reliant. They hold us back from asking for and receiving the connection that we need to scale our businesses, achieve our goals and create a bigger positive impact on the world through following our callings.

With all of this going on, it's no wonder connection is hard.

It's no wonder we're experiencing a mental health crisis around the globe.

It's no wonder over 60% of small businesses will fail before their third birthday.

And it's no wonder nearly half of all female entrepreneurs feel guilty about asking for help.

Distrust, individualism, aggression, self-doubt, that's why Connection is hard.

But it doesn't have to be this way.

In 2016, Katy and I launched The Women's Business School. Not just to teach business skills, but to teach the art of connection and introduce women to the crucial connections they need to succeed. It's gone on to be named Australia's Best Incubator for Women at the Women in Digital awards.

Why? Because with connection, incredible things can happen.

Take Georgina McEncroe, for example. George is the founder of *Shebah*, the female-only ride share service designed to be so safe, you'd happily send them to pick up your kids from school. She told me how male investors couldn't understand why on earth she'd create this service when Uber already exists. Georgina understood problems won't get solved by people who don't experience those problems. So, she turned to her community. Using equity crowd-funding and giving her community the power to be the investors, she raised $3 million from the same people her business is designed to help.

Or how about Ayumi Moore Aoki, the founder of *Women in Tech* who in just two years has launched chapters globally, partnered with the UN and held events all over the world hosted by passionate ambassadors?

Or the incredible Dr Tererai Trent, whose dream of creating generational change through education for children in Zimbabwe has now leveraged her connections to help build 11 schools and educate over 40,000 African children?

These women are incredible leaders who have built deeply connected communities of people around them. You could call them super connectors.

I've found that there are certain qualities they have in common that we can all learn to cultivate.

Relationships

One of the most important keys of building relationships is to be present. Everyone wants to feel important, seen and heard.

When I think of the quality of presence, I picture someone who you can confide in and trust, someone who listens with their heart, who holds space for you, who pauses to let you finish what you're saying; someone who isn't distracted by their phone or looking around behind you for someone more interesting to arrive. They're the people who check in that you're okay and call you just to say hello, not because they want something. This is a powerful quality we can all be better at. Combined with presence, we need curiosity, or the art of being interested in other people.

Everyone has a story, and when you're meeting new people, it's important to ask the right questions which invite people to open up and share their story. Everyone loves to talk about themselves, and if you'll give them the space to open up, it's one of the best ways to really connect deeply. The people who are good at this skill are warm and friendly and seem to make new friends easily and effortlessly. I have a friend who is so good at this. When you first meet her, you might think she's an introvert or shy and quietly spoken. Yet if you take her to an event, you'll notice she's the one who's always taking selfies with new people, making friends and talking one on one to all kinds of different people about all kinds of different things. Her open curiosity and ability to ask interesting questions allows her to easily strike up conversations and form a bond with new people.

Reciprocity

Reciprocity is the act of giving generously, knowing the favour will be returned. Not necessarily by the person you've given the favour to, or even anytime soon, but trusting when you're kind to someone, that kindness will also be returned to you. Importantly, it's not the same as doing something with the expectation of something of equal value in return or an obligation. The other important consideration is that reciprocity doesn't mean you're always giving and being taken advantage of. The magic of reciprocity is that it's a two-way street, where your time, energy and kindness is given where it is truly respected and appreciated.

Generosity doesn't have to be about big grand gestures; in fact, sometimes the smallest act of kindness can have the biggest impact. Giving our time with a phone call, opening a door to an opportunity for someone or suggesting a referral, these acts cost nothing but can mean so much. Super connectors understand the law of reciprocity, they are thoughtful, kind and generous and they know how to give, how to receive and how to ask graciously for help.

Resonance

We gravitate towards people who we like to be around. A person with positive energy, self-confidence and a great sense of humour is always someone you want to be around.

Resonance is all about your energy, and when you feel good, it literally attracts people and new opportunities to you. Einstein believed the Law of Resonance is a universal, energetic law in which our thoughts and emotions create a frequency, like a radio wave. The opposite of resonance is dissonance, and you've probably experienced the feeling of people like this who leave you feeling drained rather than energised after talking to them. This is why it's so important to surround yourself with positive, well-connected people and to ensure you're regularly engaged in the activities and experiences that make you feel good.

It's simple, feel good all day every day and you'll attract more opportunities to your life. Resonance isn't about just being happy all the time, no matter what though. Instead, it is about letting go of grudges, negative thinking, and bouncing back from disappointment and setbacks rather than dwelling on them. In business, there will always be challenges and obstacles, but how you handle them is what makes all the difference.

Super connectors are powerful because connection is great for business. By building relationships, listening, nurturing, collaborating and fostering connections rather than assets, the connection economy provides opportunities for solving problems. Such as finding profits, and redefining success in ways that benefit society as a whole and not just the few wealthy individuals at the top. It's about abundance for all and all of us winning.

Super connectors have the power to do incredible things, give back in incredible ways, and they understand that we rise by lifting others.

What inspires me is that so many of them started from a place where they felt remote, forgotten or alone, and yet now with powerful networks surrounding them they have achieved so much.

So how can we leverage the power of connection?

As entrepreneurs and business leaders, we have an opportunity to create resonance and surround ourselves with positive people. To find new ways to create deeper relationships and connections with our clients, and collaborate with other businesses who share the values of the change we want to see in the world.

If you have a platform, then why not use this platform for reciprocity, to lift others up, to give back and to give others a voice.

The connection economy provides us with a powerful force for change and unique opportunities to co-create a brighter future for us all.

My sister and I won't stop until we take our connections global, breaking down barriers for women in business everywhere as we do.

We'll get there because we will lean on, show up for, and continue to grow with our community.

We'll get there by always asking 'What can I give?' instead of 'What can I get?'

And we'll get there because when things get rough, as they inevitably will, we will ask for help. Early and often. And we'll go far, because we'll always, always go together.

PEACE MITCHELL is a TEDx speaker, author, co-founder of The Women's Business School & AusMumpreneur, Australian Ambassador of Women in Tech and Forbes.com business expert.

Peace is passionate about supporting women to reach their full potential and create the life they want to live. She has helped thousands of women achieve their dream of running a successful and profitable business and believes investing in women is the best way to change the world.

Peace Mitchell co-founded AusMumpreneur in 2009, with her sister, Katy Garner, creating Australia's #1 community for mothers in business and together they co-founded the Women's Business School in 2016 to provide entrepreneurial education for women globally. She has a community of 50,000 women and is surrounded by women who inspire her to dream bigger and follow her calling every day.

Today, her commitment is stronger than ever, to invest in the power of women to change the world.

www.thewomensbusinessschool.com

The key to winning in business is to make up your own rules

ELLE LIKOPOULOS

As a mother of four young children and a successful career in business, I am always asked, 'How do you manage to do it all?' The answer is simple, but one that usually has people perplexed at first. I play by my own rules!

We all know that catchy Dolly Parton song 'Working 9 to 5', but the reality is the idea of a primary caregiver trying to do this is as outdated as the song. Recent studies indicate the weight of caring for the children and household are still largely the women's responsibility in most 'traditional' families. As the cost-of-living rises across the globe, more and more households are reliant on two incomes to survive. Mothers are now more than ever feeling the pressure of having to juggle the impossible. You can buy all the self-help books in the world, meditate, goal set and binge watch Marie Kondo all you like. The fact of the matter is you feel overwhelmed and exhausted, because it isn't sustainable to work fulltime structured hours, along with being at every sports match, remembering to pick up dry cleaning and prepare Martha Stewart worthy roasts for dinner forever. Instead of trying to change myself and my family to fit around work, I realised it would be far more sensible to change my working schedule to weave through my family's life. By starting your own business, you begin taking control of your life and creating your own rules to play by.

Don't try to fit in

The hardest part about starting your own business is the start. Not only do you have to throw money into an idea you're not sure will even work, but you need this business to be successful to earn you an income to replace the job or position you left. Many become overwhelmed at the thought of this kind of gamble and decide the money is better spent on a holiday with the kids. As a natural gatherer and nurturer, it is not inherent in us to make bold decisions for ourselves that could impact our family. It is time, however, we break the 'Martyr mother' mould and start trusting in our own abilities more. Prior to being a mother or someone's partner, you were just you. Try to bring that version of yourself back and list all the things you are good at and enjoy. This is not a time to edit your thoughts or downplay your inner desires. By having a visual list of what makes you happy, you have a foundation or theme for your future business. If you start a business based on what you think may make you money, rather than what you're passionate about, it will not be sustainable in the long run and it is likely to be unsuccessful.

As a business broker, I have seen many people make the mistake of starting a business based on what they felt was secure rather than do something they were good at. By trying to fit into a certain mould or standard, you risk losing your creative instinct and missing the opportunity to create something unique. Your business needs to reflect you and your offerings to the market. If you start with the idea of fitting into a certain business plan, you will be back in the position you were as an employee. That's where you are trying to keep up, rather than customising to fit around you and your family's lifestyle and needs. Almost all the clients I have seen who have done that, end up burnt out and looking to sell or close within the first three years of trade. The most successful entrepreneurs are those who have been able to step outside of society standards and understand that a business is not a 'one size fits all'. Once you realise this, you see how ridiculous the idea really is!

Consider the typical schedule of your household and work out the time slots you could have to assign for your business. If you are, for example, the one who does the school drop off or pick-ups, then you should look at having your business commitments work around this. There's no point in trying to convince yourself that you can 'make it work'. It's not usually sustainable in the long run and you face being stressed and running around trying to keep up with everything around you.

You can't build a business on a trend

We've all seen on social media the business bandwagon at one point or another. When one café created giant milkshakes with towering whipped cream and confectionary, we soon found our newsfeed flooded with similar images from others following suit. Likewise, recently it seemed as though every event planner pivoted their business into creating grazing boxes delivered to your door. Visual forums such as Pinterest and Instagram are great sources for inspiration, however they can also dull your imagination and block the ability to come up with your own creative ideas. For a business to be successful, it needs people to engage. You don't necessarily need to invent something, but you do need to find your point of difference within your market.

Whilst trends can sometimes be a quick and easy spike in income, they don't last long enough to build an entire business model around them. It is therefore important to have an underlining base of which your business stands on that sets you apart. Consider the world around you and make a list of what seems to be topics of interest and passion. What is making a lot of noise? If you want to stand out from your competition and convince people to spend money with you, you need to appeal to their emotional triggers.

We all remember the big cupcake craze that took over little pop-up shops and stalls everywhere overnight. The demand for these were so high the prices soared, and franchises began selling stores for hundreds of thousands to eager buyers looking to cash in on the craze. By the time many of them bought the business or set up their business, the trend was already at the tail end. Many ended up losing their homes and life savings before they could even get a return on their investment, because the hype had moved to macarons so quickly. Depending on your business and industry, you should think about how you can associate a value important to your target demographic that can connect with them for a long-term commitment. Using grazing boxes as the example, you may wish to use ethically sourced packaging and local produce with stories of the producers or farmers to connect 'support local' and 'sustainability' movements with your product. When you start brainstorming, you will find the ideas are rather easy to come up with, provided you already have a sense of what issues are important to your demographic. Keywords on Instagram are a great tool to help you research and see what moves your buyers, as it's what AI (artificial intelligence) is doing already to keep us scrolling.

Using values rather than trends, allows your business to adapt with changing hypes whilst maintaining consistent foundations and identity for branding awareness and customer loyalty.

Spend where it counts

Putting your plans and ideas into motion and giving life to your business can be a costly exercise. There is a whole new world of products and services designed to support and nurture your delicate little newborn business, all of which sound amazing but come with a price. You need to make sure you've allocated a certain budget for the initial outlay, factoring in all your costs and cash flow needs to launch. If you start without having a firm budget in mind, it is easy to get swept up in the romance and excitement of the whole process. Remember, the ultimate objective of a business is for it to be profitable and begin generating enough revenue to allow steady annual growth for re-investment.

A budget doesn't necessarily mean you have to sacrifice the look or concept of your business, but it does mean you need to spend consciously. If, for example, you're planning to open a salon, you may consider buying one that is established already. Rather than spend $70,000 on fitting out a blank canvas, you might take over a newly built existing salon for $30,000 and save on asset costs and setup time. The money left over which you've now saved, can go towards hiring that marketing agency you like to build up your exposure.

Even if you've got a unique product or concept that doesn't exist, you may find something in a similar industry or style that you could take over and customise to fit your brief. It's all about being open-minded and flexible to ensure you open up as efficiently as possible. You can always add new things to a business that is making money, but you can never recover the money spent in a business that is struggling.

Whilst it's important to be thrifty with your money, you also need to remember that certain things come with a price tag. In my many years' experience representing the sale of businesses across every industry imaginable, there is almost always the same common factor between the businesses that fail within the first 3-5 years of trade. Can you guess it? I've run the exercise of asking first-time buyers this question, and I've yet to have someone guess correctly. The answer is, all the businesses that failed in less than five years of trading spent little to no money on hiring an accountant advisory service or a solicitor with commercial experience. The focus is always around the creativity and branding of the business, which generates instant physical or visual reinforcement that your business is coming to life. The idea of spending money out of the budget for business structuring advice or for legal advice around the many clauses in the lease you want to sign never seems feasible at first. The reality is your business can't survive on good looks alone. Your business needs solid foundations of financial structure to rest on and the legal framework to prop itself against in challenging times.

Know your best asset

The balance between business and family is a constant tug of war for most women. It usually feels like you can never get that perfect equilibrium. If you've had a great day playing with the kids and folding all your laundry, then you feel guilty for all the unread emails in your inbox, and vice versa in this hamster wheel of guilt we like to play on.

We put a lot of stress on ourselves to over compensate with our children because we have 'mum guilt' for working, and then we spend all night working from our laptops in bed over compensating on our business. In the early days of my career, this toxic wheel of guilt nearly killed me.

I was constantly trying to do everything and multitask wherever I could to avoid the feeling of letting anyone down. I got to the point where I literally worked around the clock, sending emails at 3-4 in the morning and sleeping only three hours a day to try to fit more time into my schedule. Even when I was in the toilet or shower, I felt guilty for not being efficient, so I'd clean the shower whilst I was in there or answer emails on the toilet. I couldn't allow myself any downtime without feeling like I was doing something wrong.

For a while, this schedule seemed to work. I had achieved the impossible and was perfecting every aspect of my life, or so I thought! The stress on my body caused severe weight loss to the point where I had to alter the smallest size jeans in a small cut designer store. I began getting sick more often and hospitalised several times for dehydration and exhaustion. I remember one time at the hospital, I was getting very annoyed because I had stayed overnight and I wanted to be discharged so I could get into the office. The nurse didn't let me drive and urged me to 'take the day off.' I called an Uber from the hospital and went straight to the office, wearing my clothes from the night before and my hospital bands still on my wrists.

It wasn't until I started the IVF journey with my twins, that I again thought of myself, and my body as valuable too. The need to nurture my body to conceive and then to protect this vessel that carried my babies, allowed me to reconnect with myself. I learned to slow down and realised it wasn't the end of the world to let some emails stay unread for a day. If you think your business will suffer if you're not always working on it, then you need to realise you are the most valuable asset. You need to ensure you factor in 'self-care' time and do the things you love every day. Schedule in your calendar time slots to go for a walk, get a blow wave or whatever makes you happy. Treat these time slots as client meetings and don't cancel them or reschedule. The year I slowed down and spent mainly on bedrest, pregnant and working mostly from home, I doubled my sales. When I saw the sales graph on the screen, I was shocked. I went over the figures twice in case there was a mistake. Then I thought about it, and it made sense. I was taking care of the business's best asset, and therefore could work more efficiently.

Don't catch feelings

We all know the saying 'your business is like your baby' and in a lot of ways it really does take you on a similar journey of growth and discovery like parenthood would. You spend all your time and energy devoted to creating your business and then carefully nurture and protect it, as it grows into its different stages of development. When you become a parent, we talk about seeing the world differently through your child's eyes. The same thing happens in business, as you explore relationships and the world from a newly found business perspective.

The reality is, however, that a business is really not like a child but more like that selfish, toxic ex-boyfriend you dated in high school. It's a one-sided relationship you can't really see for what it is because you are infatuated. No matter how much time and energy you put into your business, there is always room for more to give. The moment you stop giving it all your time and love, it will eventually feel neglected and betray you. It's not a forever, unconditional kind of love or relationship. Just like that ex that was cute and funny but deep down you knew he wasn't 'The One', you need to set limits and boundaries to avoid getting hurt whilst you're having fun. If the time comes where your business is no longer fulfilling you or giving you what you want, don't feel obligated to stay if you try to fix it, but it's just not working out. The most successful business people in the world have had many failures in business; in fact, most of them have had more failed businesses than successful. It is not a reflection of your worth or abilities if your business comes to a point where it no longer fulfils you or gives you what you need. Just like a breakup, it can hurt at first, but you will soon meet someone new that makes you totally forget about your heartache from 'what's his name?'

As a business broker, I can't tell you how many business owners are in total denial of the state and reality of their business. You shouldn't have to make excuses for your business as to why it's not treating you right. Sometimes certain relationships are good for that moment but not a forever thing, and when the time is up, you need to call it and move on. The more business owners have tried to force or fight this phenomenon, the more money and people around them they end up ultimately losing. Love your business, love the journey, but above all love yourself!

You've got this

Starting a business is hard work and there will always be moments where you wonder if you made the right decision. Don't let fear and uncertainty cloud your judgement and ability to make the courageous first steps. Most often the biggest regrets we have in life are not from actions we've taken, but from the actions we didn't take because we were too scared. If you have come this far, it means it's something you really want to do, so block out the negative thoughts and just dive in. It's not about the success of the business or how much money you make, in fact, you may need to make a few attempts before you get it right. Ultimately, it's the empowerment you unlock from within once you finally decide to *Back Yourself!*

ELLE LIKOPOULOS

I run one of the most successful business brokerages in the state of Victoria. In a heavily male-dominated industry, I have climbed the ranks to being one of the best-selling agents in my field. I was the first business broker in the state to be formally invited to speak in China about buying small business to foreign investors and visa migrants. I have pioneered for women within my industry, and Absolute Business Brokers is now proudly one of the few companies to have more females than men in the team amongst the business brokerages in Australia. And I have four young children, including twins who are under two years of age. My mission is to continue to empower women to scrap the notion we need to choose between our career and our families.

When I was a little girl, I used to love going into my auntie's room and playing dress up in her corporate fancy outfits. I would clip on these huge 80s chandelier earrings, wear her shiny suit and be lost in puffs of sleeves and nylon. I used to even wrap sticky tape around my nails to make them look longer and colour them red with my texta. Undoubtedly, I would have looked ridiculous, but all these years later, I still remember the rush I felt when I looked in the mirror and saw my reflection as a little girl. I felt glamorous, strong and powerful. It was as if I had put my super hero costume on and went from Bruce Wayne to Batman. I would take an old typewriter my grandmother had lying around, and I would set up a pretend office on the coffee table. I would sit on that coffee table typing with my taped red fingernails for hours, never breaking out of character.

One day, someone gifted me a doll that looked like a little baby boy. I named him Joshua, and I literally took him everywhere. He was my baby in every sense of the word to me. You'd imagine I'd forget about my career alter ego and move on to playing house with my new favourite baby doll as most children would. To the surprise and amusement of my family, I set up my coffee table office, put on my garish power suit and began typing away as I normally did. The only difference was that baby Joshua was right next to me in his little toy bed. My mother turned to me and said, 'Sweetie, you can't bring your baby into your office.' I looked up at her and innocently asked her 'Why not?'

In the 80s, women certainly had more choice to enter the workforce and hold careers than previous generations, but there was still very much a choice that women had to make between being career women or mothers. My mother laughed and explained to me that my boss probably wouldn't want a baby to be in their office and I had to leave my baby doll at home. I didn't realise it then, but I was about to make a decision in my life at that moment that broke society norms. 'No, Mummy, I'm not going to choose, I'm going to do both!' I said and went back to typing away.

Elle is a mother of four kids under ten (two of which are under 2), and runs Absolute Business Brokers, which is a family business. She is the highest earning sales agent in her firm and the first business broker to be invited by the Chinese government to speak in China to visa buyers. Elle also hosts a podcast called The Mumpreneurs Club, which is designed for career women with children and recently launched a not-for-profit support group for mums in business. Elle's role in Absolute Business Brokers is to motivate a group of agents to sell, manage the administration staff, all legal matters, and steer the direction of the brand. She is driven to succeed to prove to women there is no need to choose between career and children.

www.absolutebusinessbrokers.com.au

Part Five

Resilience through personal crisis

REBECCA CORBETT

When you are a business owner, it is difficult to separate your personal life from your business life. When things are stressful at home, or at work, it will affect the other. It is just a fact of life for a business owner. But that does not mean we have to accept it.

I have attended many professional development seminars and training, but by far the best thing I ever did was complete a resilient leadership course. I thought I would learn tips on leading a team, but what I learned about, was myself. Who I am. How I react to situations and other people.

When we know ourselves, the intricacies of our mind and what triggers us, we can put in place techniques and plans to calm our minds when faced with a personal or business crisis.

There are six domains of personal resilience. Think of all six as spokes on a wheel. They all need to be equal to ensure a smooth ride. If one is out of balance, your wheel is going to make for a bumpy ride. I am going to cover all six domains in this chapter, from the perspective of my story. My story is a roller coaster. When I was in the middle of it, some days I was not sure it would ever end. But looking back now, it perpetuated some of the biggest growth I have had personally and professionally.

PART 1

No one is coming to save you.

Resilient Domain: Tenacity and Collaboration
When I first ventured into business for myself, my husband was not onboard. In fact, I did not get much support from those closest to me at all. We'd moved to a rural town before getting married, with no family within three hours of us. There was no free babysitting for my kids aged two and four. Every minute I had away from my children was in paid childcare. I was under so much pressure to get this right and make my business a success. I did not know then that this was only the beginning of a tumultuous roller coaster.

When you first start a business, it is common to not take a wage for the first year. Generally, you will keep every dollar you make in the business and use it to leverage your business growth. For me, I was under immense pressure to take a wage from my business. And I did. But that meant I had to leverage the only asset I had–my time–to grow my business.

I attended the 'Google University' and taught myself to build a website. Instead of spending $63 on a premium template, I opted for the free version and spent days learning to custom code so I could change the colours on my site. Picture me with cans of energy drink sitting in the dark, my face illuminated only by the computer screen, awake for far too long, custom coding a website. Three days later, I emerged from my laser focus with a fully functioning website, and I expected a pat on the back from my husband. I was met with annoyance that he had to take care of the kids all weekend solo.

This was only the beginning. Soon enough I'd thrown myself so far into my business that I was spending 50-60 hours a week working in and on my business. What was supposed to give me flexibility in my life took me away from my children even more. And all the late nights in my office spurred some nasty allegations about my fidelity to my husband.

In the fight between my business and my marriage, my marriage lost. I believe it would have ended itself, eventually, but the time I spent in my business sped that process up. It taught me a lot about myself, and about business.

Humans are social creatures. We need connection and collaboration with others. Sometimes we can have a perception that our friends and family are going to be our biggest supporters. And in life that may be true. But in business, it is not uncommon for those around us to not understand the stressors we face as business owners.

When you are a business owner, no one is coming to save you. You alone will be the driving force of success in your business. It is important to look for collaboration outside your family. Find a networking event in your area, or an online business group, and reach out to others who understand. Collaboration is one of the domains of personal resilience. Without it, you will not find a balance between all six domains.

The other lesson I learned was to be persistent and tenacious in the pursuit of business. There is no need for speed or accuracy behind your tenacity. All that matters is that you learn from your mistakes, find another way, and keep going. Had I listened to the nay sayers, I would have quit my business and gone back into the world of employment. And now, after six years of backing myself and being solely responsible for my income, I am so glad I did not throw it all away.

PART 2

You can eat an entire elephant, if you take it one bite at a time.

Resilient Domain: Composure

Immediately after my separation, things got worse. I took the dog and the debt from my marriage. I had no savings. The rental I moved into had a laundry list of problems I had to fight to get fixed. I was three months into a lease on an office I could no longer afford. My employee quit, and my client list was reducing rapidly, as I was no longer giving my clients the attention they needed.

I would have had more income if I closed my business and went on welfare. I was determined to be a role model for my kids and show them that with determination and hard work, you can achieve anything. It seemed the harder I worked; the more things went wrong.

I was overwhelmed by my to-do list, both personally and for my business. I just was not coping at all. My anxiety was at an all-time high. Depression had snuck back up on me, though I was in denial about that, and I would learn later that this was the beginning of my adrenal fatigue. It just did not seem like life was going to get any easier. I was ready to give up.

The thing that saved me; breaking down every aspect of life into smaller pieces. Each morning I would wake up and list off the aspects of my life on my fingers and ask myself, 'can I do anything today to help resolve this problem?' If the answer was 'no,' then I put that issue to the back of my mind. If the answer was 'yes,' then I would do that one thing that would move me forward.

Looking at the big picture is overwhelming, much like the idea of eating an entire elephant. But breaking down into smaller steps or bites is achievable. Do not worry yourself with the tasks of tomorrow.

Today has enough worries of its own.

Even when life and business is smooth sailing, the same technique is invaluable. By breaking down your tasks, and setting yourself a timetable of all you need to get done in your week, you can maintain your composure. Maintaining your composure keeps your mind out of the fight-or-flight zone. The fight-or-flight zone is a stress response in our body designed to keep us alive. In cave men days, the surge of adrenaline we receive during this stress response, gave us the fuel we needed to escape the lion who wanted us for its dinner.

When we are overwhelmed and constantly in that stress response, it can lead to burnout. Burnout is something I heard a lot about and never thought it would happen to me. But it does eventually catch up with you. And it takes three times as long to recover as it does to reach it.

By far, the best thing I ever did for myself was implementing a job management system. I schedule in the tasks I have for the week ahead. I also set myself a rigid timetable of work time and home time. That does not mean I do not ever work on a weekend, but when I do, it is the exception and not the rule. Having the same dedication to my health, as I do for my clients, is the key to that balance.

PART 3

Be who you are, not who you think they want you to be.

Resilient Domain: Vision

It was not just my husband I faced a lack of support from. Early on in business I attended a local networking event. I was super excited and I dressed in the only uniform I owned, complete with my logo embroidered on. I had my business cards ready and had practiced my elevator pitch. I was ready to meet some other business owners and collaborate.

With that pitter patter of butterflies in my stomach, I ascended the stairs to the second level of the restaurant and straight into a room full of people I had never met. One of the first people I spoke with asked me what I do, and I gave him my best elevator pitch. He enquired about my family status, and I told him I had two children. He replied, 'Isn't it cute you get to play business while the kids are at school?' Deflated but not defeated, I brushed off the comment and moved on to a group of ladies, again, delivering my elevator pitch. One lady was in the same industry as me. She was nice enough, but told me I would never make my business a fulltime gig being a mother. Little did she know that this was indeed my fulltime gig already.

I left that event as soon as I could, drove away in my car, and once out of site, pulled over and cried my eyes out. I felt like an utter failure, and an imposter. Maybe they were right, maybe I would never be successful. I let them get in my head. But true to my stubborn and determined style, I used it as fuel to my fire and pushed on. I was determined to show them how wrong they were and grow my business to have more staff than the person who had told me I would never succeed.

I went against all the plans I had for my business and pushed for more clients. I portrayed my business as bigger than it was, and myself as the most professional person you have met. I made myself into the person I thought my potential clients wanted me to be.

It worked to a point. I doubled my client base quickly. But keeping up the façade was tiring. And hiring staff to help with the workload bought about its own headaches. Like that one time my staff member opened her own firm and tried to poach my staff while working for me. Note to self: add a non-compete clause to your employee contracts.

But my business values no longer aligned with my personal values. My work life balance was non-existent. Work consumed me. Nothing I was doing was in my original strategic plan. I'd thrown away everything I had planned in pursuit of a win against people who did not even know I was fighting them.

You cannot control the way people treat you, what they think of you, or what they say about you, but you can control your response to them. Let your actions speak louder than words and remember you alone get to choose what matters and what does not.

Having a strategic plan and knowing your business will succeed makes it easier to brush off the negativity when you're faced with it. When you are confident in your plan, and it aligns with your values, you cannot fail. It means when opportunities come along you can assess them against your plan. Will this opportunity help you get further to your goal? Or take you on another path completely?

That is not to say your plan should be rigid. Plans change and evolve, just as we evolve and grow as people. But knowing what end goal you want to achieve, can help you keep yourself and your business in check.

PART 4

Let the tech do your dirty work

Resilient Domain: Reasoning

It was a Friday afternoon, and I needed to contact four clients to book an appointment with them the next week. I knew they would not answer their phone, and I just wanted to go home. If I emailed them available times, I knew I would get double booked. I spent twenty minutes setting up the free version of Calendly (an online calendar booking system) and emailed them all a link to book in themselves for the next week.

I went home and logged off the entire weekend. Come Monday morning, all four clients had booked themselves in. My clients were not overly techy, which is why I had not implemented it sooner, but this proved it could work and my clients would use it. I paid for Calendly Monday morning and set it up correctly, and I have never looked back.

The best thing I ever did was to automate as many of my re-occurring tasks as I can. I use a scheduling tool for all my social media and podcasts. It means I can create my content in a big batch and schedule ahead for weeks. I have an email sequence that sends out the link to my calendar to book in for sessions, and reminders so I have fewer no-shows. Implementing these systems means I can work solo instead of needing an assistant. The money I would have spent on an admin assistant can now go towards other more crucial things like marketing, which is not my strong suit.

When you need to work both in and on your business, it is quite easy to get distracted and be less than productive. As a mother, there are days when my kids wake up with a mystery illness. I need to know my business is stable, even when I may not get to work that day. Automating the way your clients can book in or buy from you, means you can be making an income while you're away from your desk.

Anticipating the things that may happen in your business that can disrupt your work, and planning for them, is critical in keeping your composure during a crisis. When we flick to that fight-or-flight mode, we lose all sense of reason. You do not want to make any rash decisions in business. I have seen businesses go from success to failure over night from one bad decision.

The bonus is that in planning for a crisis, you will also have the tools you need to work fewer hours and take some time off to go on a holiday. It is a win-win in my view.

PART 5

You reap what you sow

Resilient domain: Health

There are many ways stress affects our body. For me, the stress of being a solo parent and trying to keep my business open and putting food on the table resulted in adrenal fatigue and weight gain. Not long after I had my second child, I lost 30kg and was the lightest and healthiest I had been in my entire adult life. But over time, as I stepped further into the business world and opened a second business, the way I treated my body took a nosedive.

I stopped going to yoga, I was 'too busy' for that. And the pain in my neck and shoulder from being hit by a car a few years back, slowly crept back in. Pain became an ordinary occurrence for me, and it was not unusual to down the maximum allowed amount of Ibruphen each day.

I had been feeling more pain than usual in my back for about a week, but I brushed it off as just being overdue for a chiropractic appointment. I did not think much of it. Then I awoke at 3am one Sunday morning in the worst pain I have ever felt. I did not want to wake my partner to take me to the hospital at that time in the morning, so I gritted my teeth and tried my best to get some sleep.

Monday came, and off to work I went. I had a workshop on that morning, and I did not want to let the group of ladies I was working with down. Turns out I was quite the shade of yellow, and they all were insistent I go straight to the hospital as soon as we'd finished. I went to my GP instead of the hospital and was sent for an ultrasound. I got a call twenty minutes after the scan telling me to go straight to the hospital; they were expecting me.

Turns out I had a 13mm gall stone completely blocking my gall bladder. I walked into the emergency waiting room. They came and took me in straight away. It was only then that I realised just how serious it was. I was given strong painkillers, and the head surgeon came and spoke to me about removing my gall bladder. And I was first on the list for tomorrow. I had my partner bring in my laptop cord, as the laptop had gone flat, and continued to work right up until my surgery.

I had put myself, and my health, at the bottom of the list. And my body was loudly telling me to stop. I have hit rock bottom with my health more than once now. You would think I would have learnt the first time, but it took emergency surgery for me to really stop and take stock of where I was at with life. I am not perfect, but I take small steps each day to improve my health.

We need to stop glorifying the person who works all weekend and rather praise the person who succeeds in finding a balance between work, family, and rest. Our culture of celebrating the workaholic is one of the main reasons we are seeing an increase in mental, emotional and physical burnout.

Conclusion

I went on to re-build my business after my divorce, implementing all the things I learned along the way. And a few years later, I sold that business for enough profit to get myself out of all my debt and buy a decent car. It gave me the space to go all in on my second business.

I have built that second business on much stronger foundations. It is automated where possible, without being completely impersonal. I am particularly good at sticking to my timetable and taking the time off I need for my health, and my family. And I am no longer easily rattled by others; I have my strategic plan and refer to it often. It gives me confidence to know I am on the right path.

And most importantly, I give myself the time I need to take care of myself. I regularly check in with my counsellor to keep my mental health optimal. And I do my best to eat and nourish my body with the vitamins and nutrients it needs to thrive. I am not perfect, but I take small steps every day.

I passionately believe you can achieve anything you set your mind too, no matter what your personal circumstances are. But dreams do not happen if they are only a thought.

A dream written down with a date becomes a goal, A goal broken down into steps becomes a plan. And a plan backed by action makes your dreams become a reality.

REBECCA CORBETT

When I started Tally and Tick, I did not think it would amount to anything more than a side gig. It quickly outgrew my kitchen table and became a fulltime job for me. On the outside, it looked successful. But inside, it was full of stress and the hourly rate I was making was terrible, until I backed myself, learned my lessons, and implemented change in my business.

If you told me then, that one day I would sell my business for enough money to get out of debt, and start a second successful business that allowed freedom in my work hours and location, I wouldn't have believed you.

I have taken my own experiences, plus my years of training in all things business, resilience and tech, and rolled it up into one neat little ball. I feel like I have been training all my life for this moment. I'm a Business Specialist & Trainer. I can help you build an automated system, and set up an accounting system that talks to your E-comm store. I teach business owners how to do it for themselves so they can save money and gain the skills they need to grow.

I'm honest and anti-fluff. When you work with me, you're getting tangible advice, programs and processes to help you *thrive.* I'll tell you what you need without the sales pitch. I'll take the time to find out who you are, and what you want to achieve—because success is different for everyone, and so are the steps in achieving it.

I won't sell you a solution you don't need. Or push you into using paid programs when you cannot afford it. I have been there and bootstrapped it with the best of them. I want to share the hacks I learned that helped me scale in the early days, and help you implement that paid solution when the time and situation is right.

I truly love what I do. I get to take away that stress I once felt for my clients and assist them to reach their full potential. When your personal and work values align, that's when you truly are successful.

rebeccacorbett.com.au

Achieving success through resilience in the face of adversity.

LANA KRUGER

Who doesn't dream of being successful - one day? I do, and I believe so does everyone else. All of us define and measure success differently because we are all created with unique gifts and talents. These talents and gifts ignite a 'flame' in us that makes us want to be successful. Ultimately, being successful translates into living a life of abundance, purpose and meaning.

How do you become successful? Through character!

Success is built on the foundation of character, and character is shaped through adversity. Adversity is the myriad of setbacks, hardships, or misfortune everyone in life faces. Life would certainly be a breeze if we could avoid adversity, however, we cannot and that's where resilience comes in. Resilience involves 'bouncing back' from difficult experiences and it delivers profound personal growth.

I view resilience as the 'superpower' that helped me overcome the adversities I faced at a young age. Life-changing events that unexpectedly and drastically changed my life as I knew it, saw me losing my (young) parents, eleven months apart and left me being an orphan at nineteen.

Resilience is key to any business to help us overcome the many challenges, setbacks and disappointments we face daily in our lives and in businesses. With resilience you can overcome any adversity you are faced with in business and each time you do, you emerge stronger as a leader and as a business.

'It's your reaction to adversity, not adversity itself that determines how your life's story will develop.'
DIETER F. UCHTDORF

What is your superpower?

Success follows happiness, and true happiness comes from living a life of purpose and meaning.

Let us say you have a job, family and friendships that make life great, yet you feel as though 'something is missing.' It is your inner voice calling you to find your purpose and to follow your dreams!

When you discover the ***essence*** of what you were created to be, what you and you alone were put on this earth to do with your unique gifts and talents, is when you become the best version of you.

'No one is YOU and that is your Superpower.'

Until three years ago, I had a senior management position in the corporate world which saw me rake in promotions, travel extensively for work and excelling as a sales professional. To most that would seem like a perfect life, but for me it was far from perfect. My soul was yearning for something different.

I recall, so vividly, the life-changing moment in my life that set my soul on fire, liberated me from fear, and propelled me to become relentless in my pursuit of following my dreams! It was the day I celebrated my 40th birthday. My amazing family and friends surrounded me when suddenly, all those years of feeling as though 'something is missing' ended. The answers to my questions of 'There has to be more to life than this?' and 'Why was I created?' became crystal clear.

Amidst the celebrations, there was a moment when it suddenly felt as though everything around me stopped. Time stood still. In that moment came an epiphany! I realised why I was created and that it was for doing far greater things than what I'd done with my life up to that moment. What I wanted from life was freedom, fairness, time, and being in a position from where I could empower and support others to experience the same. I wanted to take back control of my life, the time I spend with my family and the freedom to choose a career where I can make an income while making an impact.

So, I found my purpose, and now it was time to follow my dreams. I started my own company, in a male-dominant industry, one I'd been working in for over twenty years.

If you are still feeling as though 'something is missing' ask yourself these few questions, and somewhere in the answers, you are bound to find your epiphany. If you were told today you have one year left to live, what would you do with time you have left? For what do you wish they would remember you?

Believing in our hearts we have a purpose and a role in this world no one else can fill, should be enough motivation to get up and do something about it. I encourage you to celebrate yourself, everything you are, and everything you have to offer. Follow your dreams and dream big.

'Be fearless in the pursuit of what sets your soul on fire.'
JENNIFER LEE

Make it happen...

Life does not reward those who try to figure things out before acting. It rewards people who move on their desire to chase their dreams in the face of adversity. Recognise that you only get one chance to live the life of your dreams. The reality is there will NEVER be a better time than now. Start now, take the leap of faith and make it happen!

'We cannot become what we want, by remaining what we are.'
MAX DEPREE

The next day after discovering my purpose, and knowing clearly what I wanted from life, it was time to turn my dreams into reality. To create the life I was destined for, the dream that would make my life meaningful and bring me true happiness. I hadn't figured it all out, nor was I clear on all the details yet. But one thing I was certain of was that I wasn't going to sit around, waste another precious second of my life, waiting to find the answers. It was time to act!

I handed in my resignation the next day. Is that crazy or what? What made this act of boldness so risky, and one that briefly filled me with much doubt, was that I had not determined how I was going to generate an income. All I knew with certainty was that I was no longer willing to work for a 'boss.' Nor was I willing to have to ask someone's 'permission' for time to spend with my family or to get paid what I'm worth, rather than according to my gender. From that bold moment, everything thereafter just seemed to fall into place.

As Dan Sullivan said: 'You can have everything you love in life as long as you give up what you hate.'

If you have been holding back from taking the plunge into the journey, you sense will lead you to the life you have dreamed of, take comfort in knowing you are not alone. There are so many emotions that can derail us from believing we are good enough or strong enough to take bold action. It is also natural to doubt ourselves and our abilities. Then there is the fear of failure and let us not forget about guilt. The guilt that our dreams may be selfish. Take a deep look at yourself and what is holding you back, then remember this. 'When the *why* is strong enough, the *how* is easily found.'

Your dreams are in alignment with your life's purpose. You have everything you need, the gifts, talents, and strengths to fulfil this purpose. Knowing this, I urge you to find the courage, believe in yourself and start now.

'Boldness has genius, power, and
magic in it. Begin it now.'
WILLIAM HUTCHINSON MURRAY

Know Your Worth!

Know yourself, be true to yourself, and never settle for less than you deserve and dream of.

Since success follows happiness, it is important to know your worth because self-worth is vital to your happiness. Always remember you are part of a divine purpose, uniquely created, and you deserve the best life has to offer. If you are being treated like you are average, overcome it by determining your values and setting boundaries.

You get what you settle for, so aim high and surround yourself with those who see your self-worth, who love you, respect you, and who encourage you.

'Know your worth. Know the difference between what you're getting and what you deserve.'
UNKNOWN

During my career, an opportunity for a promotion, for a sales management position arose within the organisation which I was employed by at that time. This was one of the four sales management roles held in the organisation. For sixteen consecutive months leading up to the promotion for sales manager, I'd been the top performing salesperson each month, and the first team member to achieve my annual target after only eight months. I was also the only woman in the commercial team of sixteen members. At the end of the year, I was one of only four team members who achieved the annual targets.

I was so excited when I received the company's internal communications around this vacancy because that was what I aspired to since the day I joined the company. It was the natural advancement in this department, and I was certainly going to apply. The advertised remuneration on offer was extremely attractive, and the position encompassed coaching and development for the team I would be responsible for and something I am good at and have always loved. I was confident I would be the obvious choice for this position because I knew my contribution as a top performing sales member was valued by the organisation. Or so I thought.

As I'd hoped, I was successful, however, the remuneration in my new contract was far lower than what was advertised, and of that which my male colleagues were earning in the same position. It was clear my boundaries were violated, and I was not being treated the way I deserved to be treated. Knowing my worth, I recognised I was getting less than I deserve and I would not settle for this.

In business, your level of self-worth directly correlates to your level of success. This is true for anyone, but doubly so for entrepreneurs because we put so much of ourselves into our businesses. Use your values to set clear boundaries because not only will it improve your self-worth, but it will help your clients to value you more highly and make you more productive and efficient.

'Love yourself. Be clear on how you want to be treated. Know your worth. Always.'

MARYAM HASNAA

You've got this!

Courage is not the absence of fear. Brave women feel fear, but they prioritise their dreams over their fears. They overcome fear so it does not stop them from taking action, standing up against things that threaten them or the people or things they care about. Courage is the ability to do something difficult, even when there's risk.

From women with multi-million-dollar empires, to everyday mothers raising kids and trying to make ends meet, I know a lot of courageous women and if you are reading this, you are one too.

'The best way out is always through.'

ROBERT FROST

We all have courage, but only when we face adversity and overcome it, do we discover so much more about ourselves. I was nineteen when I discovered the most about myself in one day. The day I lost my mother only eleven months after my father, which meant as a nineteen-year-old with a sixteen-year-old brother, I was suddenly required to step into parenthood. Not by choice, but by design when the people who were legally selected by my parents to care for us in such a tragic event renounced themselves from this obligation. I cannot describe the level of fear I felt, knowing we both had our beautiful, bright futures ahead of us, with divine purposes to fill but that now, I was the one responsible for leading the way. All whilst having to face our life's journey alone and providing for both of us.

Courage helped me to overcome my fears and take action, the necessary action needed for taking on this responsibility and surviving. Every step I needed to take from that day on was to survive and care for my brother, and I took it with courage. When I look back and observe my life from that day, I am reminded how much everything since that day has shaped my life and the person I am today. I have no regrets, nor do I wish things turned out any different because I have grown immensely. I developed an ability to face and overcome any fear by reminding myself that if I could overcome that, I can overcome anything. In comparison, no fear I face now in life will ever be as big as that.

Whether you are required to be courageous in life or business, find your courage in all the small, everyday acts that force you to take a deep breath. Ignore the sweaty palms, plunging butterflies and the voice in your head that say, 'you can't' and do it anyway. Then watch yourself propel towards your goals and achieve your dreams.

'I know what I want, I have a goal, an opinion, I have a religion and love. Let me be myself and then I am satisfied. I know that I'm a woman, a woman with inward strength and plenty of courage.'

ANNE FRANK

Awaken the warrior

Even though there is a woman warrior inside the heart of every woman, many of us fail to find her. What is a woman worrier? A woman warrior recognises she represents a gender that has been degraded, stripped of power, usurped, and rendered invisible and silent for centuries. She is also the woman who rises above adversities and circumstances. Women warriors possess a determined spirit and a 'can do' attitude that propel their actions towards their goals.

She knows her life is not defined by her circumstances, but by her vision and inner strength.

One of my greatest mantras is, *'Life is what you make it, make it count and make it spectacular.'*

Was I going to let the fact I lost both my parents at a young age, being called an orphan, define me? Was I going to allow the fact that I do not have a degree because of stepping into 'parenthood' at nineteen determine my success in life? Could I use these unexpected, life-changing events as an excuse to be bitter or to give up on my dreams? Anyone looking in on my journey might argue that I could, but I chose not to. I chose to be better than my circumstances and the challenges from this and yes to the solution. I am not a victim of my circumstances; I am a woman warrior. I set out with the vision and dream to succeed in life, despite my past and the obstacles that came with it.

Over the years, I discovered a significant benefit in my life and in my business has been the ability to identify problems, but not to focus on the problems and more on the solutions. This has had a huge impact on keeping my levels of motivation high, and not being 'thrown' off course in my pursuit of reaching my goals. That's because focussing on the solution awakens emotions of optimism whereas the opposite emotions are evoked when focussing on problems. When friends or people I work with approach me with the words, 'We have a problem,' my instinctive response is, 'Don't come to me with problems, come to me with solutions.'

There are so many things that happen beyond our control in life, but what we can control is how we react to these things. My advice is to find a way to worry less about the things you cannot control and focus only on the things you can control. Experience taught me we have the tendency to worry about everything, even things that never eventuate.

Change your vocabulary accordingly and refuse to use the word 'problem.' I have replaced the word 'problem' with 'challenge' in my vocabulary. The mind and body respond so much more positively to the word 'challenge' than 'problem.'

'Either I will find a way, or I will make one.'

PHILIP SIDNEY

Conclusion:

To all women, mothers, and daughters, you are unique, you are beautiful, and you possess an inner strength, which along with your gifts and talents, makes you uniquely you. Remember, you were born to fulfil a divine purpose and on your journey in life; you change people's lives when they cross your path, whether you know it. Dream big and seek to live only an abundant life that brings you true happiness. Find the courage to change or leave that which does not serve you or your dreams and remember you are strong, beautiful, and worthy. You are enough. You are a woman.

'Our deepest fear is not that we are inadequate. Our deepest fear is that we are powerful beyond measure. It is our light, not our darkness that most frightens us. We ask ourselves, "Who am I to be brilliant, gorgeous, talented, fabulous?" Actually, who are you not to be? You are a child of God. Your playing small does not serve the world. There is nothing enlightened about shrinking so other people won't feel insecure around you. We are all meant to shine, as children do. We were born to make manifest the glory of God that is within us. It's not just in some of us; it's in everyone. And as we let our own light shine, we unconsciously give other people permission to do the same. As we are liberated from our own fear, our presence automatically liberates others.' - **Marianne Williamson**

LANA KRUGER, THE MEGNA GROUP

I am Lana Kruger, the Chief Executive Officer and founder of The Megna Group, a female-founded and owned logistics company in Australia. My business is an award-winning company re-imagining the supply chain for brands and e-commerce businesses.

I started in logistics over two decades ago in South Africa, where I originate from, and have since worked in three countries in senior management positions for some of the world's largest logistics companies.

After emigrating to Australia in 2011, I launched The Megna Group in 2018 – an innovative logistics company that is agile, fast-thinking, and creative.

The Megna Group provides a one-stop, total solution, in warehousing, distribution, international freight, and packaging. 'To enable brands to truly *differentiate* was what motivated me to start a logistics company that would focus on helping e-commerce brands exceed customer expectations.'

I am passionate about empowering women through my business and being an advocate for women's rights. I strive to make an impact that will contribute to reducing the gender pay gap and bring about gender equality in the workplace.

My 'safe' interests are dancing (when no one is watching), travelling, and creating memories with my family. I also have 'extreme' interests, and these consist of skydiving and deep-sea diving.

In closing, I would like to part with these inspirational words by Steve Maraboli.

www.megnagroup.com.au

Live your truth.
Express your love.
Share your enthusiasm.
Take action towards your dreams.
Walk your talk.
Dance and sing to your music.
Embrace your blessings.
Make today worth remembering.

Playing the long game

CHERIE GREGORY

'I never dreamed about success. I worked for it.'.
ESTÉE LAUDER

My eighteen-year-old son asked me something during a drive the other day.

'I'm thinking of starting up Anthem again, but considering I've tried once and it didn't work out, what are your thoughts?'

To provide you with context, my eldest two of four children completed high school via distance education. At sixteen, my son Caleb, extremely talented in design, decided to start a street-wear t-shirt label, Anthem Apparel. He designed (really great) t-shirts, had them printed, built a website and got a few orders, but because of other school and life commitments, it got put aside. That and the fact that, other than a couple of family friends, he didn't get the number of orders he was hoping for, so his motivation and enthusiasm took a hit.

I answered, 'Love, Anthem was amazing. Your designs were great. You were sixteen and knew nothing about business or marketing. But I bet you've learnt a lot of lessons for the next time around. Was it an OVERNIGHT success? No. Will it be if you try again? Probably not, but you can't start a business on the assumption it will be. You've got to play the long game. And in most cases the long, long game.'

With my husband and business partner, Peter, we have built one of Australia's premier digital agencies, Koben Digital, building websites and digital marketing solutions for some of Australia's biggest not-for-profits, government departments and international brands. We have also built a rapidly growing parenting/behavioural strategy app, Thumsters. But our entrepreneurial journey started decades ago and we've learnt many valuable (sometimes hard) lessons playing the long (long, long) game when building a successful and thriving business.

There is no such thing as overnight success

We live in an instant gratification generation. Instant food via pre-made delivery services, takeout or the trusty microwave; instant weight loss via pills or surgery; instant dating via swiping on Tinder; instant beauty through Botox and fillers; and overnight success in business, or so we are led to believe. We've all seen the ads on Facebook:

BEST FRIENDS FROM MANLY MAKE $500,000 OVER 3 MONTHS DURING PANDEMIC SELLING MOON-MUD MAN MASKS!!

Now I'm not insinuating these stories aren't true, however, having dabbled in the creation of an organic skincare range, I'll point out there are numerous high costs, including manufacturing, marketing and PR, and those ads/articles you see on Facebook are one clever form of marketing. They may have a turnover of $500,000, however manufacturing their product is likely to cost them hundreds of thousands. The PR company and Facebook ads are also likely to cost them thousands more. On top of this, there are many other costs of running the business such as staff, insurance, plant, legal etc. There's a big difference between turnover and net profit! (The money left over after all expenses are paid.) However, we see the figures and think, *Wow! They made it big in three months. So can I! Or, argh, they made it big in three months and I've been going for over a year now without that kind of success. What am I doing wrong?* And in their dismay, hopeful entrepreneurs drop off or drop out, because they assume if they haven't made it big in a matter of months, they must not be cut out for business ownership.

Understand that for a majority of entrepreneurs and business builders, though we may appear to have had overnight success, we are also likely to have experienced setbacks/hard lessons and stagnant periods. I said to my son on that drive, 'It may take you two, five or even ten years to get Anthem to a point where you can leave your fulltime job (he works as a web designer at Koben), and for some people this reality can be enough to prevent them from even starting. But think of it this way; that time will pass regardless. It would be confronting sitting there ten years from now, still with the same dream/idea/drive in your heart, to start your business/degree/saving/adventure thinking, 'I wish I'd started ten years ago.'

Get going.

I love the following quote from Henrietta C. Mears.

'It is difficult to steer a parked car. So get moving!'

If you feel like you have a great business idea, step one should always be to write it down. Getting your idea down on paper helps you to look at it both intentionally and critically. Not all ideas are good ideas, and that's ok, but some are worth pursuing. Bounce your idea off people you trust. Your friends and family are not always the best people to talk to. Find someone already running a successful business as they can look at your idea more objectively. One of my favourite things to do as a business owner is to get excited for, and encourage budding entrepreneurs. Be brave and ask people. Don't let the effort of starting or writing a business plan keep you parked. There are many great templates out there for business plans, and funnily enough, most of them don't end at the three -month mark with YOU'VE MADE IT! BUY THAT PRIVATE PLANE!

You have to spend money to make money.

During my twelve years as a stay-at-home mum, I went on a journey with health and nutrition, studying remotely with the New York based Institute of Integrative Nutrition. Through my study I learnt about a skincare technique called oil cleansing, which quickly transformed my pimple prone thirty-year-old skin into balanced, glowing skin that I loved. I could go out without wearing makeup for the first time in twenty years. It was a pretty amazing transformation! My friends and family saw my results and new found confidence and asked me to mix them up some products, which I happily did. Eventually, my husband suggested I start a business and The Oil Cleansing Company was born, with four great products: two cleansers, a night oil and a day oil. Everyone who tried them (mostly friends and family) loved them. They worked, and worked well. I was going to make millions of dollars! Overnight success was definitely on the cards. The product would basically sell itself. Wrong. The business quickly stalled because I was missing one key factor: marketing. The truth is, you can have the absolute BEST product or service known to man, but if you don't have a strong marketing plan, your target market will be oblivious. They won't even know you exist. Lack of customers can be the ultimate de-motivator, causing many to give up before your business truly has a chance to gain momentum. Here are a few tips for ALL budgets when it comes to effective marketing.

1. **Have a plan** - As with most business tasks these days, there are plenty of templates for marketing plans on the Internet, many free. Try a few out and fill them in honestly in terms of budget and resources. There is a MASSIVE difference between what you can do if you have a budget of a thousand dollars, or a budget of tens of thousands of dollars. If done cleverly, both can absolutely move your business forward. And at the end of the day, momentum is king. For example, you can run effective Facebook marketing campaigns for as little as five dollars per day and scale them as you grow.
2. **If you can, hire an expert** - If your marketing budget is substantial, and marketing is not your forte, consider the hire of a marketing specialist one of the first positions you fill. A lot of entrepreneurs make the 'it can't be too hard' mistake when it comes to marketing, but you have to remember people go to university for three plus years to learn the ins and outs of effective marketing practices and how to get you the biggest bang for your buck. In my opinion, even if you can't afford a marketing specialist to begin with, or even one on a contract basis, this should definitely be something you have on your business roadmap. Having a specialist on staff can really propel your business forward.

3. **Social Media mindfulness** - Social media has been a Godsend for small business marketing. With the Thumsters Parenting App, for the first two years, we did not have the budget to hire a dedicated marketing role. What we did do early on was to put ourselves through a social media workshop, run by a highly recommended expert in this area, Emma Williams (@sociallyem on Instagram). This taught us the basics of algorithms, engagement, growth and content. Social media can do wonders for your small business, but like any tool you must learn to use it effectively and efficiently, or it will likely lead to frustration when your numbers don't grow, or when your following does grow, but for the wrong reasons and your new followers aren't in your target market, don't engage, and ultimately don't convert to sales.
4. **A word on influencers** - I never want to hear anyone say influencers get paid a lot for doing nothing. The ones we've worked with have worked INCREDIBLY hard on behalf of Thumsters. However, a few things to note: back in the day when Instagram was fairly new and the idea of 'social influencer' was even newer, you could totally send a product to an influencer and, if they liked it, they would talk about it on their channel. Now, influencing is a multi-million-dollar business, and most influencers charge for campaigns. Not that you should never try your luck! A company I know here on the Gold Coast sent some of their kids clothing range to the Kardashians, who loved them and posted their kids wearing their gear. I guess that's what they call a 'unicorn' situation in the social media world! For most businesses, there will be a cost for influencers, and this can range from a couple of hundred, to hundreds of thousands per engagement. For most businesses starting out, influencers will fall in one of two categories: micro influencer, and large and/or 'celebrity'

influencer. Micro influencers by loose definition have around 1-100 thousand followers. Large influencers have above that, and then you move into the realm of the 'celebrity' influencers such as the Kardashians, etc. Do not discount micro-influencer campaigns. We usually run these at a rate of about 25-30 in one campaign. This costs us around the same as one larger influencer. The reason micro-influencers can be gold is, though their audience is smaller, it tends to be made up to a large extent of friends and family, or friends of friends and family. This means they already know them, know their journey, and so their recommendations have a solid base of credibility, which is GREAT for influencing. There is no denying the larger influencers get great numbers in terms of social following (in our experience), but in terms of conversion, TRYING the product/service, there is little difference in numbers. The other benefit of doing one campaign with 20-30 micro-influencers is, with everyone posting at a set time on a set day, people's feeds are flooded by reviews and information about your brand. Assuming you've done your research and the influencers chosen are all within the same social media space/target audience (e.g., In our case families and parenting), they often share a lot of the same followers. Micros are also incredibly affordable and will often post about your product long after the campaign finishes if they truly like it. The added benefit of using many influencers vs one larger influencer is the sheer volume of content and images they generate that you can reuse in future campaigns.

5. **PR** - Hiring a PR agency can be another great marketing tool. The cost will depend on what services are rendered but a 2-3-month campaign with a good agency can often land under the 10k mark. PR can be excellent for getting you

in front of your target audience in a more traditional way, such as television interviews or magazine articles. Research agencies carefully, and find one that has worked with a lot of brands in your space (beauty, clothing & fashion, family and parenting just to name a few). Authenticity is SO important today and people love to hear the story behind a brand. It fosters connection and trust. If using a PR agency is not in your marketing plan at current, there is nothing stopping you from reaching out to magazines, blog authors, pod casts etc. to see if they'll have you come and speak or tell your story. You may not have the connections a PR agency does, and THAT'S what you pay them for, but with a little confidence and research you can definitely start making them!

You are your best business partner

Consider, and then reconsider a business partner. I get it! I'm a sanguine, an extrovert, an enneagram number… (The number where you take the test over and over and immediately forget the number you are!) I love being around other people, absolutely THRIVE on it. So, having a business partner just sounds more FUN. And let's be honest, safe. Failing hurts less if you're not failing alone, am I right? Peter and I have had multiple business partnerships in three of our businesses over the years. And the only one that has EVER worked out well has been our own business partnership, the two of us. When we tried to bring in other people, or start something with another person, it has frankly ended negatively. There is only so much I can write in this chapter to guard the other people's privacy, and to be fair, I take my share of blame on why things did not work out. But there's a reason why on average 50% of partnerships fail (up to 80% for 'unstructured' partnerships.) And there are some commonalities in all three of our experiences as to why they did not end well.

We went into it for the wrong reasons.

It's more fun with someone else. We can share the workload; it feels less risky, less ALONE. These are not good reasons to seek out, or take on a business partner. These are innately selfish reasons, and in my experience, the risks to taking on a business partner FAR OUTWEIGH the risks to going it alone. A business partnership can be as close, intimate, and as personal as a marriage. Not in the physical sense of course, but in terms of time spent, energy sown, and emotional and mental involvement. If you're in partnership with your relational partner, you're probably already across all of the above when it comes to your differences, nuances and idiosyncrasies. Some business partnerships work and work well. But like personal relationships, don't jump in too quickly. You have to court; you have to date. There has to be a certain amount of business chemistry and compatibility, and you must realise that this may be a life-long partnership.

You are or may eventually be, at different life stages.

This can be a big one, if a clear set of boundaries and business structure aren't established early on. In one partnership, we had a large family with young kids in good schools, and large housing needs, while our business partner had one adult child. To keep things fair and equal, both partners were paying themselves the same wage. If we needed extra for a big bill that came along etc., the other partner would take the same. Any extra profits that were taken for those extras, had to have permission, and rightfully so. This can get difficult, awkward or frustrating for both partners. In my view, if you are not aligned financially, there will be problems. And just because you are in similar life stages now, does not mean you will be in five years' time.

Now that the business partnership is purely between my husband and I, if we want to take some of the profits out of the company for a family trip, we are able to do this without asking permission from or making it 'even' with the other partners. Of course, this can be mitigated by having strong accounting in place, solid agreements on wages and/or profit share, and great communication. If you do take on a partner, make sure this is set up from day one. Do not wait until it becomes an issue.

You have different core values.

This was a huge one for us. Peter and I have extremely strong core values in life and in business; non-negotiables on conduct and boundaries, that in fairness, we are immoveable on. It doesn't matter how well you know a person, each navigates their own individual stories in their own unique way and sometimes, unfortunately, personal struggles can cross over into their business journey, and ultimately yours. What you can usually give grace and empathy to when it's a friend or acquaintance walking a difficult path, and if needed, distance yourself from if boundaries are crossed, becomes increasingly difficult when you are intimately connected day to day through business. We have experienced these struggles in past business partnerships that did not last, due to changes in core values. This is not to say that business partnerships don't work, but like marriage, be prepared to constantly work on your business relationship, and from time to time have some extremely confronting and difficult conversations, and constantly compromise. If you are conflict adverse or communication is not a strength, I do not recommend a business partnership.

What are the alternatives?

Some of the benefits of business partnerships are: sharing the burden of capital and risk, allowing a spread of particular skillsets complimentary to your business, and the ability to bounce ideas and challenges off one another. These needs can be met in ways that don't involve taking on a business partner. With a great business plan, investment can come from family or investors. Business coaches and mentors can be hugely beneficial when it comes to support and advice. As for spreading the skill set, it will end up a lot cheaper in the long run hiring or contracting someone to do social media for example, than taking on your best friend as a partner because she is great on the 'gram and subsequently needing to split profits and pay another directors salary.

Value mindfulness

Many successful leaders in business will put a lot of their success down to resilience and mindset, and for good reason! Iron is one of the toughest compounds on earth, however the ONE thing that can destroy iron is its own rust. Like iron, the human spirit can be unbreakable, however one thing that can easily bring it crumbling down is a person's own mindset. A poor or weak mindset can be like rust.... it will eat you from the inside out, causing you to crumble and fall.

With this in mind, something I always encourage budding entrepreneurs to do is to take an honest look at, or sit down with a trusted peer or family member and have an honest conversation about your mindset. In particular, your strengths and weaknesses. There is no shame in recognising and naming our weaknesses... in fact, ironically, it takes an extraordinary amount of strength. Even the most successful business woman has vulnerable areas. When you have setbacks in business, and these are guaranteed, it is better to be aware of these vulnerabilities so you can intentionally operate from a stance of strength, rather than letting your weaknesses overwhelm you.

Some people need to take it further than just acknowledgment and enlist help to overcome some of these mindset setbacks. Coaches, faith leaders/pastors, or therapists can be a great place to start. Things that hide in the dark often fester, but bringing them out into the light allows you growth. I can't recommend highly enough dealing with these areas of susceptibility early in your business journey. Some areas to look at could be:

- **past trauma's** - childhood trauma, abuse, divorce.
- **money issues.** Most of us who aren't great with money KNOW they aren't great with money (I'll put my hand up first!) Having a great accountant, money coach, budget advisor is key here. Do NOT allow what could be a thriving and profitable business to go down hill because you are not brave enough to say 'hey, money management is just NOT my strong suit.'
- **Addictions** - gambling, alcohol, relationships. Starting a new business can be stressful, often INCREDIBLY stressful, especially if you are still at your full time job whilst building up your business before you can go full time. These periods of stress can exasperate poor coping techniques. There are plenty of community and government care organisations who are willing to help you work on any dependency issues.
- **Relationship/marriage** - as above, the added stress can affect even a rock solid marriage, and even if you are not currently experiencing issues in your relationship, seeing a councillor or therapist as a couple during the start-up phase of business can be highly beneficial. If you are currently experiencing relationship struggles, outside help is highly recommended! Having a successful marriage or a successful business does

NOT need to be an either/or, it can and should be a both/and.

- **Lack of motivation**. This one sounds silly; you'd think we'd all be motivated to work on our own businesses! But the truth is some personality types are naturally HIGHLY motivated people, and some, naturally, aren't (I most definitely fit in the latter!) Which isn't to say, like many things that don't come naturally, you can't LEARN motivation. Motivation is something a lot of us have to be quite intentional about. As with most things, health/weight loss, relationships/marriage, being intentional and setting a plan as a business owner, both in the macro (business planning) and micro (using a planner) can mean the difference between scaling or failing. One of the greatest things I did to push ME forward as a business owner, was incorporate the discipline of using a daily planner. Boss Babe does a great 90 day planner, complete with a gratitude section, goals for the day, to-do list incorporating done, delayed, delegate or delete, and a time schedule. I definitely see a massive difference in both my motivation and over all output when I am being disciplined in using my daily planner.

"Success is not final; failure is not fatal: It is the courage to continue that counts".

WINSTON S. CHURCHILL

As a new entrepreneur it's easy and natural to embark on our business journey with expectations that we will open the door and the cash will just pour in, that our business idea is so unique and so 'on point' that there is no way we can fail. Building a stable, scalable business doesn't happen overnight, maybe not even a few months.

Most from my experience, take years. This may sound discouraging, but the years go by regardless, and they will fly by when you are building something you believe in. This journey we take as business owners is not an easy one, but it can be immensely rewarding. It will have high highs and low lows, tears of joy, sadness and frustration, plenty of sleepless nights and worry, success and failure. How we move through this, scale and not fail, comes down to consistency, resilience, mindset and the support we put in place to grow both as individuals and commercially. These will help ensure we're in it for the long game. And hopefully, even the long long game.

CHERIE GREGORY is a mother of four, and with her husband Peter, is co-owner and director of Koben Digital, one of Australia's premiere digital marketing and development agencies. They partner with government clients, internationally recognised not for profits, and commercial level enterprises. Having had four kids in five years, Cherie stepped back into fulltime work after twelve years at home. She rose to the challenge of helping build Koben's reputation as an industry leader in content management using the Umbraco CMS for which she was recently awarded an MVP. Life is full and hectic for Cherie balancing family and business, so she was thrilled to be awarded a gold AusMumprenuer award in the area of business-to-business, recognising her leadership in both these areas of her life.

Cherie's true passion (besides faith, good coffee and sausage dogs) is for family and it is through this passion she launched the Thumsters Parenting App on IOS and Android. Thumsters encourages kids to make intentional, respectful behaviour decisions in line with their family's values. Thumsters is growing worldwide, specifically in the USA, and has garnered interest from the educational market. It is this interest that now sees Cherie embarking on her biggest business endeavour to date, Thumsters in schools.

A big believer in great work culture and an empathic work environment, in the office you'll find her battling it out in front of the communal Street Fighter machine, engaged in a meme or gif battle with staff, or dishing out meeting donuts. In fact, job interviews held by Cherie are famous for including these three factors.

An engaging and warm presenter/guest, Cherie loves to speak and write on the topics of family, marriage and business (she will consider a Street Fighter workshop for the right fee) and can be contacted via email: cherie@koben.com.au

www.koben.com.au

Pivoting your business

LYNDA PEDDER

'I can see the light!' The fog had cleared, and I could FINALLY see the light at the end of the tunnel! I had no idea if this 'light' was enticing me towards death or leading me to an amazing new life, but I could see it at least. I couldn't resist the powerful pull the light had. So I surrendered and followed to see where the light would take me.

When I closed my eyes and let my 'self' talk, I could not see any other future for my business except inevitable closure and bankruptcy. Despite the odds, I somehow avoided my business going bankrupt. The stress of business had contributed to five miscarriages, divorce, sale of my home and moving eight times in nine years. If your business is where mine was, you may be thinking, 'What the Hell! I have a good product or service. I am smart and enjoy my business. Why am I not smashing this? Why am I working harder than everyone I know and not making tons of money?' This was my self-talk and my reality. When I finally let my heart speak and lead, and stopped getting in my own way, the light became pure and led me towards an incredible transformation in my 'self' and my business. I started to have FUN!

Up Shit Creek without a paddle.

I had been living on borrowed time or should I say, borrowed money, for a long time and the debts had worsened. After almost fifteen years of running my business, I had to face reality. I was 'Up Shit Creek without a paddle.' So, I contemplated how I could set sail into 'Champagne Creek' instead.

I decided I was going to give it one last shot! I reassessed everything and totally pivoted my business from a place of being 74% down on sales on our regular business, to being 70% up on the previous year's sales five months later. How did I do it?

Have a reality check – don't hang on when the writing is on the wall.

I was considering whether my business would go bankrupt with the path I was on and the negative cash flow. Was it time to give up? Then the Global Pandemic arrived like a tornado, and things looked even more dire. I didn't have enough money for bills and loans. I wanted to transition to be an online retailer, but didn't think it would be fast enough to save the business. I accepted I may go bankrupt.

I am known amongst women business friends as the 'Silver Lining Queen.' I always look for some positive spin on any situation. It's something my mother taught me. There is always someone worse off than you! I laughed and said 'At least if I fail now, I can blame it on the Pandemic and not look like I failed.' Then I met with my accountant and he bluntly stated, 'It's not pretty.' I asked him for the meeting because I needed someone independent to give me a reality check. I was always convincing myself there was a good reason my figures were not great. We had plenty of sales, but small profit and negative cash flow.

When COVID started causing Governments to make Draconian decisions, I knew we needed to act quickly and decisively. I knew I wouldn't make the same decisions I did when the Global Financial Crisis (GFC) hit in 2008. Then, I had just opened a second chocolate café to franchise. The mistake I made and paid for dearly was hanging on too long. We never turned a profit. The best sales were in the opening week. It didn't matter what I did; the location was a lemon, and so we were a lemon. It would have been easier, a lot less painful, and better financially to close, but I hung on for two years. This was my biggest business lesson. We lost a lot of money, all borrowed. I didn't want to admit it was a failure. My decisions were fear driven, but I could only see that in hindsight. If we didn't save the business first, there would be no jobs for anyone.

Go hard or go home.

We had five stores' worth of Easter chocolates and had no idea how we were going to sell the eggs. Our biggest wholesale customers were airlines, hospitality companies and hotels. We lost 90% of our wholesale business overnight. We could give up or go hard.

I thought about giving up.

But giving up is not in my nature.

So, I chose to go hard.

And hard I did.

At the time, I didn't even know what the word 'pivot' meant, not in a business sense. It was a term I never used. People kept saying to me, 'I love how you have pivoted,' and I didn't understand what they meant. I had changed direction so many times in my business life, often out of desperation, but I never referred to it as pivoting. This time was no different, in terms of the desperation, but the difference was that this was not done out of fear, but with hope.

Make the decision to be decisive.

Several years prior, I made a decision to be decisive. This was one of the best decisions I ever made. What does this mean? This means I would not procrastinate and would not look back and question my decision. It meant I would make a choice and get on with it. If it turned out to be the wrong choice, then I would deal with it when I realised it was the wrong choice, laugh it off and make a new decision then. I wouldn't look back and think, 'Maybe I should have done this.' Like when you buy a car or house, it is the worst thing to keep looking at them after you have bought one. You made a decision, now move onto the next thing.

I made quick decisions, as it felt like life or death. My business was going to flourish or die. Just surviving wasn't an option for me, as I would have rather killed it off. I immediately reduced staff, wages and hours. I had three retail outlets at the time, including a factory outlet, pop-up store and a chocolate cafe. We'd been planning on an additional two pop-up stores for Easter. I made a snap decision to close the pop-up immediately and closed the café a week before Easter. I believed once we closed the café, we wouldn't reopen it. My staff knew the situation seemed dire. We all shed a tear and then got to work. Then I put all repayments on hold and asked the bank to reject direct debits.

I had tunnel vision. I blocked out all other distractions, as much as I could, being a mother of three and now having them all at home, home schooling. My only focus was to sell all our Easter products. I did not want to be stuck with a lot of Easter eggs. There was an urgency in what I needed to do, and it had a deadline.

How to pivot quickly?

Six months earlier, I realised getting rid of our online store two years prior had been a poor decision. It wasn't because we weren't selling online. I realised that with a physical retail store, people would still browse online first and then come into the store. We were missing out on sales in our physical locations because we didn't have an online store. I was contemplating this when I watched a presentation on someone's Shopify business and decided I was going to use Shopify. Within a week, I had the online store set up and active. It was basic, but I had done it and already had photos of most of our products. It was so easy compared to my previous experiences with our online shops. We got our first sale on the first night!

When the Pandemic hit, we had a grand, mind-blowing total of seventeen orders in three months and I had done barely anything else to the online store since setup. It wasn't exactly a huge success story but we, at least, had the site setup and were ready to expand online quickly. I worked hard to get all our Easter products online, found software to link with shipping, and we were ready to become an online retailer.

Ask for and accept help.

My American cousin reached out to me and asked if he could help, and I graciously accepted. Unbeknownst to me, he specialised in Facebook marketing for online Shopify stores. He helped with the Shopify setup and Facebook advertising but, more importantly, he also coached me to 'stay in my lane.' When I would get distracted by my 'bright shiny objectitis,' he would patiently listen to my ideas and then tell me to 'stay in lane 1, that is lane 3.'

Every time I have tried to simplify my life, I have done something stupid, like open another café after I swore I would never own a café again! So, to avoid making these decisions, I also surrounded myself with people who would help me stay on track and not go down these side-tracks, chasing bright shiny objects! I joined business groups and formed a women's Mastermind with ten others to keep us all accountable to our goals and support one another.

One of those women was the person who had done the Shopify presentation that inspired me to start my online store. We became good friends, and she was always willing to help when I had questions. This group was amazing and I encourage you to form one too.

I also did something I'd never done. I asked our customers for help. Before, I always thought we were just there to serve them and could never actually ask them to buy. I learnt I should be asking them to buy! When I did, I even had childhood school friends buy chocolates to support me.

Get out of your comfort zone with authenticity.

My cousin asked me for some videos he could use for Facebook marketing. I said, 'What type of video?' and he said, 'Any.' *That is totally unhelpful.* So, I sent him a mix of videos I had taken in the past, which were mediocre. He melded them together and magically came up with something better than what I'd sent him. I was shocked when product started to sell! It did work! I had tried Facebook Marketing before with another agency and had limited results. It turned out I needed better advice and material, and I needed to tell our story. I needed to get out of my comfort zone and start putting myself on camera.

I'd practiced being on video in a business Facebook group

where I felt safe and would not be criticised before I jumped into the public arena on my own business page. People probably think I am natural at it, but I really didn't want to do it. I hadn't discovered the magic yet. And I wasn't going to be fake either. I rarely wear makeup and I knew if I decided I wanted to look good on camera, I would never capture the essence of what was happening in our business. This may not be what you want to do, but I decided to be fine with this and love myself in all guises.

Customers loved me being vulnerable and honest and they bought a lot, increasing our average sale by 400%. In the past, I had focussed on being 'professional.' What I needed to do was show them who I really was and the passion I had for my product, and they would love the brand and me, and buy. Of course, there were some people who were negative, but I quickly learnt they were not my customers.

What made the difference?

The important thing was to just focus on one goal. It is so easy when you run a business to do the easy or urgent things or the things you know how to do. It is much harder to focus on the long-term and ensure your marketing is happening. I told my team my job was now marketing. Unless they needed me, I would not be there as I was working on marketing. This was the only way the business would survive.

Your job as a business owner has to be marketing.

The easy part of business is making a good product or service. The hardest thing is getting enough people to buy it. You need marketing for this and that needs to be your focus. I don't just mean spending a budget on marketing. I mean you need to be in charge and driving the marketing yourself. The great thing about the Internet and social media is that you can be 100% in charge of this. Not like when I first started and the normal avenues for marketing were expensive 'hit and miss' media strategies of radio, TV and print. I used to say marketing was 50/50. Now I know every cent I spend on marketing is bringing in revenue.

Six months from the start of the pandemic, our original wholesale customers still hadn't returned, or barely returned, yet the wholesale business had recovered to only be down 30%. This recovery was primarily because of gaining new wholesale customers, who made up 40% of the wholesale sales, who had seen my online marketing and decided they wanted to sell or use Poppy's chocolates.

Remarkably, total sales were 70% higher than the previous year and I was only just scratching the surface. Poppy's Café did better than it had been doing previously after restructuring the staff and the pay structure for the café managers. I offered the managers a base salary plus profit share, and they managed it as though it was theirs and performance improved dramatically.

How can you use this to help you and your business journey? Change is good. You can only control what is in your own four walls.

When I studied change management, I learnt you need to get people dissatisfied with where they are now, before they are motivated to change. This is why implementing change in organisations is difficult. I always see change as good. It can be scary, but not changing can be worse. Regardless of outside influences, you can only control what is going on in your four walls. I would assess what was happening in the broader economy and environment and then focus on what I could do in my own four walls.

Aside from pivoting quickly from retail stores and wholesale to online, I also personally pivoted quickly throughout that journey. I studied avatars and stories. My cousin kept talking about the customer journey, but I just didn't understand it. He kept asking what problem I was solving and I wasn't sure because I thought people love chocolate, but does it actually solve a problem? Does it? I could not see I was solving any problems as I was blinded by thinking I had to be solving some significant world changing problem. When my focus became directly on the customer and what they felt and what we did for them, things really multiplied.

How do you benefit your customers? Who is your customer?

It might sound easy to establish how we benefit our customer and who our customer is, but it was difficult because so many people like chocolate and we had a wide variety of customers. I wasn't sure who our customer was. I enlisted more help including reading some books and getting help from a specialist business. How I *saw* my business changed, and this changed my business dramatically. You need to remove yourself from inside your business and view it from outside as a customer. What is this business or product doing for me? How does it make me feel?

One thing I learnt with certainty is that you cannot have quality, service and price. You cannot be all things to all people. We stuck with our focus being quality and service and learnt to ignore those people who complained our price was too expensive, or complained about the shipping cost. They just weren't our customer. Our customers were those who were happy to pay for quality and good service, and understood that shipping quality chocolates quickly and safely costs money.

If it's meant to be, it's up to me.

Lastly, the one thing that made the biggest difference to pivoting my business was ***my mindset***. After almost fifteen years in this particular business, I knew I was the only one who could sail us up Champagne Creek. There had been many times over those years when I'd employed someone in sales or marketing and they had taken plenty of money but had not delivered results. I kept believing there was a 'knight in shining armour,' but I only got knaves. I started saying, 'If it's meant to be, it's up to me.'

Now, this no way implies you need to do everything. But what you need to realise is your most important role in business is sales and marketing. Marketing leads to sales. Without sales, you have nothing. You can focus on new products, save costs by being more efficient, but without sales, broke. I knew I was good at sales. But I just didn't like doing it. I wanted someone else to do it, until I finally realised this was THE MOST IMPORTANT thing I had to do in my business.

You must get out of your comfort zone and drive your own business.

7 tips to Pivot your business

- Have a reality check. Don't hang on when the writing is on the wall.
- Make quick and tough decisions. Make the decision to be decisive.
- Ask for and accept help. Ask for the sale.
- Get out of your comfort zone with authenticity and be vulnerable.
- Focus on one thing. Your job as a business owner has to be marketing.

- Change is good. Observe what is happening in the environment and economy, but you can only control what is in your own four walls.
- Know who your customer is and how you benefit them.
- Check your mindset. If it's meant to be, it's up to me.

LYNDA PEDDER

Lynda Pedder is a successful entrepreneur who says she has had to pivot more times than she can possibly recollect, and it wasn't until she truly backed herself that true success came.

Lynda created Poppy's Chocolate in 2005 when she had a two-year-old boy and a six-month-old girl. In 2009, she had a third child, a boy, and in 2012, her husband left. Her worst fear had come true, and she was on her own running the business and raising three children.

In 2020, Lynda has been honoured with four AusMumpreneur Awards, including a Gold Award for People's Choice, and two International Women in Business Stevie Awards for Entrepreneur of the Year in Consumer Products and Most Innovative Woman in Manufacturing. Lynda transformed her business from almost failing and a decline of 74% in sales in April 2020 to 70% growth on 2019 figures in under five months.

She was inspired to start Poppy's Chocolate because she had two passions, aside from her family, chocolate and business. Lynda said, 'My nan loved sweets and taught me to choose dessert first and then order a smaller main meal to ensure I could fit dessert in. She gave me a passion for good chocolate and sweets and we created a lot together.' Lynda says her step-dad had his own business, and she loved the idea of having her own business.

These passions came together when Lynda found a gap in the market after she encouraged her husband to be more romantic by suggesting he gift her some delicious quality chocolates. She laughingly says, 'I created my own chocolates, romance, and business.'

Lynda also has an unusual love for life that she says is because her father and uncle both died at thirty-four and her mother was diagnosed with early onset dementia at just sixty years old.

Lynda has immense gratitude for being alive and wants to make the most of everyday she has. She also has grit and determination to do as much as she can whilst she is here.

Poppy's Chocolate focus has shifted from primarily being a wholesaler to being the best online chocolate shop in Australia. Poppy's now brings joy into homes Australia wide. 'We think of ourselves as Happiness Creators,' says Lynda. Poppy's Chocolate's focus on creating an amazing customer experience, setting them apart from the competition.

http://www.lyndapedder.com/
www.poppyschocolate.com.au

Trust (Yourself and the world around you.)

SARAH WALKERDEN

Trust. It's one of the most important things to have, when starting or growing a business. At least in my mind. And from what I have learnt along my business journey.

Because none of this is particularly easy. Business is not just about 'tactics' and learning what you physically need to do. It's also a journey of personal growth and an inner mindset game.

I never knew that though when I first started over ten years ago. I merely thought you built a great website, told as many people as possible to 'buy your stuff' and they'd come flocking. In the case of my first business, being eCommerce, we literally thought it was a matter of ordering in stock, adding those products to the website, waiting for orders to appear and then shipping those items out.

Turns out, there's so much more to it than that. Business growth is almost never a straight line. You may launch with a bang and score that first rush of sales or clients, and then receive radio silence soon after. You might see steady growth for several months, and then hit a plateau that you can't quite creep over. And you might even go months without a single sale.

This puts you on a bit of a rollercoaster. And it's the 'down' times where you can start to doubt yourself and your business. Trust, however, is what will come to your rescue. Often, that's all we can do. We must place trust in ourselves, our mission, our business and our future; to trust other people around us and trust the universe too. Hopefully, this chapter can help you see how powerful it can be to simply trust. How the tiniest bit of trust can turn things around almost instantly.

And the most important thing of all? To learn to trust yourself.

It's all happening for you (Even when it sucks!)

Believe it or not, everything tends to happen for a reason. It might not seem that way when everything is going to hell. When you're in the thick of a challenging time, it almost seems as though everyone (universe included) is out to get you. That's not generally the case, however. Speaking from experience, I've seen far too much evidence that the universe seems to have a master plan for every one of us. Trouble is, many of us don't realise this, and aren't trusting enough to listen.

As they say, this isn't my first 'rodeo'. And by that, I mean, I'm now on to my second major business. The first, quite frankly, failed. Yet, I shouldn't really say that. Part of it worked really rather well. We tried to expand it in entirely the wrong way (and somehow ended up creating a life we really didn't want).

As I alluded to in my introduction, my husband and I built up a small eCommerce store, selling horse products and gear. We both were keen horse owners and riders. We ran it initially part-time around my corporate career and hubby's part-time work. It turned into quite a successful little brand.

Then, we had our first child. Despite being in a position where I had to go back to the corporate world, I knew I couldn't keep working full time in the city for too long. (We'd moved to our dream property in the country, a 2.5 hour commute each way, each day, wasn't much fun.) So, we thought, let's turn our growing part-time online business into a fulltime physical business.

We thought it was going to be our ticket to living a life of freedom under our own steam. With me running our business locally and ditching that horrid city commute and corporate stress. It seemed on the surface to be a great (and terribly exciting) idea. Trouble was, we knew nothing about establishing a physical retail store. We didn't do our research into the local market, nor did we really have the required upfront capital.

That aside, we bought a block of land, got council permits, built a commercial premises and opened the doors (something we're still incredibly proud of, as I don't think anyone around us thought we could). And we ran that business (physical and online) for two years before we finally gave up.

The toll it took on us as a family, however, was immense. I worked in the shop six days a week, with one part-time staff member. My husband still worked part-time, including weekends, so we could keep afloat financially. Our two kids were tiny (two and five), and when they weren't at childcare or school, they were stuck in the shop with me (and were always exhausted and cranky). It sent us all crazy, and we literally were tied down to that darn shop without a break or any reprieve. And it never really earned us any money for our efforts. In fact, the business just seemed to drain money, left, right and centre.

When I finally pulled the pin and called it quits, we were all done in. Magically though, giving up on that business was the best thing we ever did. I don't regret giving it a go for a single second because we learnt so much in the process. And it showed us what we really wanted and needed as a family. We went into business for more freedom and flexibility. The shop didn't provide any of that.

And because it failed, I finally put myself on the RIGHT path towards freedom. Despite our dire financial situation, and despite me being on the brink of a breakdown, somehow, I started a new business. Copywriting and websites. It's what I'd learnt to do so well in the corporate world, and it's given me and our family the freedom we craved. Now, we can see the shop was never meant to be. And all the struggle happened FOR us. It put me on the right path towards a business I really enjoy and gives our family the freedom we've always wanted.

So, know that even bad experiences, extreme challenges or perceived 'failures' in business give us valuable information and lessons to learn. If you can keep persisting and keep trusting, everything will work out how it needs to.

Instincts are worth more than 'experts'

('Cause nothing is more valuable than trusting yourself.)

When you traipse down this business path, you'll inevitably encounter lots of 'experts.' Some experts will offer advice when you don't even ask for it. Others you will purposely seek to help you with parts of the puzzle you're not good at, or need extra help with.

Either way, you always need to trust your own instincts FIRST.

I'm sure you probably know what I mean when I say 'instincts' or 'intuition' or 'gut feeling'. It's that little voice inside your head, or that unexplainable 'feeling' that guides you down a certain path towards taking a certain action. The question is, however, are you listening to yours?

See, no one else is you or knows your business as well as you. And you can't run your business according to what everyone else thinks you should do. It won't work. Your business is always (or should be) a direct representation of you. It needs to be authentic or no one will believe in you or what you offer.

Your instincts come first. It has to be right for you.

One of my first mentors, right at the beginning of my new 'copywriting' business journey, is an amazing lady and businesswoman. She perhaps wasn't quite suited to me at the time though, as her focus was helping women establish courses and a learning style business.

I wasn't up to that stage though. I just wanted to sell my website copywriting packages to people who would pay me more than $50 per page. It took me almost six months to see that though, as I was blinded a little by her enthusiasm and confidence, and didn't want to let her down by choosing a different path.

In that six months, I didn't get particularly far with my business. I gained a bit of traction, but I trusted her more than I was trusting myself, going off on unprofitable tangents in trying to create courses when all I really needed was to establish myself as a solid copywriter first. There's another little lesson right there.

Until the little voice in my head practically started screaming, 'But, I just want to write copy, not teach it yet!'

It wasn't until I found an actual COPYWRITING group and mentor and trusted my own instincts to take the leap in that direction instead, that my business really exploded. Over the past couple of years building up my copywriting business, I've discovered I have my biggest breakthroughs when I trust my own instincts. The online business world is so darn noisy with so much advice and so many opinions. And while taking expert advice IS a smart thing to do, you always need to balance that by listening in to what your instincts are telling you.

You're more capable and resourceful than you might think

(It's amazing what you can do when challenged. You just need to start.)

You really don't know what you're capable of until you're put in a situation that requires you to dig deep. Chances are, you're more resourceful and capable than you might think. At the start of your business journey, you'll probably have some set beliefs around what you can and can't do. You might worry you don't know certain aspects of business or you don't have the necessary skills. You're also likely to focus on what you CAN'T do or DON'T know, too.

That can stop you from starting your business, and it can stop you from really giving it your all. In reality though, you'll get so much further if you trust you'll have what you need, when you need it and just go for it.

I never knew just how capable I could be when the muck hit the fan. When our retail store collapsed in a heap (taking me with it) we were in a pretty dire financial situation. We were badly in debt, with no income to cover our expenses incurred from having a mortgage on our shop premises and other important bills. Hubby's part-time work was barely enough to cover our mortgage and expenses at home. Somehow, we managed to feed ourselves and the kids.

Despite having our commercial premises advertised both for lease and for sale, we were struggling to find any interest, so that wasn't going to save us in a hurry. And, in the meantime, we were practically free-falling towards bankruptcy (and no, that's not me being melodramatic).

As it turned out though, I'm extremely stubborn. I couldn't accept the worst was about to happen to us. That this could be our final chapter in the business world. So, I found the strength to forge ahead with my little copywriting business. I literally worked around the clock. Bit by bit, the clients and work started flowing. I also caught the eye of a prominent digital marketing agency owner, who started funnelling work my way (and who kindly gave me a much-needed boost of confidence).

I also listed our eCommerce business for sale. After a few headaches, several months later it sold to great new owners, and the proceeds got us out of the worst of our financial troubles.

Finally, eleven months after deciding to close our retail store, we sold our commercial premises. However, I'd already helped us out of trouble with the success of my new business. The sale though meant we finally had a clean slate to move forward, without the expense of a property we no longer needed. And it officially marked the start of our new lives.

While I am not proud of how much trouble we got ourselves into with our first business, I'm darn proud of how I found the strength to fight back and fight our way out. Because believe me, all I could do was trust that I could and that I would. The odds were against me. Family and friends were somewhat panicked on our behalf, yet I focused forward, and it worked.

And if little old me can perform such an amazing feat of endurance, survival and revival, so can you. It's amazing just how much we CAN DO when we absolutely need to. So, while I hope you do not have to go through what we did, please trust that you can fight your way through anything too.

Learning to trust others

(You can't walk the business path entirely alone.)

While you may start your business alone, real growth and real results require you to have extra help and support. You will need to lean on your partner, family, and friends, so you can handle the mental and emotional load. You will also need to find outside help who can take some of the task load off your shoulders.

Relying on others though takes REAL trust. When we build a business, it's literally our baby. And it's easy to become quite precious about how things are done and to have the desire to micromanage every single little detail. It's also incredibly tempting to not share your struggles with those close to you. You might worry they'll lose faith in you if you're struggling. You might worry that it will burden them.

The trick with this is to find the RIGHT people who you can trust.

Emotional Support

First, you need at least one person who you can talk to about your mental and emotional load when it comes to business. For me, it's my husband. As he runs his own business too, he gets the whole business thing (whereas the vast majority of our family and friends do not). We often bounce ideas around together and talk things through, which can be a massive relief and spark amazing ideas.

And most importantly, if I get a little frazzled and overwhelmed and question my entire business existence, he can lend a friendly ear and lovingly tell me to snap out of my self-doubt.

Expert Support

Even though I told you earlier to always listen and trust yourself FIRST, you'll still need the occasional business mentor, or expert, or a community of like-minded businesspeople to learn from.

Getting advice from people who are further down the business path than I am has been really crucial for me. (It's something I NEVER did in my first business.) Someone more experienced can offer different perspectives and ideas you may not stumble across on your own. And they can fast-track your growth and help you reach your goals quicker.

Outsourcing Support

There will come a time when you won't be able to do everything that your business needs you to do. This could be because of time constraints or knowledge constraints. This is where you need to think about outsourcing, whether that's your admin, your accounts, your website development or of course, your copywriting.

Bringing people in to help you with your business is a massive leap of faith and trust. Yet when you do, you'll find that you breathe a huge sigh of relief. You'll also hopefully get much better results.

I recently found two amazing junior copywriters to help me when things get really busy. I didn't necessarily need them right now, but knowing they're there for when I DO need them gives me a lot more confidence. But I know I can now grow further and keep up with extra demand. And if I get hit by writers' block (yes, copywriters get that too), I've got them there to help me with fresh ideas and concepts.

So, once you've learnt to trust the universe, trust yourself, trust how truly capable you are, and therefore trust your business, it's time to outsource and bring other people and support systems in.

Trust that success will come

(Even when you can't see it yet.)

Success is inevitable, providing you don't quit. It may not come in the form you first expect. It may not come with the first business you create (I'm the perfect case study for that one). It may not be the first offer you promote. In fact, you could try a thousand different offers to no avail.

Yet it could be 'Offer 1001' that finally works.

All you can do is keep putting one foot after another, keep throwing yourself 'out there' and keep trusting. Because you just never know who might be watching. Or just when the next sale will come. You might be doing all the right things; posting on social media, networking, blogging, advertising, with very little results. You might start questioning your business, your strategy, your tactics, your execution, your copy, your graphics and your entire reason for existing.

Then boom! Suddenly, out of nowhere, things take off. A client shows up. A collaboration opportunity falls into your lap. Business explodes. Or maybe you just get one bit of traction, which spurs you on to find your next bit of traction.

It's definitely been that way for me. I've had little traction for months and then suddenly been contacted by a major marketing agency wanting to hand me all their client copywriting work. Or there's no work for weeks, when suddenly I score a new client with a nice, juicy $5,000 project.

There's always plenty of moments when you feel like no one is listening to you and things just aren't working. Particularly, when you're in the first few years of a business, income and success can be a little inconsistent (or so I've found). As you progress and build your profile and fine-tune your offers, you're likely to find the inconsistency lessens and you can rely on being able to bring in a certain number of clients and income each month. In the meantime, though, trust that success is out there and you're on track to find it.

The trick with this is to take the next best step forward; whether that's brainstorming a new offer, or to write a particular social media post with a different approach, or to reach out to someone who can help. Keep taking those 'next best steps' and soon, things will start falling into place for you.

Amazing opportunities seem to come out of nowhere. And success often seems to just sneak up on you, all of a sudden. The trick is to trust the process and to never give up.

Conclusion

I can imagine some of this may challenge you as I'm asking you to trust (ha-ha) a concept that is a little more intangible than the latest and greatest marketing strategy or tactic. It's a mindset shift first that will hopefully help guide you forward in the right ways.

Hopefully, however, it gives you a little hope. Hopefully, it encourages you to really start trusting yourself and believing in yourself. We're all entirely capable of building our own successful businesses, so long as we can open ourselves up to trust and give it a go.

Yet even trust is a balancing act. You need the right amount of it, with the right priorities. With my eCommerce and retail business, I began innocently by trusting everyone else and their opinions rather than myself. Trouble is, that led to a lack of boundaries and a lack of clear direction. When that approach got me into trouble, I lost trust completely. In everyone and everything. I didn't trust myself to make the right decisions, and I didn't trust anyone else to help me. And being in that place was not much fun at all.

Having trust in yourself and your instincts is the starting point. Trusting the world around you is also necessary. Then, you can start trusting other people and letting them in to help you. Providing, you don't stop listening to your instincts throughout the process.

Trusting is not always easy. But it makes such a massive difference to your business journey. And if you don't yet feel able to trust yourself or your ability to grab a firm hold of the opportunities out there, you will just have to learn from my stories and trust me.

SARAH WALKERDEN

In my family, academic achievement and a city-based corporate career has always been heralded as the pinnacle of success. I, however, loved horses and from the age of ten, was determined to buy and live on my own farm.

Now, as 'The Rural Copywriter', I've firmly established myself as a digital marketing messaging and strategy ace. I help rural and regional businesses win scores of adoring customers and boost their Google rankings.

My strict 'no fluff, no bull-dust' approach creates straight-shooting SEO Website Copy that cultivates real results, helping 'agri' and other rural businesses to flourish. I've never wanted to lead a 'normal' life. I've always wanted to live a life of freedom, flexibility and fun. To not be tied down to a 9-to-5 job. And to have more impact on the world.

Together, with my husband, we're creating the life WE want to lead. Our kids have the freedom and the space to run, explore and learn about nature and farming. We're not yet what we would consider 'rich' or 'wealthy' but we're comfortable. And we believe the best is yet to come.

Finally, I'll leave you with my business vision. It's why I do what I do…

- To help rural businesses thrive, regardless of location.
- To support the future of Australian Agriculture.
- To support rural and remote communities.
- To empower rural business leaders to chase their wildest dreams and build a life of freedom, flexibility and fun for themselves and their families, from anywhere they so choose.

Sarah Walkerden, The Rural Copywriter
Website: https://www.theruralcopywriter.com.au
Facebook: www.facebook.com/theruralcopywriter

The Art of Collaboration & Partnerships – We're Better Together

SANDRA SPADANUDA

I learnt early on in my career that to make change, real meaningful change, I needed to back myself with a tribe of passionate individuals willing to support me to achieve my goals; a community willing to support my dreams and my vision. And that's exactly what I did.

'There is nothing stronger, more powerful or with the potential for greater success than a collective, connected group–a tribe–of strong women. Those who empower each other, build each other up and do so with complete love, passion and unwavering support.'

I am a strong believer in women supporting each other and raising each other up, which inspired me to write the above quote recently during a late-night light-bulb moment. Connection is a superpower.

I've always been a dreamer and a believer in the greater good. I knew from a young age I wanted to change the world. And I always felt it was my calling in life to help others.

I didn't always know or understand what that would look like or how I would do it, but my biggest passion has been working as a professional youth worker. I'm not sure there has ever been a single day where what I was doing ever felt like work.

Over the years, this passion and love for my work has evolved and grown. It's no longer just about youth work, it has become so much more. I am incredibly fortunate to share my life passion with my husband, Dave, and together as youth workers, we have become passionate advocates for suicide awareness and prevention. But always with a tribe of incredible individuals backing us.

As skilled, qualified or experienced as you may be individually, I assure you, there is so much added value and benefit when you work with others.

Whether you're a small business owner, an executive company CEO, a director on the board of a charity you're passionate about, or a not-for-profit sector employee, whatever your position, whichever company or organisation you work for, this much is clear; networking, collaboration and partnerships have the potential to ultimately make or break you.

So why a partner? Why a collaborative project? Why not just do it solo and reap the benefits as an individual? Why not take the credit on your own?

The answer is simple… WE ARE BETTER TOGETHER. It's a fact!

And when you get those wins, no matter how big or small, sharing that with those who share your hard work, vision and dreams is an amazing feeling. The triumphs are amplified when you're able to share the reward of your achievements with others.

I have always prided myself on my ability to network, collaborate, and form partnerships. I often struggle to identify my own strengths. (Secretly, we all have fears, setbacks and self-doubt.) But one thing I have realised over the years is I love to network and build relationships.

I've been fortunate enough to have worked extensively within multidisciplinary teams, partnerships, and through collaborative processes. But I have also lost count of the times I have watched creative, innovative and potentially life-changing projects fail before they have even begun. All purely out of individual people's desire to work solo, as opposed to reaching out for help and working in collaboration.

There is not, and never should be, any shame in asking for help when we need it. While we may be experts in our own individual ways, the added value in working with others is priceless.

Your tribe is so much more than just your business partners, collaborators and workmates. It's about your personal community too, and those we have in every aspect of our lives, like our family, partners, husbands, wives, friends and our supporters.

I have had some of the most inspirational, supportive and motivational individuals back me on my journey. They have given me the courage, motivation, and strength to face every challenge that has been thrown at me head on!

1. Shared Values... Shared Vision.

No matter the partnership or collaboration you are considering, it's so important whoever you bring on board understands and shares your values and passion. And that together, you're able to mutually agree on your vision, mission, objectives and goals.

When choosing who you'll collaborate with, or how they will fit in with your plans, be honest with yourself and your potential partner about your personal vision, and how their skills and vision will align with yours. *Values and Vision are key to shaping your business culture and inspiring your employees, partners, and stakeholders.*

When I think of partnerships, collaboration, and networking, I almost instantaneously think 'teamwork.' Vision is so important, but equally (if not more) important is *Shared Vision*. Whether at a management level or involving your team of staff, if you have the objective of energising your team, gaining their commitment and providing a clear sense of direction, it's definitely worth involving them in the creative process. It then has the incredible power to move from 'my vision' to '*Our Vision.*'

Dave and I together co-founded *Blue Beanie Projects* (BBP) in 2015.

In all my years working in youth services and as a business owner, what we together envisaged and created was a success I'd never expected, experienced or imagined. We worked towards achieving this together passionately, because our vision was shared.

We created *BBP* in memory of Bluey, who we sadly lost to suicide. He took his own life, only weeks after the youth service in his local community, (of which he was an active participant and volunteer), was defunded. It was shut down because of the belief that the community's suicide epidemic was under control. Bluey is only one of the many we lose to suicide every year.

The *Blue Beanie* team believe, with access to the appropriate professional services for young people, we can help reduce rates of youth suicide in regional and remote areas across Australia. We are made up of a dedicated group of volunteers who are professional, qualified, skilled, experienced and passionate youth workers. *Blue Beanie* services are aimed at building children and young people's self-esteem, confidence, resilience, social and emotional wellbeing and connection to community.

One of our key projects has been the development and design of our own merchandise and clothing line. How do we market and show our latest designs to the world? BRAND AMBASSADORS and INFLUENCERS! Individuals with great social media presence and following, but above all else, *we look for people who truly believe in our cause and support our vision*. Individuals who, through their social media following, can represent and uphold the integrity and values of our organisation. We don't look for people with the highest number of followers. We look for individuals whose vision and values align with ours.

That is only one example of the many types of partnerships and collaborative initiatives we are part of through *Blue Beanie*. We are continually receiving EOI's (Expressions of Interest) from potential volunteers, project partners, sponsors, businesses, and youth services to collaborate with us. Each time we meet someone new, or recruit a new volunteer, or partake in more formal partnership activities, we carefully choose who we are working with.

We ask ourselves

- Do they share our vision?
- Do they understand our passion?
- Are they truly supportive of our cause?

2. Strengths, Weaknesses and Complimentary Skill Sets.

'Great things in business are never done by one person. They're done by a team of people.'
STEVE JOBS

As many of us do when building our teams, it's ideal business practice to balance the skills of individual employees with the complimentary abilities of others. This way, each team member plays a unique role through the use of their individual strengths. It's much the same when working in partnership arrangements or through collaborative initiatives and projects.

The beauty of partnerships and collaboration is the multitude of diverse skills and experience each individual brings to the table. We all have our own strengths and weaknesses, and with the right partnership, your complimentary skill sets will only benefit your business, your potential for further growth and development, and will ultimately benefit your customers and clients.

The youth service sector is diverse. People enter the field of 'working with young people' in a range of different roles and through multiple different avenues. But right from the outset, it is the responsibility of each service provider entering any collaborative project to be realistic about what it is they can provide. Or perhaps in your case, the business owner, and at which point it is best to refer or pass on to a more suitably qualified organisation or individual.

I have lived and worked in the glorious Pilbara region of Western Australia for coming up to ten years. In that time, I have had the opportunity of working collaboratively with so many partners, such as youth service providers, clothing retailers, hairdressers, makeup artists, photographers, community members, and elders. But most importantly and key to what we do – young people.

The reality of the youth sector is that so many individuals play an integral part in how we shape and deliver the best service possible, to the young people we support.

When I first arrived in Karratha, I was looking for any volunteer opportunities where I could commit some time outside of my fulltime job, and to get to know my new community a little better. While I worked fulltime, I would spend my afternoons, evenings and weekends volunteering and working with young people.

Back in 2013, when we first commenced Karratha's 'Friday Late Night' initiative at our local youth centre, we saw almost instantaneously the true meaning of a one-stop shop for young people in Karratha. This initiative brought together such a diverse range of service providers. Youth Work case managers, Social and Emotional Wellbeing Support Workers, Sport, Recreation and Activity officers, Crisis Youth Accommodation Staff, and even government department staff working with young people.

A one-stop shop model allowed for young people to get to know workers from each organisation, making it easier for them to access and connect with the relevant support.

Our joint projects grew, expanded and evolved. We were so successful in our collaborative approach we were invited to sit on a panel as keynote speakers at the state youth affairs conference. We each shared our story of how a collective group of non-government, local government and state government service providers, worked so well collectively to support young people.

3. Define Roles, Responsibilities and Expectations.

So, you've found your business partner, your vision and their's align, you've identified each of your own strengths, weaknesses and complimentary skill sets; now, to clearly define each of your roles.

I can't stress enough that the discussions and agreements around role definitions are important to be had right from the outset. This establishes clear responsibility and accountability in line with your company's or organisation's vision and goals.

Personally, I am all about Job Description Forms (JDF's). The list of benefits of having JDF's are seemingly endless to me.

Something I realised in my time as a business professional is that no matter your role within an organisation, however big or small, whether paid or voluntary, and yes even for the business owner or director themselves, JDF's are ***ESSENTIAL***. They clearly define and outline each person's role, should include your organisation's vision and mission, and ultimately can hold people accountable for their responsibilities.

It's also important for customers, clients, and employees who benefit from knowing who handles what aspects of the business.

My husband and I together embarked on a new venture four years ago, when we bought a busy café / restaurant in Karratha. My husband is a trade-qualified (and super experienced) Chef, so it wasn't completely new territory to us.

We were so overjoyed about finally owning our own café we didn't slow down, in the beginning, to clearly identify each of our roles as a 'husband and wife' team.

Despite both of our extensive and combined experiences, we didn't even think to stop and create JDF's for ourselves. That was something we realised and learnt from quickly. But these are the simple things you don't stop to think about when you're going into a business partnership with your spouse.

Little things began popping up, like staff answering to two owners. My time commitment was limited because I was working my own fulltime job elsewhere. And the realisation we weren't super humans able to do it all alone because I was working my own.

So, we pivoted and restructured our business model. My husband took on the roles of Executive Chef and Managing Director, taking responsibility for overseeing and supervising all kitchen operations and staff. I took on the role of Director of Marketing, Communications and HR; and we created a new Venue Manager position to take on responsibility of daily management, and all front of house operations, including rostering.

As we navigated our way through our new business, we identified changes that were needed, and over the years, we adapted as we needed to. For example, over time, we decided the HR portfolio would be better suited sitting under Dave's management, as he could commit to the time needed. We also adapted and changed our interview and recruitment processes, allowing me the opportunity to move away from Café HR activities and to focus on my other commitments.

JDF's don't have to be rigid and set-in-stone, they can be living, breathing, ever-evolving documents that are continually reviewed. Sometimes position descriptions change, as business models change and grow.

No matter who you are partnering with, even your own husband or wife, it's imperative you create clear job descriptions, defining each individual person's role and responsibilities.

4. Communicate often.

Communication is fundamental to any successful partnership or collaboration, but it's not just about team meetings, emails or phone calls. It's not necessarily about the methods of communication. It's also about *how* we communicate with each other. Partners and collaborators should be honest, transparent, and above all else, respectful.

When setting up your partnership arrangement, whether you are going into business as formal partners, or you are collaborating on specific projects where a Memorandum of Understanding (MOU) is created, the 'how' behind communication should be established from the beginning.

Effective communication helps foster a good working relationship between your partners, collaborators and staff, which improves team morale and efficiency.

- Establish regular meetings.
- Identify and utilise the most appropriately suited communication platforms for your particular business model.
- Be honest and transparent with each other.
- Make a commitment to be mutually respectful.
- Agree to handle any issues, disagreements or grievances early on and promptly.
- Do what you say you will. Take your commitments seriously and meet deadlines you've agreed to.
- Set boundaries. Be clear with each other around your working styles and be respectful of each other's personal life.

In 2017 *BBP* developed The Pilbara Shine Project, in collaboration and through consultation with a group of young people who had a vision to develop and grow the Pilbara region's first all-inclusive Modelling Academy for children and young people.

It has taken a collective group of countless individuals to support the development of this project, where communication with young people and stakeholders has been key.

The vision was an all-inclusive, non-discriminatory project. Open to children and young people of all shapes, sizes, genders, ethnicities and ages between 5-25.

What started as a small idea has since turned into an incredible journey. Never in a million years did any of us believe we would come as far as we have:

- Over 1200 contacts with children and young people.
- Delivered fifty-five workshops.
- Produced fourteen fashion shows and five photo shoots with one of our young male models recently published in a fashion magazine.

Young people are empowered by their involvement in project planning, fashion show production, liaison with clothing retailers, promotional activities, hair, makeup, styling and choreography. They are, with the support of Youth Workers and Mentors, our key 'communicators'.

What's truly incredible about what we do is that we are volunteers. We have survived with the ongoing support and through in-kind contributions and donations from our generous community of local businesses, service providers and volunteers. Communication between ourselves and our key stakeholders has been instrumental to our success.

We encourage all children and young people to participate, including those with disabilities; mental health difficulties; complex behaviours; young people considered at risk; disengaged; disadvantaged; and those from low socio-economic backgrounds.

We offer what we believe is a truly unique project and service. The Project is facilitated by a unique group of volunteers; they are both professional and qualified youth workers, and modelling and fashion industry professionals.

We are program facilitators, but as professional youth workers, we also have the skills, education, experience and knowledge to deal with difficult-to-manage behaviours. We have the skills and abilities to engage some of even the most hard-to-reach young people in our community.

This enables us to ensure inclusivity and to reduce the numbers of vulnerable and disengaged young people becoming further isolated, withdrawn, and disconnected from our communities. We have accepted into the Project young people who are, or had been excluded from attending other services, because of difficult-to-manage behaviours. By providing them the opportunity to be involved in a pro-social activity, we aim to support their return to and reintegration with services where they'd previously been excluded.

We are connected and knowledgeable about our community. To this day, through our Volunteers and Directors of our Board, we consult and continually communicate with the true experts in our field. They are young people in our community - our Youth Project Consultants and Youth Project Leaders.

This incredible project has survived through continual communication, internally within our own team and the young people with whom we work, also through effective communication with so many external key stakeholders who share our vision.

5. Put it in writing

No matter how long you've known the person, or how good of a friend they are, or how well you think you've done to verbally agree something, everything you discuss and agree on should be documented.

Whether it's a simple case of two youth support agencies collaborating and creating an MOU to define each agency's role, or a more legally binding contractual partnership between business partners, my bottom-line advice is *document, document, document.*

This goes for anything. Any agreements, business plans, vision and mission statements, goals, strategic plans, JDF's, MOU's, meeting minutes, policies and procedures, and handover notes. *Document everything.*

Through *Blue Beanie*, so much of what we do has required consistent and professional documentation. Garment registers and agreements when partnering with clothing retailers for fashion shows and photo shoots; participation consent forms; photo and video consent forms; referral forms; meeting minutes; and policies and procedures.

Through *Soul*, it's been something as simple as JDF's, having our staff read and commit to complying with our business policies and procedures, and having all staff read, agree to and follow the procedures and expectations, as outlined in our staff handbook.

In closing this chapter, my message of *wisdom* is simple.

Nobody is perfect. No one individual has life perfectly together. We all have our faults, insecurities, and self-doubt. We all have bad days where all we want to do is give up, no matter how confident we may seem to the outside world.

And you know what? That's absolutely ok.

We all have, at some point (no matter how mild or severe), had a case of good old imposter syndrome.

Stay true to you, true to your passion, and as women and mothers continue to support, uplift and encourage one another.

I have wasted too many years working with toxic

individuals who don't believe in the combined power of women. I genuinely love the feeling of meeting strong women who are not afraid to compliment and support each other.

My goal in life and how I interact with others is to make a change and be the difference I want to see in the world. I'm talking, it's our duty to do whatever we need to advocate for what we are truly passionate about (diplomatically, of course). If you're ever afforded the opportunity or given the platform, please, '*Let Free Speech Be.*'

No matter your role, no matter your background, whatever your platform, speak your truth and act on your passion and carefully select who makes up your tribe.

'We must shift the culture and thinking of humankind... Let's move from thinking "What can I get?" to "What can I GIVE?"'

SANDRA SPADANUDA

My husband and I are foster carers, bringing into our home and caring for some of the state's most vulnerable children and young people. The decision for us to foster was a well thought out and planned one. We always felt bringing a child into the world wasn't for us. We were the type wanting to care for children in need of homes and families, a decision likely heavily influenced by our own work with young people. It was just a better fit for us, and our circumstances.

It makes me no less of a mother. People often ask why I don't have or want children of my own. I always politely reply with 'they are our own.'

'Not being biologically related to a child, doesn't make you any less of a parent. Being a real parent isn't in the DNA, it's in the heart.'-

MOTHERHOOD: THE UNCUT TRUTH

I have worked in the Youth and Community Services sector of Australia for twenty-two years. And I've been involved in various youth and community development programs, projects and services in Perth, South East Queensland and the Kimberley and Pilbara regions of Western Australia.

I am particularly passionate about the development and sustainability of professional youth work practice in regional and remote areas. I have designed and managed multi award-winning Youth Services and Projects in some of WA's most remote and isolated communities. And I have also, together with my chef husband, owned and operated award-winning Karratha based cafe 'Soul' since January 2017, taking on the role of Director of Marketing, Communications and Public Relations.

I co-founded *Blue Beanie Projects* in 2015, a not-for-profit health promotion charity working with 5-25year olds. Our motto is 'Spirit of Youth – Strong, Resilient, Empowered.'

We believe, with access to appropriate *professional* services, delivered by suitably qualified and experienced youth workers, we can help reduce the staggering rates of youth suicide in regional and remote locations.

My youth work journey has never been about personal fame, recognition or photo opportunities. I am a fairly humble human who isn't too great when it comes to recognition, praise, or compliments. I do what I do out of pure passion and love. But through my journey and involvement in the AusMumpreneur community, I realise it's ok to accept the praise and congrats.

Last year, I was recognised for my community contributions (which honestly, I still find difficult to mention); I was named City of Karratha's Citizen of the Year; and Karratha Chamber of Commerce Business Woman of the Year. I was Winner of the Pilbara Community Service Awards Outstanding Demonstration of Leadership award; and together with my husband was named as one of Karratha's fifteen most influential people.

My youth work journey is far from over. My passion for what I do will continue for a long time yet.

SANDRA SPADANUDA

Sandra has worked in the Youth and Community Services sector for 22 years and is particularly passionate about the development and sustainability of professional Youth Work practice in Regional and Remote areas. Sandra has designed and managed multi award winning Youth Services & Projects in some of WA's most remote and isolated communities. She also, together with her Chef husband, has owned and operated award winning Karratha based cafe "Soul" since January 2017.

She Co-Founded Blue Beanie Projects in 2015, a not for profit health promotion charity working with 5-25 year olds, aimed at building children and young people's self esteem, confidence, resilience, social and emotional wellbeing, health and connection to community.

In 2019, Sandra was recognised for her outstanding leadership skills and contributions to community; named City of Karratha's Citizen of the Year; Karratha Chamber of Commerce Business Woman of the Year; Winner of the Pilbara Community Service Awards' Outstanding Demonstration of Leadership award; and was together with her husband was named as one of Karratha's 15 most influential people.

bluebeanieprojects.com.au

Giving Back

Proceeds from the sale of 'Back Yourself' go to providing women with scholarships to enable them to receive support, mentoring and education through The Women's Business School.

We believe that investing in women is the most powerful way to change the world and these scholarships provide opportunities for deserving women to receive the support they need to succeed.

www.ingramcontent.com/pod-product-compliance
Lightning Source LLC
Chambersburg PA
CBHW030232120726
47903CB00005B/1458

* 9 7 8 0 6 4 5 0 3 7 1 9 7 *